TEARS AND FLOWERS

UNIVERSITY PRESS OF FLORIDA

Florida A&M University, Tallahassee
Florida Atlantic University, Boca Raton
Florida Gulf Coast University, Ft. Myers
Florida International University, Miami
Florida State University, Tallahassee
New College of Florida, Sarasota
University of Central Florida, Orlando
University of Florida, Gainesville
University of North Florida, Jacksonville
University of South Florida, Tampa
University of West Florida, Pensacola

TEARS AND FLOWERS
A Poet of Migration in Old Key West

Feliciano Castro

Edited by Joy Castro and Rhi Johnson

Translated by Rhi Johnson

UNIVERSITY PRESS OF FLORIDA

Gainesville/Tallahassee/Tampa/Boca Raton
Pensacola/Orlando/Miami/Jacksonville/Ft. Myers/Sarasota

Publication of this work made possible by a Sustaining the Humanities through the American Rescue Plan grant from the National Endowment for the Humanities.

Copyright 2024 by Joy Castro and Rhi Johnson
All rights reserved
Published in the United States of America

29 28 27 26 25 24   6 5 4 3 2 1

Library of Congress Cataloging-in-Publication Data
Names: Castro, Feliciano, 1892–1982, author. | Castro, Joy, editor, writer
   of introduction. | Johnson, Rhi, translator, editor, writer of
   introduction. | Castro, Feliciano, 1892–1982. Lágrimas y flores. |
   Castro, Feliciano, 1892–1982. Lágrimas y flores. English.
Title: Tears and flowers : a poet of migration in old Key West / Feliciano
   Castro ; introduced and edited by Joy Castro and Rhi Johnson ;
   translated by Rhi Johnson.
Description: Gainesville : University Press of Florida, 2024. | Includes
   bibliographical references.
Identifiers: LCCN 2024012235 (print) | LCCN 2024012236 (ebook) | ISBN
   9780813079134 (hardback) | ISBN 9780813080703 (paperback) | ISBN
   9780813070810 (pdf) | ISBN 9780813073415 (ebook)
Subjects: LCSH: Castro, Feliciano, 1892–1982—Translations into English. |
   BISAC: POETRY / Caribbean & Latin American | LITERARY CRITICISM /
   Caribbean & Latin American | LCGFT: Poetry.
Classification: LCC PQ7079.C25 L3413 2024 (print) | LCC PQ7079.C25
   (ebook) | DDC 861/.62—dc23/eng/20240525
LC record available at https://lccn.loc.gov/2024012235
LC ebook record available at https://lccn.loc.gov/2024012236

The University Press of Florida is the scholarly publishing agency for the State University System of Florida, comprising Florida A&M University, Florida Atlantic University, Florida Gulf Coast University, Florida International University, Florida State University, New College of Florida, University of Central Florida, University of Florida, University of North Florida, University of South Florida, and University of West Florida.

University Press of Florida
2046 NE Waldo Road
Suite 2100
Gainesville, FL 32609
http://upress.ufl.edu

CONTENTS

List of Illustrations   ix
Gratitude   xi
On the Origin of the Manuscript   xiii
  Joy Castro
Translator's Note   xvii
  Rhi Johnson
Introduction: Feliciano Castro, Cuban Key West, and the Dawn of U.S. Empire   1
  Joy Castro and Rhi Johnson

LÁGRIMAS Y FLORES
A manera de prólogo / By Way of a Prologue   33

LÁGRIMAS
Mi madre y mi bandera / My Mother and My Flag   38
El alma de Martí / The Soul of Martí   40
Lágrimas / Tears   42
¡Mentira! / Lie!   46
La jauria / The Pack of Hounds   48
¿Por qué callas? / Why Do You Hold Your Tongue?   50
El hombre que infama / The Man Who Defames   52
Es un iris tu voz / Your Voice Is an Iris   54
A mi padre / To My Father   56
Una patria azul / A Blue Patria   58
Yo tengo aquí en mi cuarto . . . / I Have Here in My Room . . .   62
Las palmas / The Palms   66
El tiempo / Time   68
La eterna queja / The Eternal Complaint   72
La escuela / School   74
Página gris / Gray Page   78

El derrumbe universal / The Universal Collapse   80
La barquilla y el alma / The Little Boat and the Soul   84
Mis versos / My Verses   86
Mis ilusiones / My Daydreams   88
¡Cuba y mi amada! / Cuba and My Beloved!   92
El pescador / The Fisherman   96
Paisaje nocturno / Nocturnal Landscape   104
En la ausencia / In Absence   106
¿Por qué despertarla? . . . / Why Wake Her? . . .   108
El Angelus / The Angelus   112
Soñaba / I Used to Dream   114
La mano del amigo / The Hand of a Friend   118
¿Te acuerdas? / Do You Remember?   120
Yo / Self   124
En la playa / On the Beach   126
F. Domínguez Pérez   130
El dos de noviembre / The Second of November   132
¿ . . . . ?   136
España: ¡Salve, bandera mía! / Spain: Hail, Flag of Mine!   140
Año viejo/Año nuevo / Old Year/New Year   144
Cuba   146
El grito de Yara / The Cry of Yara   150
¡Cubanos, proseguid! / Cubans, Carry On!   160
Bodas de plata del Centro Español de Tampa / The Silver Anniversary of the Spanish Center in Tampa   164
Mensaje de lágrimas / Message of Tears   168

FLORES

Mi ofrenda / My Offering   176
A mis hermanas / To My Sisters   180
A las obreritas / To the Factory Girls   182
Quisiera . . . / I Should Like . . .   186
¿Por qué te escribo? / Why Do I Write to You?   188
Rimas / Rhymes   190
A Dulce María Bravo   194
A Antonia Martínez   196

A "Conchita" Saenz   198
Tu debieras tener . . . / You Ought to Have . . .   200
A Graciela Corbett   202
A "Teresita" Colón   204
A Célida Bravo   206
A Josefina López   208
A Rosa María López   210
A Sofía Pérez Rolo   212
En el baile / At the Dance   214
A Graciela Avalo   216
Tu boca / Your Mouth   218
A Delia López   220
A Celia Avalo   222
Tu caricia / Your Caress   224
A "Consuelito" Rivero   226
Estela Rodríguez   228
La amada mía / My Beloved   230
Ofrenda póstuma / Posthumous Offering   234
A Ofelia Rivero   236
A América Cermeño   238
A Adelaida Pinet   240
A Rosalía Vila   242
A Heliodora Toledo   244
A Ofelia Quesada   246
En el teatro / In the Theater   248
A. Cermeño—R. Miqueli   250
A Agnelia López   252
A Rosa Sibila   254
A Gloria Sibila   256
A Julieta Raga   258
A Dalia Viera   260
A María Boza   262
A Carolina Rivero   264
A la Sra. P. Rolo de Simón   266
A Estrella Bravo   268
A Eponine P. Rolo   270

A Edelmira Acosta   272
Tus ojos / Your Eyes   274
A Elisa Salgado   276
A "Angelita" Machin   278
Con besos y flores / With Kisses and Flowers   280
No olvides mis cantares . . . / Don't Forget My Songs . . .   282
A Mariana Salgado   286
Tus ojos / Your Eyes   288
Homenaje / Homage   290
Última página / Final Page   294
NOTAS / NOTES   296

Appendix 1. The Social World of *Lágrimas y flores*   299
Appendix 2. Meter and Verse Forms   309
Endnotes   315
Works Consulted   331

ILLUSTRATIONS

Illustrations follow page 171.

1. Front cover of *Lágrimas y flores*
2. Feliciano Castro circa 1918, photo included in *Lágrimas y flores*
3. Enlargement of printing press information
4. Back cover of *Lágrimas y flores*
5. Section-dividing page of *Lágrimas y flores*

GRATITUDE

The authors would like to thank organizers James López and Denis Rey and all the scholars of the 2019 NEH Summer Institute "José Martí and the Immigrant Communities of Florida in Cuban Independence and the Dawn of the American Century," where this project was born. For their belief in and support of the project, Stephanye Hunter, Nicole Guidotti-Hernández, and Esther Allen. For reading early drafts of the translations, Irene Gómez Castellano, Nuria Alishio Caballero, and Sam Krieg. For her care and attention, Kel Pero. For funding support that helped make this project possible, the College of Arts and Sciences at the University of Nebraska–Lincoln.

ON THE ORIGIN OF THE MANUSCRIPT

Joy Castro

My grandfather, as I knew him, was a silent man. When we visited my grandparents' house on Elizabeth Street in Key West in the 1970s and '80s, he sat in a brown upholstered rocker in the TV room all morning, listening to Spanish-language radio and doing Spanish search-a-words, circling the long diagonal streaks of letters with a pen.

At noon, Papi would clomp out to the kitchen, where my grandmother had been cooking since six a.m., and sit down, surrounded by all the aunts and uncles and grandchildren and whoever was working in the print shop—usually Uncle Mario, I guess—and we'd devour the spread of garlic roast pork or ropa vieja or papas rellenas with ground beef or picadillo, always with plenty of hot gold maduros and black beans and rice on the side. We children chattered in English while my father and aunts and grandmother switched back and forth between languages, but even when the conversation slid to Spanish, Papi hardly spoke. After lunch, he'd retire to the TV room to resume his search-a-words until my grandmother, finished with her housework, was ready to watch *Mod Squad* (which I watched with her) and soap operas (which I didn't), at which point he would rise heavily from his rocking chair, sigh, and clomp back to his room, a bedroom separate from hers at the very back of the house.

I rarely remember seeing him in the evenings when we'd come in, still all wild and rambunctious after a hot day swimming at the beach or fishing from the docks. Tired, Papi kept to himself. Already forty-seven years old when my father was born in 1939, he seemed nothing short of ancient to me. Dignified, remote, and aloof, he was separated from us children by old age and a language barrier he deplored.

When it was time for us to leave—to return to Miami or London or West Virginia, wherever we were living at the time—he would gesture me toward him, embrace me awkwardly, and press a folded dollar bill into my hand.

"Remember Papi," he said every time. They were the only words he ever spoke to me, *remember* the only English I ever heard him utter. Every time, a tear would run down his cheek.

I was fourteen when he died in 1982. My cousins and I were hushed and respectful at the funeral, and it was sad watching the older people be sad together, but—though it sounds cruel—not much of a sense of grief seemed to imbue our generation, to be honest. Papi had simply been too much of a stranger to us.

A few years later, my father showed me a book of poems Papi had once published. Fragile, softcover. I was surprised. I was in college then, studying early twentieth-century British and U.S. literature—high modernism, Dada, free verse—and quietly struggling with the challenges of being a first-generation scholarship girl, a Latina at an almost all-white school, before people talked about such things. We were working-class people. No one in my extended family had been to college. My university had no courses in Latinx literature, no Latinx professors, and no Latinx students whom I knew; my only Latino friend was a fellow food server at the restaurant where I waited tables. I read Sandra Cisneros, Julia Alvarez, Esmeralda Santiago, and Judith Ortiz Cofer on my own.

When I opened my father's copy of *Lágrimas y flores,* the regular stanzas of Papi's poems looked old-fashioned to me, like Longfellow or Whittier, poets our professors had taught us to abjure. With my rocky Spanish, I painstakingly translated a few of his sonnets, only to find that their content, too, seemed flowery and old-fashioned: endless praise of beautiful women, with imagery I found entirely over the top. There were poems about Cuba and Spain and politics, too, but I didn't know any of the references. If that stuff were important, wouldn't I have heard of it? I had no context, no frame.

Hearts and flowers, I thought. *Ugh.* Didn't everyone's grandfather leave behind some sentimental nonsense or other? I dismissed my Galician Cuban American grandfather's poetic work, as U.S. writers and literary critics had been dismissing sentiment since Nathaniel Hawthorne damned his mob of scribbling women in 1855.

I finished three degrees in literature focusing on anglophone modernism; I loved its experimentation, political rebellions, and cool rigors. For my dissertation, advised by an all-white graduate committee, I recovered the work of a white U.S. modernist, Margery Latimer, a leftist-feminist-antiracist who'd published alongside Joyce, Faulkner, and Stein, but married Harlem Renaissance writer Jean Toomer, died in childbirth, and subsequently been forgotten.

Anglophone modernism was important, the academy swore, and Latimer had been, I thought, unjustly left out.

The irony is painful.

In 2002, the year I was going up for tenure at a small college, my father died by suicide. Papi's book was among his things, along with equally fragile copies of *Mis Recuerdos,* a book I'd never seen before: Juan Pérez Rolo's eyewitness account of the nineteenth- and early twentieth-century insurgent Cuban community in Key West, a rebel base in the anticolonial fight against Spain. Pérez Rolo had been Papi's father-in-law, my father's grandfather—my great-grandfather, who had died three decades before my birth.

Curious about the period, of which I'd learned nothing in any history course, I kept my ears open over the next few years, but I was busy raising a son, teaching my classes, and writing books—not to mention coping with the grief of losing my father—and Cuban Key West was more of an idle curiosity than a research interest. I'd imbibed—along with the cultural value of humility—the message my father had believed too despairingly and deeply: we were nothing, nobody. Irrelevant. In a white supremacist culture, we were simply also-rans, failures at the American Dream. Even within Latinx and Cuban American history, the nineteenth-century story of the utopian, antiracist, pro-labor rebel community of Key West was invisible, entirely eclipsed by the post-1959 story of well-to-do exiles fleeing Communism and the waves who followed them—a right-wing, pro-capitalist narrative that my older relatives did not embrace. I knew nothing of that previous, nineteenth-century Cuban American history at the time, believing that my ancestors had come to Key West as economic migrants only, not antiracist political rebels against Spain's imperial domination of Cuba.

In 2019, I ran by chance across an announcement for a month-long National Endowment for the Humanities summer institute at the University of Tampa: "José Martí and the Immigrant Communities of Florida in Cuban Independence and the Dawn of the American Century," focusing on the tobacco towns of Tampa and Key West—the nichest niche I could imagine, and exactly what I'd been longing for. My breath caught. At last, a chance to learn about the Cuban community in Key West in the nineteenth century, to put some flesh on the scant bones of the Key West history I knew.

Packing for a month in Tampa, I took Papi's book with me, in case any scholar there might be able to offer clarity on whether it had historical value or literary merit. My hope was the slenderest of threads.

And what a month it was! I will be forever grateful to organizers James López and Denis Rey, as well as to Kenya Dworkin, Esther Allen, and a host of other scholars who lectured to us and shared their work in dozens of generous conversations. Our reading list was extensive, too, and being introduced to the work of historians Gerald Poyo and Ada Ferrer was, especially, a revelation.

But it's the young poetry scholar Rhi Johnson, a translator of Galician nineteenth-century poetry, to whom I am immeasurably grateful. They were still only completing their PhD at the time, but everything they said in our daily seminars struck me as richly synthetic, comprehensive, and brilliantly insightful. When they expressed a willingness to look at *Lágrimas y flores*, I held my breath, and when they later stood before me, eyes alight, I felt thrilled without knowing why.

Collaborating with Rhi on this project has been a gift, an education, an honor, and a pleasure. This recovery of Feliciano Castro's literary contributions could not have happened without their deep knowledge of the period, their immediate recognition of the manuscript's value, and their deft and patient labor with its intricacies. I cannot sufficiently express my gratitude for their generosity and faith, the elegance and intelligence of their translations, and the diligence of their meticulous research.

Similarly, my gratitude to editor Stephanye Hunter for her belief in the literary, intellectual, and historical value of this particular project—an unusual acquisition for the University Press of Florida, which rarely publishes either poetry or bilingual texts—is immense, and her congeniality, grace, and kindness have been likewise. This book could not exist without her profound commitment to expanding and complicating the canon of Floridian literature.

"Remember Papi," my grandfather used to tell me. It has taken me more than four decades to realize and re-member his legacy, to piece together our family's and our people's torn heritage, and to begin to restore their gifts to the world.

Better late, he might have said, than not at all.

TRANSLATOR'S NOTE

Rhi Johnson

I wasn't in Key West when I first read *Lágrimas y flores*, but I was in a Florida cigar town that had joined that sister city in funding the final Cuban independence war. It seemed like even the air was redolent with the confluence of labor history, truly effective mutual aid from a historical high point of capitalist bootstraps individualism, and the optimistic foment of a revolution. We were there, thanks to James López and Denis Rey, to revel in the historical specificity of these communities, to join in the work of raising their profiles on a national and academic level. It was one of those magical moments when everything becomes subsumed into the shared energy of learning together. When Joy told me about her grandfather and about *Lágrimas y flores* one evening, I flowed over with excitement at being one of the first people in a century to encounter his words. I asked if I could read it, and with some reticence—either about sharing this family treasure at all, or due to insecurity about its content and quality, I wasn't sure—she agreed.

My impressions that night, reading this book for the first time in that place, with the humid summer air scented by heavy blooms and heavier rains, were of spinning golden orbs at once planets and jewel-bright eyes. The particular and perfect flower arrangements of the late nineteenth century. The loss and longing that starts early and stays late in Galician verse. Echoes of poets I love—of Bécquer, of Carolina Coronado, of Antonio Machado. It fit between and among—and, to an extent, outside of—a whole series of literary traditions and movements, all with youthful energy, a generous dash of pride, and a rapturous pleasure in human beauty. I overflowed with praise to Joy the next day, and gave her my English version of Feliciano's sonnet to "The Soul of Martí," the poem that most definitively fit within our curriculum in Tampa. I decided to translate some pieces or some sections of the book, just for her, so that she could experience some of his work as an aesthetic experience, rather than an arduous one with a dictionary as intermediary.

And as this project grew from that modest and private goal, a process during which it was a constant on a sea of personal and global upheaval, my affection for Feliciano Castro increased: for his openheartedness, for his sentimentality, and most particularly for the euphony of his verses. For their rhythm—assisted but not solely granted by his mastery of form—and the way that, in the tradition of Espronceda, the soundscape of the poetry adds to their worldbuilding. That feeling, that attention to cadence and consonants, to musicality, was the main structural element that I worked to bring into the English—though not necessarily in the same way that these soundscapes would be built in English poetry—in this volume, to maintain that pleasure in reading or hearing.

Even though a large part of the showcase of skill in this collection is the manipulation of Spanish meter, and despite constantly tapping my fingers through syllable counts as I worked on this manuscript, to offer the translation of the text that is truest to its meaning I had to lay a lot of the formal structure aside: meter with great frequency, and rhyme almost entirely. There are some poems where I could convince the counts to come true, like "Time" ["El tiempo"] with its sixteen-syllable lines marked by a middle caesura, or "The Soul of Martí" ["El alma de Martí"], which measures up and even manages to rhyme. These little triumphs, probably not readily noticed by a reader not accustomed to counting beats, are scattered throughout the collection.

One element of the Spanish verse that I do frequently maintain, and that is much less common in English, is hyperbaton, or the agrammatical shifting in word order or sentence structure to achieve an effect. That effect could be in the sound, creating internal rhyme, resonance, or alliteration, or in the meaning of a verse or stanza: the creation of puzzles that draw new connections or build narrative tension. Take, for example, this stanza from the sonnet "To Consuelito Rivero":

> Yo quisiera en estrofas melodiosas
> y a despecho de Venus arrogante,
> la reina sobre un trono de diamante
> proclamarte de todas las hermosas.

> [I should like, in melodious stanzas
> and to spite arrogant Venus,
> the queen on a throne of diamonds
> to proclaim you amongst all beauties.]

If the grammar were "correct" in this stanza, we would know from the beginning, in both languages, that it is the addressee of this poem who is being proclaimed a queen. And yet, the beauty of the stanza is that on reading it, the third line sounds like it is a description of Venus, and it isn't until the much belated "to proclaim you" that that association shifts, snubbing the goddess of love in the structure of the text as well as its content. In another sonnet, "To Rosa María López," the combination of hyperbaton and enjambment shows the mental process of moving from the effect that the addressee has on the poetic voice (internal) to processing how it is actually a part of her (external):

> Mujer bella: ¿de dónde tú surgiste,
> que así cambias la triste remembranza,
> y así truecas en horas de bonanza
> las horas de nostalgia? . . . ¿Por qué existe
>
> en tu ser esa llama bienhechora
> que, vertiendo su luz consoladora,
> dá a mis versos la dúlcida armonía? . . .
>
> [Lovely woman: from what place did you appear,
> that in this way you can so change a sad remembrance,
> and so turn to hours of fertile bounty
> my hours of nostalgia? . . . Why does it exist,
>
> central to your being, that philanthropic
> flame, which on pouring forth its comforting light
> gives to my verses a dulcet harmony?]

His recognition causes the overflowing of one verse into the next—a formal parallelism for his new capacity (in the following stanza) to overflow with verses rather than tears, and an instantiation of the function of sonnet form. This kind of puzzle and play with the structure of language can be off-putting, uncomfortable, or confusing, until the payoffs start rolling in. And to an extent, that discomfort is in itself a positive thing, as it can encourage us to embrace a kind of beauty that is not the one that we know or expect or understand.

On a more technical note, I made the choice to regularize the text to contemporary spelling and accentuation, and to correct minor errors in Castro's text. As he says in the Notes at the end of the volume, "the good sense of the reader will correct" errors that he is sure the volume must, owing to the circumstances of its publication, contain. In the same vein, Castro very occasionally uses an extra phoneme or a non-standard form of a word to fit the meter, which I have not retained in the English. For example: *desfortunanza* which means *misfortunehood,* doubling the noun endings to hit the rhyme and the syllable count for the line. There are several times where he uses *dúlcida* rather than *dulce,* both to retain meter, and, I posit, because this is a somewhat standard alternate form in Spanish-language poetry of the nineteenth Century. For me, these stumbles, or exertions of creative license in constructing words, are part of the charm of this collection, this first staking of a claim on literary ground with a full book of poems, gathered from previous newspaper publications, written new, and compiled in some haste for the salving of a bruised dignity.

There are certain things in the translation of Spanish into English that always cause subtle shifts in meaning, or mean that a translator's interpretation of the text and aesthetic preferences will have an impact. If one could lay one language next to another and perfectly transpose them, translation would not be an art, and language itself would be much less rich. A lot of these omnipresent issues seem very technical and grammatical, even though they have a profound aesthetic impact.

Without turning this into a language acquisition class, I'll give a couple of examples that I hope will be illuminative to English speakers who are approaching this text. In Spanish, the infinitive form of a verb (in English, the form with "to" added in front, like "to be") can be used as a noun. This matters in poetry particularly, because it gives extra options for rhyme and meter. For example, the three words *canto* (noun, llano, masculine) *canción* (noun, agudo, feminine) and *cantar* (noun, agudo, masculine) all mean *song,* without even considering other synonyms. Additionally, one conjugated verb in Spanish can need a whole stack of words in English to replace it, since we add more words rather than complicating the form of a verb. So "Cantaba" needs "I was singing" *or* "I used to sing."

The last of the common challenges that I'll mention is that gender is very concrete in Spanish, although the work of creatives and activists from the last decades are starting to undo the prosaic truth of that statement. This has two main impacts on poetry. First, knowing when a noun should be a "she," and when it should be an "it." Boats can be "she" easily enough, but flowers? The second is how to make these articulations when English would not default to a gendered form, and indeed is made more awkward by the use of one. An example of this is the title of the poem "The Factory Girls," originally "Las obreritas." This title highlighted not only that it is talking exclusively about female workers (the "neutral" or "mixed company" form of a noun is always the masculine, so "Los obreros"), but also that they are given a diminutive, signifying endearment, smallness, youth, or a patronizing tone. If youth, then "The working girls," except that doesn't work in English at all, as it signifies a particular profession. Not girls, then, but women: "The Little Women Workers." Are they re-editing Alcott's novel, or releasing a longer cut of Gerwig's film? Just "The Workers" takes away both of the specifics given by that *-itas* suffix. The answer, for me, was to recur to a thematically similar song trope within anglophone folk music, which maintains those specificities, and also connects the labor of the cigar factories in Key West to the mills of the northeast.

There are a couple of concrete choices that I made in the translation of this text that go beyond these common themes in Spanish-to-English translation. One is *patria*. I decided to maintain the word *patria* untranslated, leaning into its presence in extant English lexicons as a loan word. The reason for this is not meter, but rather that patria means too much more than any single English translation to work across the whole text, and translating it sometimes as one thing and sometimes as another loses the regularity with which it shows up (some thirty times) in this book of poems by a man who had either too many homelands, or, by the abstractions of time, distance, and geography, none at all. Patria is homeland, and motherland, and fatherland. It also goes beyond the level of a nation, in the way that its cognate, *patriotism*, doesn't really. One can feel that their patria is their city (either birth or adopted), or their region. Particularly around struggles for independence or in times of political upheaval, the term patria is often used to speak about a nation or a place that is beloved and to which one feels allegiance, but that does not yet exist as a geopolitical entity. In the revolutionary communities of Key West and Tampa, the idea of patria was also a solemn invocation and a promise, and one that lasted well beyond the end of the war in Cuba. Cigar workers regularly donated one full day's wages per week to the cause, along with heavy fundraising in social and political organizations. That day was the "día de la patria" [day for the patria]: it embodied the potential of what a liberated Republic of Cuba, following the ideals of Martí, could one day be.

Like belonging, like sorrow, and like song, the idea of a separate, beautiful, pleasurable, oneiric reality runs the length and breadth of *Lágrimas y flores*. This alternate reality is constructed through both a series of heavily used words, and through the subjunctive mood. The latter allows for hypotheticals: constructions like "if I *were able,* I *would . . .*" allow for potential, without having to instantiate it. Castro also uses the verb *fingir* [to feign or pretend] thirty times in the volume, and invokes drunkenness or an altered consciousness a further fifteen (through *embriaguez* in all its forms). There are also sixty-five occurrences of dreaming, across its noun *sueño,* verb *soñar,* and personified noun *soñador/a* forms. The largest factor in the creation of this other world, however, is the use of two synonyms, *ensueño* (thirty instances) and *ilusión* (used sixty-five times in the text).

Because *ilusión* appears so many times in the text, I wanted to give it a reasonably constant translation in English, where possible. This seems like it should be easy: it looks like *illusion,* after all. And yet, that is the least common of its uses, particularly in this period, in Spanish. *Ilusión* means a hope or a wish, and furthermore, one that is particularly desired. It means the sense of pleasure that someone can feel about another someone or something. It is a thrill and eagerness, often used as an exclamation. And it is a daydream, which is where I landed with it for this book.

Its synonym, *ensueño,* common enough to also hold steady in some form, also means *daydream*. But to use that for both would deaden the musicality of the difference. So I landed on *fantasy* for *ensueño,* again, in those instances where it fits the meaning. The thing is that any words I chose for these two terms would automatically be reductive. Because *daydream,* while it builds the dreamworld that I need it to invoke, does not also offer excitement, hopeful optimism, and all the rest that is contained in *ilusión*. And, despite his omnipresent sorrow and longing, Castro's poetry is also drenched in that youthful optimism, alongside a naïveté that belies his already-rich life experience. I hope that this harmony of sentiment reaches across the years and through my work, and that these poems offer both a glimpse into his world, and an escape into an ilusión.

Introduction

Feliciano Castro, Cuban Key West, and the Dawn of U.S. Empire

Joy Castro and Rhi Johnson

In 1917, in the midst of Europe's Great War, a jobless young poet on his way from Tampa to Havana stopped briefly in Key West. He left the steamship and dined in a restaurant, where he overheard that a local cigar factory was seeking a *lector*, a professional reader.

Lectores were eloquent, well-educated orators who read aloud in cigar factories from high wooden platforms for hours each day to keep the workers—as many as five hundred cigar rollers—entertained. Because the tobacco laborers themselves, not the factory owners, auditioned, hired, fired, and paid the lectores, this entertainment was quite the opposite of a pacifying palliative for the exploited. Rather, in addition to swashbuckling adventure tales like Alexandre Dumas's *The Count of Monte Cristo* and great humanist novels such as Victor Hugo's *Les Miserables*, lectores read the local, national, and international news each day as well as recent (and subversive) political theory, including the work of Karl Marx, Friedrich Engels, and Russian anarchist Mikhail Bakunin. The Cuban communities of late nineteenth- and early twentieth-century Florida were anticolonial, anti-imperial, proudly pro-labor, profoundly anti-racist, and devoted to liberation of all kinds. Lectores, many of whom also wrote for the transnational Spanish-language press, were the intellectual rockstars of their day, delivering patriotic poems aloud at important social occasions and debating politics in the evenings in local cafés while crowds gathered to listen. As such, lectores occupied significant positions of cultural prestige in the Cuban communities of Florida—and a young, single lector also carried a certain level of romantic cachet.

Feliciano Castro, then twenty-four years old, had nothing awaiting him in Havana. His godfather and patron Rosendo López, after years of exceptional generosity, had died, leaving Feliciano without inheritance or prospects.

Born Feliciano Castro Verde in 1892 into a struggling farm family in Galicia—one of Spain's two most poverty-stricken autonomous communities, from which most Spanish emigrants to the New World flowed—Castro was nine years old when López took the boy across the Atlantic to his home in Old Havana near the Torreón, a massive seventeenth-century watchtower, and brought him up as his own. López also provided him with a classical European education, sending young Feliciano to Rome at age fourteen to study at the Pontifical Spanish College of St. Joseph, a Jesuit seminary in the Palazzo Altemps. St. Joseph's, which became Castro's home for the next five years, had been founded to train Spaniards for the priesthood, a vocation for which Castro was notably ill-suited. Yet he revered his teachers and reveled in the intellectual stimulation of his coursework, particularly in literature and history. At nineteen, he finished his education and returned to Havana to rejoin his godfather, who unexpectedly passed away, leaving his ward at financial loose ends.

Havana, moreover, was also the site of romantic loss for Castro. According to the newspaper *Diario de la Marina,* the young man apparently married Eloísa Vázquez there in May 1914 ("De Colón")—only to divorce the following year ("Sobre," "Demanda").

In 1916, Castro headed to Tampa, perhaps seeking a fresh start among its sizable Cuban and Spanish communities, but was able to procure only a job writing for *Bohemia* for $15—a little over $300 in today's terms—per month, hardly a livable income for even a single man alone. His attempt to seek his fortune had yielded meager results.

Even so, he had reason to believe that a lector position in a Key West factory was possible. His long sojourn in Rome and his rigorous education by the Jesuits had left him fluent in French and Italian as well as Spanish, and he was deeply conversant with history, science, and literary traditions. Young and vigorous, he was capable of the factory position's physical demands.[1]

And Key West offered the promise of a blank slate.

A lush tropical island abundant with wildlife, Key West was a tiny paradise, home to flocks of flamingoes, turtles, small Key deer, and iguanas, where fragrant frangipani, poinciana, and hibiscus flowers grew wild, and the island's markets teemed with varieties of seafood and fresh fruit. By the early years of the twentieth century, moreover, the booming cigar industry and its deep-water port had made Key West one of Florida's most prosperous towns, and cigar workers were among the highest-paid laborers in the state of Florida (Mormino and Pozzetta, *Immigrant* 68). A map of Key West published in 1884 shows shipyards, large mercantile establishments, several churches, a naval base, numerous factories, a convent, a town hall, a saltworks adjacent to Key West's two natural salt ponds, and hundreds of houses, from small workers' cottages to mansions ("Bird's eye").

In the early twentieth century, Key West still occupied, as it had for decades, one point on the so-called Tobacco Triangle of three cities—Havana, Tampa, and Key West—that formed the core of a global cigar industry that produced hundreds of millions of cigars each year; by 1915, twenty-nine cigar factories operated in Key West (Westfall 65). The three cities were also linked by a decades-long revolutionary commitment to liberate Cuba from Spain's imperial power, and since the 1860s, Key West had been a haven for Cuban nationalist rebels fleeing the chaos of revolutionary war on their home soil.[2] In the relative safety offered by Key West, they raised funds and gathered munitions for *Cuba Libre*. A rich and diverse local print culture supported this focus on Cuban independence, providing venues for its vigorous written expression: between 1880 and 1918, at least twenty daily and weekly Spanish-language newspapers flourished in Key West alone (Kanellos and Martell 285). Spanish expatriates sincerely devoted to Cuban freedom, of whom there were many, were warmly welcomed by the Cuban exile community.

Moreover, the residents of Key West were highly mobile and cosmopolitan. Well before the Florida Overseas Railroad connected their small island to the Floridian mainland in 1912, steamships ran regularly on routes that linked the tiny island to Havana, Tampa, New Orleans, and New York. Only four miles long and a little over a mile wide, Key West was nonetheless a center of industry, commerce, and politics. Much as Havana's heavily fortified harbor in Cuba, the "Pearl of the Antilles," had served for centuries as the gathering place of Spanish galleons before they set off across the Atlantic with stolen Latin American treasure, Key West, too, functioned as a gateway, a Caribbean entrepôt, a link between Havana's tobacco wealth and the United States.

The signing of The Treaty of Paris in 1898 ended the Spanish-Cuban-American war, forcing Spain to relinquish its last remaining colonial possessions in the so-called New World—Cuba, Puerto Rico, the Philippines, and Guam—yet Cuba's de facto liberation was short-lived, for Spain's colonial dominion was swiftly replaced by the political and economic domination of the United States,[3] fulfilling the fears of Cuba's liberation poet and national hero José Martí: "The hour is near when [Latin America, including Cuba] will be approached by an enterprising and forceful nation that will demand intimate relations with her, though it does not know her and disdains her" (295). His prediction was correct, and Cubans watched the unfolding situation closely. Even when Cuba followed the lead of the United States during the first World War, becoming one of the only Latin American countries to join the Allies, the political consciousness of Cuban American exiles in Florida and New York remained focused on the political drama unfolding just ninety miles south of Key West's shores.

It was in this environment that Feliciano Castro auditioned for the workers of the Eduardo Hidalgo Gato Factory, one of Key West's oldest cigar manufacturers, and, in 1917, its largest. Successful, he was hired and began reading aloud to cigar rollers.

It was a heady atmosphere. Politically au courant, the workers struck often themselves and were aware of strikes, labor protests, and liberation movements around the world, as well as Latin American, Spanish, and U.S. politics. Well-paid due to successful union organizing—and both contributing to and benefiting from local Cuban mutual aid societies that provided high-quality education and healthcare—the cigar rollers "considered themselves an elite group" of skilled artisans who absorbed and vigorously debated the ideas, culture, and controversies of their moment (Westfall 55). They actively shaped contemporary discourse, too, by pounding their *chavetas*, small cigar knives, upon the wooden worktables—their form of applause—which signaled to the lectores their approval and endorsement of particular passages. The lectores—many of whom also wrote for the international Cuban press—could then swiftly incorporate the reactions of the workers into their own arguments, capturing the mood of the masses, and Spanish-language newspapers printed in Havana were read by the wealthy Cuban independence community in New York City. In this way, political ideas circulated rapidly and freely among manual laborers and intellectual elites and between large urban centers and Key West. Lectores were a key conduit for that circulation.

Castro's three-hour shifts each day at the Gato Factory not only left him time for other pursuits but earned him the unprecedented amount of $140 a month, over $2700 in today's terms—an increase in his income so considerable that, in addition to writing journalism for *Florida,* a local weekly

(Kanellos and Martell 193), he soon purchased a half-interest in a local printing concern, Taller Tipográfico, where he learned the trade. Taller Tipográfico was owned by Juan Pérez Rolo—a connection that proved fortuitous in more ways than one.

An older Cuban émigré who had moved to Key West in 1869, Pérez Rolo was himself a writer of sorts. A child when he emigrated from Havana, fleeing the bloodshed of the Ten Years' War, Pérez Rolo became a printer, married, and raised a family on the little island. Late in life he wrote *Mis Recuerdos* [*My Memories*], an eyewitness account that records not only the conflicts (including pistol duels) of the growing Cuban settlement in Key West but also the founding of various societies, schools, and clubs—particularly the San Carlos Institute—designed with the purpose of keeping Cuban culture alive on U.S. soil while gathering and funneling funds and munitions back home to support the revolutionary cause. A lifelong patriot, Pérez Rolo evidently warmed to the young Castro's erudition and zeal for the cause of Cuban liberty.

In 1918, Taller Tipográfico published *Lágrimas y flores,* Castro's volume of political and romantic verses, and in 1920, Castro married Pérez Rolo's daughter Sofia, to whom one of the poems in *Lágrimas y flores* is dedicated, and who had herself written poems as a child ("De Key West"). They had a son, Mario, and Castro founded The Florida Press, which handled much of the Spanish-language printing on the island. In 1926, Castro was named the honorary vice consul to Spain for Key West and Monroe County, and in 1934 he became the administrator of a Spanish-language newspaper, *Cayo Hueso* [Key West].

After Sofia died in childbirth, he married her younger sister Virginia, with whom he had a daughter, Leticia, and another son, Libano. His position in the community grew: in 1937 he was unanimously elected as an honorary member of The Social Club Martí in Key West, and in 1943, he was installed as the secretary of the Dr. Félix Varela Masonic Lodge, which was named after a key founder of the Cuban independence movement in the United States ("Three").

The following year, after having rented various apartments since his arrival in Key West, he purchased a two-story house at 311 Elizabeth Street ("Key West"). With their three children, the Castros occupied the lower floor of the house and soon had two more daughters, Lourdes and Linda, while they rented the upper floor to other families for additional income.

At the end of the driveway stood a small building that housed The Florida Press, which Castro ran for the next several decades with the help of his sons Mario and Libano. Survived by his wife, four of his children, eleven grandchildren, and the eloquent poetic outpouring of *Lágrimas y flores,* he died in 1982.

The Transnational Literary Context of *Lágrimas y flores*

While clearly influenced by nineteenth-century Romanticism, Castro's 1918 collection of ninety-six formal poems locates his aesthetic firmly within Latin American literature's Modernismo movement, which was the precursor to other literary Modernisms around the world. The paratextual dedications and intertextual allusions of *Lágrimas y flores* also situate Castro among a transnational network of contemporary Latin American writers who knew and admired each other's work, describing a web of literary influence that fluidly transgressed national borders.

Ignited by the 1888 publication of *Azul,* Rubén Darío's groundbreaking collection of essays and poetry, Modernismo was one of the first literary movements to spread influence from the Americas to Europe in a first wave composed not only of Darío but also Cubans José Martí—whose 1891 *Versos sencillos* [*Simple verses*] is another of the foundational texts of the movement—and Julián del Casal and Mexican Manuel Gutiérez Nájera. Their work, as well as that of those who followed them both in Latin America and Spain, reacted against the realism and naturalism of the earlier nineteenth century, prizing art for art's sake, intellectual erudition (including a fascination with history and science), and an exacting devotion to the technicalities of poetic craft—all characteristics of Castro's poetry. Moreover, in the long wake of the revolutions for independence across Latin America led by Simón Bolívar, the nineteenth century's philosophical preoccupation with nation-building, and the subsequent growth in awareness of and fascination with the hybridized specificity of varied syncretic blends of Spanish cultural values with different nations' Indigenous populations, Modernismo also included a strong strand of patriotism—another clear preoccupation of Castro's, whose poetic patriotic fervor embraced both Cuba and Spain and instantiated the influence of both cultures within U.S. society in Tampa and Key West.

Lágrimas y flores also demonstrates Castro's connections to a web of contemporary writers in Latin America. Various poems are dedicated, for example, to Salvador Turcios, a noted Honduran poet and statesman; Rogelio Miqueli, an editor who was Castro's close friend in Key West; Octavio Monteresy, a lively Cuban literary critic who wrote plays for the local theater in Key West and reviewed *Lágrimas y flores* in the Cuban press; and Arturo Doreste, a Canarian Cuban poet and journalist. The year before Castro's *Lágrimas y flores* appeared, Doreste, in his own debut collection of poems, *Mis sueños y mis rosas* [My Dreams and My Roses], dedicated his poem "La voz piadosa" [The Pious Voice] to Castro.

Through direct references and concrete intertexts within the poems, moreover, Castro's volume interacts with the literary world of its day, demonstrating influences from his larger literary milieu, from Romanticism through Modernismo, that swirled on both sides of the Atlantic. His texts allude to work by Mexican poets Manuel Acuña and Juan de Dios Peza, and they mention José Martí, a clear influence upon his political worldview, by name. In Castro's construction of sea and nation can be read the impact of Cuban Romantics José María Heredia and Gertrudis Gómez de Avellaneda, and his work also resonates thematically with that of his Cuban contemporary, modernist Julián del Casal. Perhaps the two most apparent influences on his work are the Nicaraguan progenitor of Modernismo, Rubén Darío, and the postromantic Gustavo Adolfo Bécquer, the emblematic Sevillian poet whose infatuation with eyes and the potential creative force of poetry echoes throughout Castro's volume. Other poets from Andalucía who impact his style include the transitional Romantic Alberto Lista and Antonio Machado.

These Andalusian authors are not odd interlopers—not in Castro's corpus specifically, in the literary world in Cuba generally, or in Cuban and Galician communities elsewhere in the Americas—for the networks of communication and literary community that we can see among Havana, Key West, and Tampa existed transatlantically as well, even in the wake of independence conflicts.[4] Not only would Castro have likely passed through Seville on his way to and from Rome, but a large percentage of Galician émigrés went first to Andalucía, and Cádiz particularly, before crossing the Atlantic to Cuba. Multiple literary magazines, notably *La Ilustración Española y Americana*, brought together the work of authors from many nations. The expatriate Galician community in Havana devoted newspapers to its former patria, and in fact was responsible for the first printing of Galician poet Rosalía de Castro's (no relation) second book of verse in Galician (*Follas novas*, 1880). The circulation of workers from Spain to the Americas, and the transatlantic and intercontinental familial ties they forged, reinforced similar kinds of relationships extant from the colonial period and led to a rich, transnational, highly communicative literary community of which Castro was an enthusiastic member.

The Poems of *Lágrimas y flores*

The collection's direct and simple title (*Tears and Flowers*) indicates its clear bipartite structure and thematic organization. Its steady focus on Cuban and Latin American political and cultural affairs asks us to expand our conception of the concerns of U.S. modernist poetry.

The forty-two poems of the first section, *Lágrimas* [*Tears*], focus primarily on politics, patriotism, and conflict, a sphere that might traditionally be described as masculinized, yet the texts are suffused with expressions of intense emotion. As such, the *Lágrimas* poems lean heavily on Castro's Romantic roots, offering a truly vulnerable exploration of how the subject interacts emotionally with his world: in the tradition of Spanish poetry, a particular articulation of Romantic masculinity is embodied through a capacity and a willingness to cry. Distinct from the petimetre, the flaneur, or the dandy, which often entail superficial performance, this deeply Romantic version of masculinity is rooted in the same kind of vulnerability the poet here displays. The *Lágrimas* poems explore the nostalgic grief of migration and exile, including the loss of parents; the triumphs and suffering of history and war; the virtues of patriotism, education, and erudition; and the perils—both literal and metaphorical—of the sea.

In this vein, the poems in *Lágrimas* locate the collection firmly within the Cuban American literary tradition of exile,[5] rendering heart-wrenching moments of familial loss, as in the collection's opening sonnet "My Mother and My Flag," the sonnet "To My Father," and the collection's two poems—each of seventeen quatrains—containing the word *tears* in their titles, "Tears," and "Message of Tears." Several of the poems express a kind of anguished longing for companionship, as well as a sense of despair at the possibility that true closeness will never be found.

In keeping with the intensely nationalistic values of Latin American Modernismo, the poems in the *Lágrimas* section avow the poet's deeply felt patriotism, a political and sentimental loyalty that embraces both his home country of Spain and his adopted nation, Cuba. In these poems, both countries' flags are employed as meaningful symbols of lasting devotion, and the military heroism of figures in defense of both nations is celebrated.[6] By also invoking the Cuban and Spanish communities of the Floridian cities of Tampa and Key West, Castro unifies various geopolitical sites in a transnational solidarity that links all those who had been galvanized and shaped by the cause of Cuba Libre. A sequence of seven explicitly political poems deploys an encyclopedic welter of specific historical details to assert a kind of Hispanic/Latinx patriotic grandeur, both flourishing the poet's erudition via his extensive knowledge of history and establishing his political engagement with the liberation efforts of his own time.

In addition to Castro's patriotic engagement of Cuban and Spanish history, various poems in the *Lágrimas* section explore the loneliness and thrill of ocean voyages, as in the long meditation "A Blue Patria," in which "los mares" [the seas], despite their "tormentas" [storms] and "abismos" [abysses], are nonetheless "la patria de la vida venturosa" [the patria of a life full of adventure] that promises "nuevas auroras con sus esperanzas bellas" [new dawnings with their lovely hopefulness] intact. The dedication of "Cuba and My Beloved!," which reads, "On Board the 'Barcelona,' 1917," suggests that the poem may have even been composed while in transit.

The symbolic importance of the sea voyage to Castro—who first traversed the Atlantic from Spain to Cuba as a young child, made at least two additional transatlantic crossings during his adolescence, and subsequently crossed the Florida Straits many times throughout his life—is evident in his metaphor of a "barquilla" [little boat] for the human soul that must strenuously and virtuously navigate "el mar de la vida" [the sea of life], with all its dangers, romantic temptations, and vast potential. Several poems, including "A Blue Patria" and "The Fisherman," gesture toward this metaphor, and "The Little Boat and the Soul" spells it out plainly, emphasizing the isolation and vulnerability of the small craft against "the ominous waves."

As an antidote to loneliness and the perils of change, Castro repeatedly deploys the image of the bird's nest (*nido*, which occurs twenty times in the collection) to represent the safe haven of domestic bliss, a refuge filled with romantic pleasures, sensuous comforts, and the emotional security of fidelity. Though the title character of "The Fisherman" forsakes his home, loving wife, and little children for the temptations of the sea, numerous other figures throughout the collection choose romantic devotion and the emotional rewards of family life. For example, in the collection's only occasional poem to have been written in honor of a wedding, "A. Cermeño—R. Miqueli," which occurs in the *Flores* section, the speaker praises the couple for having created "un nido de paz y de amor" [a nest of peace and of love], wishing them a well-deserved "vida de mieles" [life of honey], "de eternas caricias" [of eternal caresses].

Three other poems in *Flores* describe the body of the beloved as itself "a nest," asserting eroticism's potential function as a welcome escape from the rigors and painful travails of existence. "Don't Forget My Songs . . . ," a passionate poem of eight sestets dedicated to "Consuelito" Rivero, addresses its recipient as "Mujer nido de ensueños" [Woman, nest of daydreams], while the undedicated "My Beloved" describes the lover's body as a "gentil nido de amores" [kind nest for loves]. The speaker of "To Sofía Pérez Rolo" (the young woman whom Castro would later marry) declares her body, too, a "gentil nido de amores" [a pleasing nest for lovers].

In his longest articulation of the nest metaphor, "I Have Here in My Room," which occurs in the *Lágrimas* section, as befits its tone of unfulfilled longing, Castro's speaker "envidi[a]" [envie(s)] the "pájaros muy bellos que se aman y se quieren" [very lovely birds who love and hold each other dear], two "fieles compañeros" [faithful companions] who enjoy the kind of bliss his own fortunes have thus far failed to furnish. The fact that the speaker describes the domesticated lovebirds as dwelling "en [su] cuarto" [in (his) room], moreover—not in his house, cottage, or cabin—resonates with the lonely reality of life for many migrant Galician workers at the turn of the century. In Tampa, as Ana Varela-Lago notes, boardinghouses sheltered fully one-third of Spanish immigrants, "reflecting the demographics of this mobile workforce, made up primarily of single men, or married men with families in Spain" (39). Castro's poem, which laments the speaker's "long hours of pain," ends on a note of yearning:

¡Si yo tuviese un nido y un ser que comprendiera
los sueños que he forjado con férvida pasión,
en vez de mis tristezas bendita paz sintiera
y en vez de un llanto fuera mi vida una ilusión.

[If only I had a nest and someone who could understand
the dreams that I have forged with fervent passion,
instead of my sadness I would feel a blessed peace
and instead of tears, my life too would be a daydream.]

Openly sentimental and tender as well as erotic, and essentially conventional in their moral vision of faithful monogamous love, the verses of *Lágrimas y flores* both depict the poet as bird—the singer, free to fly on the wings of imagination ("el bardo" [the bard] is a bird, one who longs to be "el pájaro cantando tu hermosura" [the bird that sings of nothing but your beauty])—and offer such poetic spirits the promise of a refuge, a home, where solace and pleasure can safely be found. The microcosm of marriage and family offers an intimate arena for the expression of loyalty and fidelity, those virtues of character that play out macropolitically in poems such as "The Cry of Yara," "Cubans, Carry On!," and "Silver Anniversary of the Spanish Center in Tampa," which urge readers to sustain their devotion to patria, holding up as models of valor those who have sacrificed for nation and liberty.

Following Modernismo's emphasis on erudition, in his eleven-quatrain paean "La Escuela" ["School"], Castro vaunts the great value of formal education as a "faro luminoso" [luminous lighthouse], praising institutions of knowledge as places of refuge and intellectual salvation—as the Jesuit seminary he attended, the Pontifical Spanish College of St. Joseph in Rome, may well have been for him. Also suffusing his work are the liturgical language and practice inculcated by his Jesuitical education, as in his sonnet "The Angelus," which refers to a Catholic prayer commemorating the incarnation of Christ. In this poem, a "labriego feliz" [happy farmer], ending his laboring day with prayer, hears the tolling of a church bell and cries, "¡Ave, María!" The angelus itself, moreover, is the bell rung thrice daily at times of prayer—that is, it signifies a form of community-focused physical labor that is tied to both music and spirituality. Even poems that are not directly about faith are steeped in religious imagery. In "Your Voice Is an Iris," which expresses gratitude for the poetry of F. Domínguez Pérez, to whom the sonnet is dedicated, the description of the speaker's apparently secular dark night of the soul is nonetheless shaped by Catholic concepts ("tenebrario" [spiritual darkness], "calvario" [Calvary]). While Castro himself joined the Freemasons—a group famously opposed to Catholicism—it is clear that the remnants of his early education exerted a powerful hold upon his imagination and lingered in his work. Though evidently not all the precepts of a school that trained young men for the priesthood spoke to Castro's romantic leanings, the rich education he received in history, rhetoric, and science infuses his poetry. His long political poems, such as "Spain: Hail, Flag of Mine!," "Cuba: Hail, Beloved Flag!," and "The Cry of Yara," are themselves an education, impressively recounting arcane details of Spanish and Cuban histories of defense and rebellion.

Intriguingly, despite the 1918 date of the book's release, references to the First World War are scant in the volume. Only "Universal Collapse," a long lament of war and inhumanity, may focus upon it. Yet many of the images in "Universal Collapse" that, for readers of Anglophone modernism, would naturally evoke the wastelands of World War I—"siguen roncos los cañones . . . / vomitando la metralla con fatídico clamor / . . . y una mole ensangrentada finge el campo en derredor" [the hoarse cannons / keep on vomiting shrapnel with an ominous clamor / . . . and the countryside seems a bloody mass]—could apply equally well to the recent devastation of Cuba under the horrific regime of General Valeriano Weyler, sent by Spain in 1896 to crush the ongoing rebel insurgency. The poem's geopolitical referents seem deliberately vague, as if leaving space for comparisons between European and Caribbean desolation. The poem's dedication to Santiago García, who was born in Sancti Spiritus, Cuba in 1881 and migrated to Key West in 1911 and would thus have witnessed the impact of Valeriano's reconcentration camps and mass starvation, suggests that this slippage is not coincidental.

Alluding to World War I with the lightest of touches is "The Cry of Yara," an occasional poem, the composition of which is temporally fixed by its headnote, "Poem read in 'San Carlos'"—the San Carlos Institute, the hub of Cuban American social, political, and educational life in Key West—"at the Celebration of the 10th of October." In Cuban communities, annual celebrations of the tenth of October commemorate the declaration of Cuban independence and the end of slavery by rebel fighter and plantation owner Carlos Manuel de Céspedes in 1868, and Castro had apparently been asked to write and deliver a poem for the occasion in Key West. He responded with enthusiasm: in nineteen stanzas of ten lines each, "The Cry of Yara" offers both an overview of the past and a hopeful look toward the future.

The reference to World War I occurs late in the poem, after a detailed rendering of the Cuban independence uprising. Cuba was one of the only Latin American countries to enter the war, a political anomaly among the Allies. As historian Ada Ferrer notes, "On April 7, 1917, Cuban president Mario [García] Menocal declared war on Germany. The declaration came one day after Woodrow Wilson's" (217). This quick echoing of the lead of the United States followed Menocal's general pattern of leaping to support U.S. political and economic interests in Cuba—to his own great financial advantage, and at the expense of his fellow Cubans. Menocal served as a willing handmaiden to U.S. imperial ambitions.

The seventeenth stanza of "The Cry of Yara" directly refers to Menocal only as "el héroe de las Tunas" [the hero of Tunas]. That is, the poem contextualizes him only vis-à-vis his admirable acquittal in a pivotal Cuban independence battle, the successful seizure of the city of Las Tunas from Spain in 1897, rather than either by his name or by any of his actions in the intervening two decades—a telling omission, given the veritable roll call of Cuban heroes that precedes the passage: Céspedes, Martí, Agramonte, Aguilera, Sanguily. It is as if Castro, aware of Menocal's highly mixed reputation due to his cooperation with U.S. imperialist exploitation, hesitated to memorialize him any more explicitly in the poem, though he does establish Cuba's current direction, and by extension its leadership, as a positive: "Y al valiente que hoy dirige / la nave ya rescatada / de la patria libertada" [And to the valiant who today directs / the ship now rescued / of the liberated patria]. Referring to the then-raging Great War in Europe simply as "otra guerra" [another war], the stanza expresses the hope that Menocal will repel any "huestes importunes / intentan campear" [inopportune armies / that attempt to campaign] on Cuban soil, and that, in so doing, he will rise to the level of "otro Martí" [another Martí].

In prioritizing Cuba's political security, not European concerns, and in refraining from lionizing Menocal, a collaborator with U.S. imperialist ambitions who had undermined the vision of Cuba Libre, Castro differentiates his political agenda from that of anglophone modernists and centers a different set of geopolitical concerns at the heart of his work.

Flores, the second section of the book, takes a significant turn, celebrating the beauties, delights, and comforts of the world of women through the language of floral imagery. To title this section after flowers is also to affirm Castro's connection to his new homeland, Florida; twice he uses the adjective *florida,* meaning flowery or in bloom, and the poems employ a variety of flowers—roses, polianthes (tuberoses), lilies, and irises—to signify the loveliness and purity of women, mentioning roses, for example, dozens of times, including numerous references to flowers' petals and perfume, and using the word *flower* itself over a hundred times throughout the collection.

Castro's deployment of this motif participates in a well-established visual and literary trope of the period, for by the end of the nineteenth century, visual representations of women always included flowers, women were often referred to *as* flowers in literary texts and the titles of paintings, and the metonymy between women and flowers signified their erotic desirability, value, virginity, suitability for matrimony, and availability to viewers or readers.[7]

While José Martí celebrated Cuban womanhood in the abstract, Castro's verses extol the allure and beauties of dozens of particular women, whom he honors by name in the poems' titles or dedications. Though initially seeming perhaps quite chaste to a twenty-first-century reader, the poems use delicately erotic imagery that springs from the tropical settings Castro knew well: the women's figures have the grace and poise of palm trees, the scent of roses flows from their lips, and their eyes dazzle like "inmensos dos diamantes" [two immense diamonds] shining "en destellos de amor" [in the glitter of love]. While praising the way that women's souls "guarda[n] de lirio la pureza" [keep the lily's purity], the poet nonetheless manages to smuggle in references to such things as "las gotas del rocío / en el húmedo cáliz de las rosas" [the drops of dew / in the humid chalice of a rose], alluding suggestively to female sexual arousal.

In keeping with Modernismo's great enthusiasm for scientific erudition, Castro employs unusually specific language to describe the beauties of women. For a poet to write, *Her eyes are like stars* or *She's as lovely as a rose* may be relatively commonplace, yet it is quite another thing to pen a line like, "tú robaste a los mundos siderales / dos estrellas: tus ojos seductores" [you stole from the sidereal worlds / two stars: your seductive eyes], or to "[pensar] en las flores de besos nimbadas, / pues ellas parecen tu imagen copiar" [think about the flowers nimbused by kisses, / because they seem to copy your image], or to describe a kiss as an "ósculos de amor" [osculation of love]. Another example of Castro's blending of the sentimental with the scientific is the word *iris*, which appears ten times in the collection. In Spanish, as in English, this word has definitions related to the refraction or polarization of light, anatomy, and, of course, flowers. In fact, the first definition of iris in the *OED* is "a rainbow-like or iridescent appearance; a circle or halo of prismatic colours; a combination or alternation of brilliant colours," even though that is not the most common usage today. It is also, of course, a part of the eye, invoking Bécquer and the gaze, discussed below. Yet most contemporary readers probably default to the flower—as, indeed, most of Castro's readers would have done, or perhaps to the rainbow (as *arco iris* means *rainbow* in Spanish). When Castro deploys this word, however, he is intentionally layering commonplace and uncommon definitions.

Many of the poems nod to the tradition of courtly love, for the speaker gallantly offers his verses as tribute, often noting his work's unworthiness in the face of the women's dazzling beauty, mystery, and sweetness. The thirteen-quatrain poem that opens *Flores*, titled "My Offering" and dedicated "To Dulce María Bravo, devotedly," announces in its first stanza the speaker's intention "tejer con mis estrofas muy bello un pedestal" [to weave with my stanzas so lovely a pedestal] for its addressee's exquisite beauty. In the sonnet "To Celia Avalo," the speaker "rindiérale homenaje a tu hermosura: / un himno le cantara a tu pureza. / . . . te ofreciera mi cántico, de hinojos" [would render homage to your loveliness: / I would sing a hymn there to your purity . . . I would offer you my canticle, on my knees]. In "Homage," the penultimate poem in the collection, dedicated "To Señorita Zenaida Barcia, Queen of Charm in Tampa," the final stanzas confess the speaker's lack of sufficient skill: "muy pobre fué mi lira, no pudo cadenciosa / verter la grata esencia de un verso todo amor" [very poor was my lyre; it could not find the rhythm / to spill forth the pleasing essence of a verse all made of love]. He pleads with his "Reina bella" [lovely queen] to nonetheless accept his inadequate "homenaje" [tribute] as heartfelt.

While the vast majority of the poems in *Flores* are dedicated to specific individuals, other verses, such as "The Factory Girls," "At the Dance," and "In the Theater," explore feminized social settings through a romantic, erotic lens as the speaker observes women. Throughout *Flores*, too, the power of the gaze, both the speaker's and the women's, is frequently explored, a preoccupation evident in the diction. Two different poems—dedicated to two different women—are titled "Your eyes," and the phrase *your eyes* occurs two dozen times in the collection, with *gaze*, *see*, and *look* also making frequent appearances. Castro's investigation of the gaze in his work seems to dialogue with Bécquer's ability to find the nature of poetry itself in the reflection of his own eye in his lover's:

¿Qué es poesía?, dices, mientras clavas
en mi pupila tu pupila azul,
¡Qué es poesía! ¿Y tú me lo preguntas?
Poesía . . . eres tú. (Bécquer)

[What is poetry? You say as you fix
on my pupil your pupil of blue,
What is poetry! And you ask this of me?
Poetry . . . are you.]

Throughout Castro's romantic poems, the speaker both observes women keenly and is himself compelled by the power of their own insistent gazes.

In *Flores*, Castro's extensive use of musical imagery works in the service of love and admiration—the poet's songs are offerings to the many beautiful and virtuous women of his acquaintance—and the collection as a whole manifests a deep concern with musicality, not only in the exacting craftsmanship of its form but also in its content—and explicitly so: the word *song* appears eighty-five times, *lyre* two dozen times, and *harp* a dozen times. There are five mentions of violins, six canticles, and seven hymns, while three poems refer to barcarolles, the songs sung by Venetian gondoliers.

There are a dozen references to musical notes and one to "los dulces arpegios del amor" [the sweet arpeggios of love]. In *Lágrimas,* the musical allusions intensify the elegiac tone, referring to the speaker's "canción entristecida" [mournful song], "arpa del dolor" [harp of pain], "canto funeral" [funereal song], "cantar entristecido" [saddened song], and so forth, and the section's focus on the various achievements of men is echoed in the dedication of one poem ("The Eternal Complaint") to Jan Kubelik (1880–1940), the internationally renowned Czech composer and violinist, whom Castro names a kindred spirit. In *Flores,* the self-conscious musicality of the work becomes even more explicit as the focus shifts to songs of praise, amplifying and transforming the thread that begins in *Lágrimas.*

While each of the poems in *Lágrimas y flores* stands elegantly on its own, Castro's arrangement of the individual verses within the collection as a whole also describes a subtle narrative arc with a clear developmental throughline, charting a shift in the psychological stance of the implied author.

The first three poems of *Lágrimas*—"My Mother and My Flag," "The Soul of Martí," and "Tears"—establish the moral identity of the implied poet as firmly rooted in a twinned devotion to his mother and his patria, via the symbol of the flag—and specifically, both the flag of Spain, Castro's country of origin, and the flag of Cuba, his beloved adopted home since boyhood. In the collection's opening verse, the sonnet "My Mother and My Flag," the speaker's mother bids him farewell, offering advice that foreshadows future conflict: "en el mundo hallarás mucho veneno, / pero el alma que es buena lo resiste" [in this world, much poison in your path will fall / but the soul that is righteous can withstand it]. She urges him to, when discouraged, envision "tu bandera" [your flag], describing it as "rojo y gualdo" [red and gold], colors that mark it as the flag of Spain, which functions as a synecdoche for "la patria los amores" [the comfort of a patria]. Though as a migrant he will have no access to his mother's embodied love, the fidelity to patria must serve to suffice as a source of honor and solace. His mother's final words exhort him to offer the tribute of "tus versos" [your verses] to his flag whenever his "camino de espinas está lleno" [way ahead should be filled with thorns]. The second poem, the sonnet "The Soul of Martí," describes a vision the speaker has when "muy niño" [very young] of an unidentified "tremolar victoriosa una bandera" [flag waving, victorious], bearing "franjas de perla y de diamante" [stripes of pearl and diamond] as well as "la estrella y el triángulo" [the star and the triangle]. Only later in life, after the nation's liberation, and with the benefit of mature political awareness, does he see that "el triángulo, las franjas y la Estrella" [the triangle, the stripes, and the star] mark the flag of a free Cuba. His allegiance—mystically conceived during the innocence of youth—has expanded to include a new patria. Composed in seventeen quatrains, "Tears," the third poem, is a cry of grief: the poet's long lament when, after searching in vain for his mother, he can find only her tomb.

Only after establishing at length, then, the emotional intensity of his deeply held commitment to family and patria, does the implied poet, in the sequence of four sonnets that follows ("Lie!," "The Pack of Hounds," "Why Do You Hold Your Tongue?," and "The Man Who Defames"), describe an egregious challenge to his honor. This challenge is the charge of plagiarism (already mentioned in his foreword, "By Way of a Prologue," just pages earlier). This sonnet sequence, though revealing, does not represent either Castro's strongest poetic work or the main themes of the book as a whole. Rather, it defends him against what were apparently charges of plagiarism leveled by his contemporaries: "no más de cuatro seres enfermos de vanidad y delirio de grandeza, intentaron, sin haberlo obtenido, hacer creer que mis versos eran de otro" [no fewer than four men, sick with vanity and delusions of grandeur, have ineffectually attempted to intimate that my verses belong to another]. The sonnet sequence functions, too, as a kind of bravura performance of nonchalant skill: *Plagiarism? Look, you scoundrels, at what I can toss off at the drop of a hat.* By publishing in book form his poems that had appeared in periodicals in Tampa and Key West—and, perhaps, some given privately to friends or circulated among small social groups—from 1916 to 1918, he stakes his claim to their originality. Thanks to the collection's first three poems about home and country, readers approach this defense-of-honor sonnet sequence with an awareness of how deeply felt the implied poet's commitment is to both his mother and his dual patrias.

"Lie!," the first of the four sonnets, immediately codes the plagiarism charge as directly attacking the speaker's loyalty, linking it explicitly to the previous poems: "Yo no sé con qué fin se me ha tildado / de ofensor de mi madre y mi bandera, / porque en versos de amor el alma entera / a mi enseña y mi madre les he dado" [I do know not to what end I have been branded / an offense to my mother and my flag, / because I have given in verses of love / to my standard [flag] and my mother all my soul]. The sonnet closes by reiterating the profound innocence, intensity, and purity of his commitment: "A mi enseña y mi madre idolatrada / yo les dí mi canción enamorada, / como el hijo a la madre le da un beso" [To my standard (flag) and my idolized mother / I gave my loving song, / like a child to his mother gives a kiss].

All four of the sonnets decry the vitriol and spite of the speaker's false accusers, and in so doing, Castro again flourishes his literary erudition, for his use of "baba" [drool] four times in "The Pack of Hounds" in reference to gossip maligning his poetry is a likely allusion to Clarín's 1884 Realist masterpiece *La Regenta* [*The Regent's Wife*], where a general dislike of sentimental poetry—and a specific dislike of José Zorilla's *Don Juan Tenorio*—is negatively coded as drool from the slimy lips of gossips. In deploying this allusion, Castro defends not only his own work and stature as a poet, but also the profound value of sentimental poetry.

In "The Pack of Hounds," the speaker asserts his determination to rise above the controversy: to "boga firme el bajel de mis canciones" "de la paz . . . a las regiones" [row firm the little ship of my songs toward the regions of peace]. It is this "row[ing]" that the remainder of the book then describes, for the ensuing thirty-seven poems in *Lágrimas* are devoted to the praise of those figures, near and far, alive and dead, who have comforted and consoled the poet, from personal friends (Domingo Milord, Rogelio Miqueli, Octavio Monteresy, Leandro de Torres) to admired musicians (Jan Kubelik) to writers (Arturo Doreste, José Martí, F. Domínguez Pérez) to liberation heroes of history (Ignacio Agramonte, Francisco Vicente Aguilera, Carlos Manuel de Céspedes, Julio Sanguily)—a kind of patria of the soul. The fifty-four poems in *Flores* then limn at length the comforting allurements of women, whose soothing caresses and exquisite beauty console and entice the poet with charms both maternal and erotic.

Only after immersing his consciousness in both forms of solace—the masculine realm of friendship, artistic achievement, and patriotic heroism, and the domestic sphere of arousal and pleasure, rendered psychologically safe by women's purity and fidelity—can the implied poet proclaim, in the closing poem of the collection, the sonnet "Final Page," that upon the completion of his process of "llamando a mi espíritu sereno / cada vez que una página escribía" [I cried out for a serene spirit / each time that I wrote a page], his "conciencia una cruz asemejaba" [conscience began to resemble a cross], symbol of Christlike forgiveness, "portadora de paz entre *sus brazos*" [bearing peace *in her arms*] (emphasis ours). After dwelling so long and so creatively amid the noble men and beautiful, caressing women he admires, the implied poet can at last, in the collection's final line, "darle el perdón al que me odiaba" [pardon those who hated me].

For Castro, then, *Lágrimas y flores* was a project driven by honor, by the urge to clear and defend his good name—which he is quick to declare in the afterword as "the only thing I inherited from my family," allying himself economically with laborers despite his elite education. While these paratextual and textual inclusions—the notes defending his honor and these weaker sonnets—may throw the collection slightly off-kilter in terms of tone, theme, and aesthetic quality, literary history is fortunate that a young man's honor was so stung, for none of the other three books that Castro may also have published—*Flores inmarchitas,* which may have appeared prior to 1918; *Horas de nostalgia,* supposedly in press at the time *Lágrimas y flores* appeared; and *La Ruta negra,* which was then in preparation—has yet been located.

We hope that future researchers will be able to find copies of these titles. Unfortunately, a paper trail in libraries and archives that could have led to our discovery of Castro's other volumes of poetry does not—to our knowledge and despite assiduous investigation—exist, though we hope some future scholarly sleuth might uncover its traces. Neither could we locate the charges of plagiarism to which Castro's indignant preface responds, nor any reviews of Castro's other books.

An exhaustive search of available digital archives and bibliographic resources rendered the newspaper publications of only 11 of the poems published in *Lágrimas y flores*. These, along with eight poems not in the collection, were published in the first volume of the Tampa magazine *Bohemia*, in the fall of 1916.[8] Of the poems reprinted from *Bohemia*—several accompanied by detailed illustrations—the new versions range from exact copies (as for "The Angelus"), to changes of only a couple of words or a new dedicatee (e.g., "My Verses" or "Why Wake Her?"), to almost entirely distinct versions of what are clearly the same poems (e.g., "Don't Forget My Songs" or "Time!"). While it may seem strange that so few original versions are extant, the archives of the Spanish-language press in Florida's immigrant communities are unfortunately far more ephemeral than many scholars in more canonical fields might realize. Works like *Lágrimas y flores* and the periodical output of the Cuban community in early twentieth-century Key West and Tampa were not considered worthy of even preservation, much less study, until recent decades. It is a precarious archive—more hole than net—that needs continued and immediate care and attention.[9]

We offer here this edition and translation of the sole copy of *Lágrimas y flores* in our possession, in the hope that it might become a useful resource for those who desire a fuller picture of poetic production in the twentieth century. In fact, we possess this single, fragile, crumbling copy of Castro's book itself only because it happened to be—eighty-four years after its publication—among the effects of a deceased relative of one of the editors. No copies are housed in the Library of Congress or any other registry or archive. No copies have as yet been discovered in other library collections. Even though Castro's book was published by a press (and his poetry is clearly in conversation with that of his contemporaries), Taller Tipográfico was not a press connected to larger distribution networks.

We regret these gaps in the historical record, a troubling aspect of the challenge of reconstructing a literary history long deemed insignificant by dominant cultural institutions in the United States, and we encourage future scholars to avail themselves of resources that may yet emerge.

The Achievement of Castro's *Lágrimas y flores*

Literary critics schooled in anglophone high modernist poetry—the classics of Ezra Pound, T.S. Eliot, H.D., Marianne Moore, Mina Loy, and William Carlos Williams, with their predispositions toward free verse, archetypal scaffoldings, allusions to ancient and medieval texts, and careful deployment of everyday diction—might be hard pressed, at first glance, to find in Castro's devotion to meter, rhyme, sonnets, and other inherited forms any evidence of an aesthetic response to Pound's famous dictum, "Make it new," and the experimentation of Anglo-American high modernists like Pound and Eliot has long held sway in the academy, such that even the stylistically brilliant, politically engaged, and immensely popular work of early twentieth-century U.S. formalist poets such as Edna St. Vincent Millay and Robert Frost has sometimes met with critical dismissal, despite the modernity of their thematic preoccupations, due to its reliance on inherited forms.

Yet there has been an enormous amount of recent critical revaluation of the many twentieth-century English-language poets who made rhyme and meter a central characteristic of their work, and many anglophone poetic traditions and contemporary practices are fully aligned with Castro's preference for traditional forms. For example, *The Lyric*, the oldest literary magazine in the United States still being published, was founded in 1921 and has always been dedicated entirely to formal poetry, while over a century later in *The New Yorker,* Adam Gopnik surveyed "The Rules of Rhyme," noting that most poems published in that taste-making magazine during the mid-twentieth century were formally structured. One major characteristic of the U.S. poetry of the past three decades, moreover, is a vigorous return to formalism and a renewed investigation of its possibilities: the magazine *The New Formalist* flourished from 2000 to 2010, and formalism marks the work of prominent contemporary poets from Dana Gioia to Brigit Pegeen Kelly to Boris Dralyuk, whose debut collection *My Hollywood,* which appeared in 2022, begins—like Castro's *Lágrimas y flores*—with a sonnet and features an exploration of intricate formal dimensions and constraints.

While Castro's clear preference for formal verse can be seen, then, to situate his work amid a significant body of contemporary U.S. anglophone poetry, his preoccupation with inherited forms—and his dazzling technical achievements within those forms—also urges our consideration of his oeuvre in conversation with the Spanish-language poetic tradition within which it most keenly resonates.

The poetic urge of Modernismo is intrinsically linked to the diversity in meter and rhyme patterns of Spanish poetry and its long history of using different kinds of meter for different kinds of work or to set different tones. Indeed, the poets of Latin American Modernismo looked to that history, drawing on the work of Spanish Baroque poets like Luis de Góngora and Francisco de Quevedo, and on the broad array of forms offered by that tradition: from the power and importance granted by the serious and elevated royal octave and the stately alexandrine (in Spanish, fourteen syllables in two hemistichs, rather than the French twelve, and used in Spain since the thirteenth century with Gonzalo de Berceo's *Milagros de nuestra señora* in *cuaderna vía*), to the sprightly, playful tone verse in *arte menor*—lines of fewer than eight syllables—or the lilting narration offered by the *romance* (eight-syllable lines with assonant rhyme only on even lines).

Nineteenth-century Romanticism saw another explosion in the creative application of meter, as playwrights like the Duke of Rivas and José Zorilla, as well as romantic and postromantic poets like José de Espronceda, Gertrudis Gómez de Avellaneda, Carolina Coronado, Rosalía de Castro, Gustavo Adolfo Bécquer, and their Latin American contemporaries engaged consciously in play and experimentation with the form of their poetry. In Espronceda's masterpiece *El estudiante de Salamanca* [*The Student of Salamanca*], not only does the use of meter form much of the characterization of the female lead, but the shaping of the lines itself also depicts narrative elements of the work, as lines twist back and forth to intimate the spiral staircase that the male lead descends before his life is snuffed out in a series of shrinking lines: from twelve syllables "En cuanto a ese espectro que decís mi esposa" [And as to that ghost whom you call my bride] (v. 842), down to two as he dies: "leve, / breve / son" [light / bright / sound] (vv. 986–88).

Modernismo, exploding in 1888, ushered in a new wave of experimentation, one colored by the movement's defining urge to revel in high culture and in the intricacies of literary expression. This rejuvenation of poetry across the Hispanic world is what John Kronik calls the fulfillment of the promise made by Romanticism (Romero Luque 116). The early decades of Modernismo are marked by a proliferation of new ways of using traditional verse forms, and it was not until the final years of the movement, after WWI, that free verse came to the fore. However, that hallmark of anglophone Modernism, an importation into English by avant-garde British and U.S. poets in the 1910s of the French *vers libre* form from the 1880s, did have its first flowering in the Spanish-language tradition at the outset of the movement, as is evinced by parts of Darío's 1903 anti-imperialist ode "A Roosevelt."

Yet most of Darío's work, and definitely that which sparked Modernismo, is intimately concerned with meter. On the composition of his poetry, Darío said that he always obeyed "al divino imperio de la música, música de las ideas, música de los verbos" [the divine Empire of music; the music of ideas, the music of words], a devotion Castro clearly shared. Darío's Colombian contemporary José Asunción Silva was said to be willing to "sacrificar un mundo para pulir un verso" [sacrifice a world to polish a line] (qtd. in Navarro 399). Innovations in this era, apart from the movement into free verse, were particularly concerned with stretching the boundaries of definitions by, for example, using a very traditional form like the alexandrine or the *romance* but shifting the number of syllables to change it into something new. It may seem that this shifting within an established form would make it no longer an alexandrine, given the detailed discussion of structure above, but Modernismo's love of making things new rejects that supposition.

Before entering into the use of meter in *Lágrimas y flores,* there are a few specific elements regarding the complexities of the structure of Spanish verse that the uninitiated will find useful. Unlike the English tradition's use of metrical feet (the iambic pentameter being of course the most famous), Spanish meter relies almost exclusively on syllables, and pays particular attention to the stress of words. Verse forms with eight or fewer syllables per line are *arte menor*, with their rhyme indicated in lowercase; those with more than eight syllables per line are *arte mayor* and are designated in uppercase.

Line length, the number of syllables itself, is impacted by a couple of technical elements. The first, the consistent use of the synalepha, comes from the Latin tradition: where one word ends in a vowel and the next begins in one, those vowels combine to make one syllable (*que estabas* = *ques/ta/bas*). This also happens when the vowels are divided by an always-silent *h*, except when followed by a diphthong. While two strong or accented vowels next to each other within a word remain separate, diphthongs of one strong and one weak vowel count together as one (*traían* = *tra/í/an*, but *emociones* = *e/mo/cio/nes*).

The element of Spanish verse that most affects meter, however, is that for the count of the syllables *each line* is considered to end with the stress on its penultimate syllable. Most Spanish words have this stress naturally, so generally, or in *versos llanos*, you can count as you would in English. However, where the final word in the line ends on the stressed syllable, or is only one syllable in length, this is a *verso agudo*, and one syllable must be added to the count. The spectrum extends in the other direction, so that a line ending in a word with the stress in the antepenultimate syllable, a *verso esdrújulo*, loses one syllable in the count.

Whether a line is llano, agudo, or esdrújulo also influences the rhyme, as the part of a word that must rhyme begins at the stressed syllable, so words with a standard stress rhyme from the second-to-last syllable, as English speakers expect, but those that end in a stressed syllable only rhyme in that last syllable. Additionally, while English has only one class of rhyme, Spanish has two. The first is consonant rhyme, the kind of rhyme that English speakers expect: all of the sounds in the ending of the word match (*lily* and *silly* / *lirio* and *martirio*). The second is assonant rhyme, where only the vowels match (*palma* and *canta*, for example, share an assonant rhyme on a-a, but do not match in their consonants: lm-nt). For those interested in the poetic form in this volume, the combination of rhyme and the use of versos agudos, with their stress on the final written syllable, is critical.

Of the ninety-six poems in *Lágrimas y flores*, sixty are sonnets—a form so traditional that its association with Modernismo may be surprising to those more familiar with the anglophone tradition. It is true that the sonnet form was first used in Spain in the mid-fifteenth century, had its first real bloom in the sixteenth century, and, from then until Modernismo began, maintained a standard of eleven syllables and a fixed rhyme scheme in the quatrains of ABBA ABBA, with most tercets following a CDC DCD pattern, with a couple of less-common variations. Within Modernismo, however, prescriptions of the form loosen, without diluting its power, and it achieves a new versatility (Romero Luque 116).

The Spanish Modernist sonnet encompasses line lengths from six to sixteen syllables, with a particular emphasis on the alexandrine sonnet (fourteen syllables in two even hemistiches), the form of half of the ten sonnets that Darío included in the second edition of *Azul* (1890), including "Caupolicán," which describes the great Mapuche war leader. While Castro's many sonnets include only two that diverge from the eleven-syllable standard, he does indulge with great gusto in the other major change in the sonnet form during this period: shifts in rhyme, owing both to the influence of Parnassianism and the exploratory urge of the Modernist spirit. Castro uses twelve distinct variations on the sonnet form in the traditional hendecasyllabic form, as well as one decasyllabic variation (used twice). The sheer number of sonnet variations Castro uses speaks not only of his knowledge of the stature of the form within the contemporary literary movement but also to his international experience and education.

The thirty-six non-sonnets in the volume use an astonishing seventeen distinct meters: fourteen in arte mayor, three in arte menor. Castro's most common meter, used in six poems, is an *alejandrino agudo en cuarteto* (a quatrain of fourteen-syllable alexandrines, with chained rhyme marked by the second and fourth lines ending on the stressed syllable), followed by the *cuarteto real* (royal quatrain) in five. While the most common lengths of lines in Spanish verse are eight and eleven syllables, Castro tends toward longer lengths, with fourteen of his poems using line lengths of twelve or more syllables, a tendency that signals toward a more elevated, formal register.

Like the content of his poetry, the form of Castro's poetry demonstrates his allegiance to the aesthetic principles of both Romanticism and Modernismo. Perhaps the most cultivated verse form in Modernismo is the alexandrine (including an expanded definition of the form to encompass line lengths from nine to twelve syllables). See, for example, the first lines of Darío's *Sonatina* (1895):

> La princesa está triste . . . ¿qué tendrá la princesa?
> los suspiros se escapan de su boca de fresa . . .[10]

[The princess is sad . . . what could be wrong with her?
the sighs escape from her mouth of strawberry . . .]

As the lines divide naturally into two halves, each offers a separate experience for the senses; this kind of divided line allows for a unified but dialectical experience, not unlike the function of the sonnet form, but without the restriction on length. In *Lágrimas y flores,* the alexandrine is used six times in poems ranging from the most sentimental ("I Have Here in My Room . . .") to Castro's most strident invocations of political activity ("Cubans, Carry On!"). Indeed, following in the line of modernist thinking, we could group all of his work that uses hemistiches under the broader definition of a modernist alexandrine, thus including lines ranging from ten syllables long ("Why Do I Write to You?") to sixteen ("A Blue Patria").

One other main tenet of Castro's poetic form firmly settles it in the Romantic/Modernist tradition: the use of rhyme that depends on versos agudos. Nineteen (more than half) of the non-sonnets in the collection and thirteen of the sonnets use the verso agudo as a main component of their meter. While versos agudos have always existed, as there are certain classes of words in Spanish that end on the last syllable (infinitive and some conjugations of verbs, monosyllabic words, certain word families), and the rhyme between agudo and llano lines was the subject of debate in the Renaissance, the function of this kind of rhyme structure was further classified in the eighteenth century. Ignacio Luzán, the author of the Spanish Enlightenment's treatise on poetry, *La Poética* [Poetics] (1737), held that aguda stanzas or rhymes were all but a necessity in poetry destined to be sung, and that this type of structure was also a positive quality in lighthearted verses (Domínguez Capparós 181). This kind of rhyme dominated in hymns and cantatas through the first part of the nineteenth century, before this stricture started to loosen (Navarro 380), though the musicality that Luzán saw in the verso agudo continued, as in, for example, Espronceda's series of poems to societal outsiders (pirates, Cossacks, a man condemned to death), which uses rima aguda.

The use of the agudo also influences stanza structure: having certain lines of the stanza consistently agudo causes structural subdivision, as in "On the Beach," where the septets are divided between the two speakers, and that division is assisted by the use of the agudo on lines four and seven. This intentional use of the agudo to subdivide stanzas also began in the eighteenth century and was first associated with the musical connection

Luzán articulated. As the form was useful, its general use outpaced this specific association (Domínguez Caparrós 69). Castro uses stanzas agudas in forms ranging from sixteen-syllable quatrains to the *octavilla* (different from an *octava* because it is arte menor). Across this volume, the use of this stanza structure gives a sense of lightness and of music to the rhythm and cadence of Castro's verses, as here, where we have a sixteen-syllable quatrain in which the use of rima aguda brings a sing-song lilt to a stately verse:

> Una patria azul, muy bella con sus brisas y su bruma,
> esa bruma que parece de los cielos regio tul;
> una patria donde flotan, cual partículas de espuma
> los ensueños, las quimeras, embriagándose de azul.

> [A blue patria, oh so lovely with her breezes and her brume,
> her fog that is like a splendid royal tulle that veils the heavens;
> a patria where float, like so many particles of seafoam,
> every daydream, every fantasy, getting themselves drunk on blue.]

Relatively popular in both Romantic and Modernist poetry, this kind of strophic structure was, along with polymetric experimentation, one of the main Romantic formal tendencies joyfully taken up in Modernismo (Navarro 447). And yet, even with that popularity, its use in Castro's work is still startling in its frequency, and when combined with the volume's thematic focus on the auditory and Castro's assertion that his poetry is a "little boat of songs," this type of rhyme and stanza structure is the physical manifestation of that musicality.

One poem in the collection particularly encapsulates Castro's *ars poetica,* and its structure is utterly unique. That poem, appropriately enough, is "My Verses," a poem about the poems in the volume and his thoughts on poetry itself. "My Verses" is composed of quatrains that alternate lines of twelve and six syllables, where the six-syllable lines are agudo. The poem's strophic rhyme is consonant on the hexasyllables and assonant on the dodecasyllables. While the combination of verses of different lengths is not uncommon—and, with seven- and eleven-syllable lines, is quite common indeed—and was increasingly characteristic from Romanticism to Modernismo, Castro's combination of hexasyllables and dodecasyllables is basically unheard of. Antonio Machado, a Sevillian poet of the Generation of '98, has one poem that combines verses of these lengths: "Fue una clara tarde, triste y soñolienta" [It was a clear afternoon, sad and somnolent]

(1907), but it does not use the verse lengths in a pattern. The poem "El beso" by Alberto Lista (2: 239–41), a transitional figure between Spanish Rococo or Neoclassical poetry and Romanticism, uses alternating six- and twelve-syllable lines with assonant rhyme on even lines, like "My Verses," but unlike "My Verses," it uses assonant rhyme traditionally: it continues through the poem without change, and the odd lines are unrhymed.

This combining of consonant and assonant rhyme—apart from a few examples at the very beginning of the history of Spanish verse—simply is not done. For a poet writing during Modernismo, this poem is the ultimate *Look what I can do!:* an assertion of the poet's engagement with the ongoing Modernist project, of his own mastery and skill, and of his boldness in playing with poetry. "Mis versos" does things that are not things, because it can. So while there are some pieces in the volume that are a bit formulaic, or where he has to add a phoneme to a word to make the meter fit, or where he seemingly accidentally uses the wrong rhyme pattern in one stanza, Castro was clearly both skilled and deeply invested in the creativity that Spanish poetry conventions allowed him.

The Cultural Function of the Poems: Mapping a Lost Latinx World

Even so, Castro was not satisfied with his work. His own sense of the collection's primary aesthetic weakness relates to the plagiarism charge against which it functions to defend his authorial prowess. In his afterword ("Notes"), Castro disclaims what he sees as "the repetitions and dissonances that must be found in this little book, principally in its second part," due to the circumstances that led to its printing—his rushed desire to set the record of authorship straight. Indeed, in the *Flores* section of the book, there is significant repetition, almost as if he possessed a collection of stock images and phrases regarding women's beauty and virtue that he simply inserted, upon request, into pleasing variations upon the sonnet form. As a result, a few of the poems feel obligatory, performative, even rote.

Yet even this quality is intriguing, because it demonstrates the social use to which such poems were put at the time. Some were composed to be employed as tokens of love by other suitors less verbally gifted, as "To América Cermeño" makes explicit in its second stanza:

> Yo quisiera de esencias infinitas,
> al tejer estos versos perfumarlos,
> porque sé que has de oír tú recitarlos
> por tu amado, de amor en vuestras citas.

[I should like with infinite essences,
on weaving these verses, to perfume them,
because I know that you must hear them recited
by your lover, full of love when you meet.]

This poem tactfully refrains from waxing lyrical about its recipient's lips, eyes, or other specific charms, and it offers its gifts of general praise to its interlocutor "sweetly" rather than passionately. Indeed, falling a few pages later in the collection is Castro's poem in celebration of Cermeño's marriage to Rogelio Miqueli, a Key West editor who was apparently Castro's close personal friend; they traveled together to Havana at least once ("El Puerto" 11).

Other poems were requested and collected as tokens of feminine social status for autograph albums, a custom popular since the nineteenth century among middle-class young women. In these little books, friends and admirers inscribed their praise and promises of friendship.[11] Four of the poems in the "Flores" section are noted as having been composed for such a purpose. Among these four, however, lies an intriguing distinction.

Three of the poems—all denoted with the line "In her album" just after their titles—follow the sonnet form: "To Dulce María Bravo," "To Célida Bravo," and "To Estella Bravo." All pleasant and accomplished, none of these three sonnets is particularly remarkable. The fact that the three recipients share a surname, moreover, gestures at the probable social situation that provoked the poems' composition, suggesting that the three young women were perhaps sisters or cousins, each requesting what the other had received.

Yet a fourth poem composed for a similar venue, marked as being "In the album of 'Consuelito' Rivero" (who is also directly addressed in a separate sonnet), follows a quite different verse form, and its title offers the passionate plaint, "Don't Forget My Songs." At eight sestets, "Don't Forget My Songs" is significantly longer than the other poems, and its language is laden with desire: "Mujer de mis ensueños, imagen seductora," [Lady of my daydreams, seductive image], it begins, "más bella que los rayos divinos de la aurora, / conjunto primoroso de nítida ilusión" [more lovely than the divine rays of the dawn, / exquisite ensemble of sharply drawn dreams]. The speaker refers to his own "alma enamorada" [enamored soul] and the "loca" [madness] that drives his "férvida cancion" [fervent song]. For Castro, formal deviation can signal specificity and emotional intensity, a release from the rhetorical obligations of social performance.

Indeed, much can be deduced from *Lágrimas y flores* about the social world of Cuban Tampa and Key West during the late 1910s. A revealing outline of the culture and its circulation of ideas emerges from Castro's many dedications of poems to specific individuals he knew and writers he admired, along with his headnotes designating the institutions and events for which he wrote occasional poems and the intertextual allusions included in the poems themselves. This detailed accounting of the people who surrounded Castro, their institutions, and their literary work offers invaluable insight into the social architecture of the interlocking Cuban and Hispanic exile and migrant communities of the early twentieth century. As such, *Lágrimas y flores* can serve as a rich resource for cultural and social historians of the period.

Three poems in the *Lágrimas* section, for example, are tied directly to key locations in the communities of tobacco towns. "The Cry of Yara" was read at the San Carlos Institute in Key West, as mentioned above, while "Cubans, Carry On!" was composed in honor of the founding of the Cuba Society there. One poem is titled simply "Silver Anniversary of the Spanish Center in Tampa." In *Flores,* the long poem "Homage" is dedicated to "To Srita. Zenaida Barcia, Queen of Charm in Tampa," referring to a kind of newspaper contest, common during the period, in which subscribers voted on the appeal and, often, level of community engagement of eligible young women.

The *Lágrimas* section includes poems dedicated to twelve men, including Canarian Cuban poet, journalist Arturo Doreste, and noted Honduran poet Salvador Turcios, as well as Key West residents Santiago García and Rogelio Miqueli. It also includes one poem, "Nocturnal Landscape," dedicated by name to a woman: Sra. A. de P. Rolo, the "excellent writer," who was apparently Castro's future mother-in-law, Antonia Pérez Rolo, the wife of his business partner. Among the fifty-four poems of the *Flores* section are verses dedicated by name to forty-three specific women, several of whom appear to fall (via their shared surnames) into nine different family groups. An alert reader can trace intriguing patterns.

Given the dozens of individuals to whom he dedicated poems, an interesting omission in this regard is Castro's business partner at Taller Tipográfico, Juan Pérez Rolo, who would soon become his father-in-law. No poem is dedicated to him. Yet we know the relationship between the two men remained one of great mutual appreciation and respect, for much later in his chronicle of Cuban Key West's early years, *Mis Recuerdos,* Pérez Rolo printed the following appreciation, which establishes the esteemed role

Castro occupied within the Cuban community in Key West. Describing the efforts to sustain the San Carlos Institute, which had functioned for decades as the center of Cuban exile life on the island and undergone multiple reconstructions, Pérez Rolo writes:

> Another fervent Spanish defender of San Carlos, like . . . so many others who have identified with the Cuban colony of the Key, was Sr. Feliciano Castro, constant fighter for good causes. In *Florida,* a local Cuban weekly, of which he was Director, and in different newspapers of Havana, above all in *La Prensa,* of which he was a Correspondent, he fought valiant campaigns for San Carlos and its construction, perhaps as no one has done it, with so much fervor and enthusiasm. Feliciano Castro is a man all heart, without caring ever for personal sacrifice, as long as it does well to his fellow beings. So I cannot cease to dedicate these lines to him, even if it is only as recognition of his labor for San Carlos and for the benefit of this town, where he is loved and respected. Today he is Viceconsul of Spain in Key West, a position to which he was elevated by the government of his country, doing justice to his personal merits. Castro doesn't only honor his patria, but also the community where he resides. (42)

Pérez Rolo's emphasis on multiple allegiances well befits Castro, a writer and worker who dwelled for decades in the United States but whose passionate loyalties to both of his original homelands never wavered.

A child of Spain who lived in Havana and Rome, an adult who thrived for over sixty years within the Cuban émigré community of Key West, a classically educated poet who worked in factories and print shops, Feliciano Castro complicates in his poetic production the vexing issues of nation, class, gender, culture, labor, exile, politics, romance, and desire that trouble our landscape today. His work, recovered in this volume over a hundred years after its publication, offers a way for contemporary scholars to enter into the aesthetic and cultural world of Florida's Latinx immigrant communities at a time when that history has never been more valued or more valuable in understanding the construction of U.S. identity.

LÁGRIMAS Y FLORES

Feliciano Castro

TALLER TIPOGRÁFICO DE CASTRO Y ROLO

Calle Southard 421
Key West, Florida, U.S.A.

A MANERA DE PRÓLOGO

Próximo a ver la luz mi libro *Horas de nostalgia*, opté por la paralización de su impresión, para publicar la presente obrita.

No menos que un dardo significa este librito, una vez que en torno mío surgió algo así como una jauría pequeña, insignificante de cerebros enfermos, muy pobres de espíritu y en contacto siempre con la inmundicia.

Lágrimas y flores contiene mis poesías que publiqué en Tampa y Key West en 1916, 17 y 18, en cuyo intervalo, no más de cuatro seres enfermos de vanidad y delirio de grandeza, intentaron, sin haberlo obtenido, hacer creer que mis versos eran de otro.

Sereno, pero adolorida el alma, oí los insultos de los pobres enfermos de espíritu.

Impasible, dirigí mi bajel hacia tierras de paz, y, a cada momento tuvo que romper las olas de baba, que, impotentes, querían mi naufragio. No he ganado aún la playa y, quien sabe, antes tronche el huracán mis alas.

Pero quiero que el público sensate que me ha leído sepa que no lo he burlado; hijo humilde del trabajo presente este librito, humilde también y pobre quizás, pero siempre propio, nacido al calor del trabajo y humedecido con el mismo sudor que rocía el pan de cada día.

Ahora es el momento oportuno para que de mis versos no quede más que la ceniza, en fuerza de crítica por todo el que a criticar tenga derecho; ahora es el instante propicio para obscurecer mi obra y empobrecer la inteligencia del autor de estos versos; pero es asimismo la hora por mi esperada para decir en voz alta que quien se atrevió a proclamar que mis versos eran robados, mintió gratuitamente, descaradamente.

Ahora es cuando los hombres los menos cívicos y lo más cínicos deben ir de puerta en puerta repartiendo la baba destilada por lo que obligaran o por lo menos consintieran que escribiesen seres indefensos a su custodia encomendados, trocándose en autómatas.

Ahora, y no antes, es llegado el tiempo de que periódicos que ostentan el título de defensores del obrero, lancen gratuitamente inculpaciones, merecedoras de ser pronunciadas por cualquiera menos por hombres dignos, directores de periódicos consagrados a dignificar el trabajo; hombres que tuvieron ocasión de conocer personalmente y ver como supo distinguirlos el autor humilde de este libro . . .

Sé perfectamente que mis versos son de escaso fondo literario, por eso espero resignado la crítica de los críticos, pero del fondo de mi alma arranco el mentís enérgico del hombre humilde entre la jauría de los menos cívicos y lo más cínicos y bastardos, que en su delirio mezcla de saña, hablaron de acusarme ante los tribunales de justicia por ladrón literario, por haber robado—decían, yo no sé por qué—los versos que este librito contiene.

A los tribunales de justicia nombro yo en estas líneas, para ampararme, como hombre justo, en ellos, cuando gratuitamente se pisotee mi dignidad por los viles que, no atreviéndose a dar la cara, desde la sombra insultan, por insultar, al que intenta dignificarse sin miras de lucro exento de orgullo, sin envidia de nada ni de nadie y del todo desafecto de pasión literaria.

No me sería factible responder de vilezas y cobardías fraguadas en la sombra para adulterar trabajos míos, como no podría autor alguno responder de la intención villana que para adulterar sus obras, abrigasen los imbéciles que circundan a los autores . . .

En franca armonía con mi sentir y proceder, a pesar de sus calumnias, recomiendo a mis detractores lean la última página de este librito, que armoniza con mi credo único: Perdonar al que ofende sin saber lo que hace, y erigir en mi pecho un altar de justicia para el semejante, profesando un religión individual: el trabajo.

F. CASTRO.

BY WAY OF A PROLOGUE

Despite the imminence of the publication of my book *Hours of Nostalgia*, I have had to freeze its progress to publish this little work.

This little book is no less than a pointed riposte, a return volley against those who have surged up against me, in their seeming a pack of hounds: insignificant, sick of mind, with weak spirits and an ever-present taint of corruption.

Tears and Flowers contains the poetry that I have published in Tampa and Key West from 1916 to 1918. During this interval, for all its brevity, no fewer than four men, sick with vanity and delusions of grandeur, have ineffectually attempted to intimate that my verses belong to another.

Outwardly serene, but pained in my very soul, I have heard these insults from men so sick in their spirits.

Implacable, I have steered my ship ever toward peaceful shores, though at each moment it was forced to plow through waves of drivel and drool that, impotent, ever desired that I should wreck. I am yet to find the safety of the beach. Who knows, perhaps before I do, the hurricane of their words will shear away my wings.

But I want my prudent public, my readers, to know that I have not tricked them. I, a humble son of labor, present this little book—itself humble, and perhaps a poor offering, but always my own, born in the heat of real work and watered with the same sweat that dews my daily bread.

Now perhaps, in this opportune moment, the force of the critique of those with the right to criticize will leave nothing of my verses but their ashes. In this propitious moment, perhaps I cast shadows on my work and impoverish the intelligence of the author of these verses, but it is also the long-awaited time for me to declare aloud that whoever dared to proclaim that my verses were stolen lied, gratuitously and brazenly.

Now those least civic and most cynical of men should go door to door, sharing out the drivel distilled by what they obliged—or at least allowed—the defenseless beings entrusted to their custody to write, transforming men into automatons.

Now, and not before, the time is arrived in which newspapers that ostent the title of defenders of the worker may launch indictments for no good reason, worthy of being pronounced by anyone but decent men, directors of newspapers consecrated to the dignity of labor; men who had occasion to know the author of this humble book personally and to see how he, for his part, could tell them apart . . .

I know very well that my verses are of slight literary basis; because of this I await resignedly the critique of critics, but from the deepest part of my soul I rip out the forceful repudiation of the humble man in the midst of the wild pack of hounds: the least civilized and the most cynical and spurious, who in their delirious mix of viciousness, spoke of accusing me before the tribunals of justice as a literary thief, for having stolen—they said, and I don't know why—the verses that this book contains.

I call on those same tribunals of justice in these lines, to protect myself in them, as a just man, when my dignity is gratuitously stepped on by the vile ones who, not daring to say it to my face, insult me from the shadows, just to be insulting to the one who attempts to build his dignity without a view to profit, without pride, without jealousy of anything or anyone, and in all indifferent to literary passion.

It would not be feasible for me to respond to the array of vileness and cowardice forged in the shadows to vitiate my works, just as no author can respond to the villainous intent that, to vitiate their work, is embraced by the imbeciles who surround the author . . .

In frank harmony with my feelings and my conduct, in spite of their calumnies, I recommend that my detractors read the last page of this little book, which harmonizes with my sole credo: to pardon he who offends not knowing what he does, and to erect in my heart an altar of justice for the same, professing thereby an individual religion: that of labor.

F. CASTRO.

LÁGRIMAS

Mi madre y mi bandera

   Hijo mío, al partir,—me dijo triste—
mi madre, y me estrechó contra su seno:
en el mundo hallarás mucho veneno,
pero el alma que es buena lo resiste.

   Nunca olvides que el día en que partiste
un consejo te di: que fueras bueno;
si el camino de espinas está lleno,
no me culpes a mi; tú lo emprendiste.

   Hijo mío, sé bueno, y si en las horas
de la ausencia, quizá mientras tu lloras,
rojo y gualdo un pendón te apareciera,

   Mira en él de la patria los amores,[12]
y unido con tus versos y tus flores,
dale un beso de amor, que es tu bandera.

My Mother and My Flag

My son, upon your leaving—my dear mother[13]
told me, saddened, as she clutched me to her breast:
in this world, much poison in your path will fall
but the soul that is righteous can withstand it.

Never forget that on the day of your leaving,
I gave you counsel: to be good above all;
and if the way ahead should be filled with thorns
don't look to me, for it is the path you charted.

My son, be good, and if ever, in the hours
of your absence, perhaps if ever you cry,
a pennant of red and gold should appear to you,

Look to it for the comfort of a patria,
and along with your verses and your flowers,
give it a kiss of love, for it is your flag.[14]

El alma de Martí

Para el Sr. Domingo Milord.

Una tarde escuchando la palmera
que cantaba y gemía acariciante,
sobre el ala del viento vi flotante
tremolar victoriosa una bandera.

Yo muy niño, quizás no comprendiera
lo que en listas de cielo vi ondeante,
ni las franjas de perla y de diamante,
ni la estrella y el triángulo siquiera.

Han pasado los años, y otro día,
al oír la palmera que gemía,
aquello que ignoraba comprendí:

Son—me dijo gentil la palma bella—
el triángulo, las franjas y la Estrella
un pedazo del alma de Martí.

The Soul of Martí

For Sr. Domingo Milord.[15]

 One afternoon, listening to the palm tree
caress me with its singing and groaning,
I saw on the wings of the wind, floating,
a flag waving, victorious, above me.[16]

 I, very young, perhaps could not be aware
of what in swathes of blue I saw aflutter;
nor what the stripes of pearl and diamond were,
nor even the star and the triangle there.

 The years they have passed by, til the other day,
hearing the palm tree as it groaned in its way,
that which once I disregarded, I could see.

 Those three, the triangle, the stripes, and the star,
—or so the lovely palm told me, gently—are
a fragment from out the soul of our Martí.

Lágrimas

   En alas del recuerdo bendecido,
que borra la fatídica distancia
alcé mi vuelo hacia el hogar querido
donde entre flores me arrulló la infancia.

   Hastiado de la ausencia el pecho mío
se lanzó tras la flor de la esperanza,
lo mismo que la nube que se lanza
tras la huella del sol en el vacío.

   "Y llegué a mi región encantadora,
como la alondra que al espacio sube
en pos del primer rayo de la aurora
que nimba de oro la flotante nube . . ."

   Presintiendo no sé que negra noche
abrí las puertas del jardín querido;
¡pero sus flores que arrulló el olvido
cerraran todas su oloroso broche!

   Llegué a la estancia de la augusta calma,
donde mi madre me arrullara un día;
¡pero, muy negra, la encontré vacía,
tan negra y triste como estaba mi alma!!

   El nido de mis gratas ilusiones
era tétrica estancia de amargura;
¡la delicada flor de su hermosura
la troncharan los recios aquilones!

   Buscando aquella flor fui tristemente
hasta la tumba de mi madre amada;
fúnebres notas entoné doliente;
lloró mi lira de sufrir cansada.

   Lloró en el extraño funeral gemido
que del triste cementerio el eco llena,
en las lóbregas tumbas repetido,
cuando en la obscura soledad resuena . . .

Tears

    On the wings of blessed memory
which blots out all fateful distance
I rode in flight toward that beloved home
where among flowers, my childhood lulled me.

    Wearied by its absence, my heart
flung itself after the flower of hope,
just as a cloud may throw itself
after a trace of sun in the void.

    "And I came to that enchanting region,
like the lark that rises into space
in pursuit of the first ray of the dawn
that nimbuses in gold the floating clouds . . ."[17]

    A feeling of foreboding in the black unknown one night
led me to the gate of my dear garden;
but lulled to sleep by sweet oblivion,
each flower there had furled its fragrant blooms!

    I made my way to the lands of august calm,
where once my mother sang me lullabies;
but, all in darkness, I found it empty,
as black and as sad as was my soul!

    The nest that sheltered my sweet daydreams
was the bleak estate of bitter loss;
the delicate flower of its beauty
shredded now by the cruel north wind!

    In search of that flower I went sadly
toward the tomb of my beloved mother;
intoning funeral notes of sorrow;
my lyre, worn down with suffering, wept.

    It cried in that strange mournful whine
that echoes through all sad graveyards,
repeats forever in gloomy tombs,
resounds in their somber solitude . . .

Entonces yo creí que no existiera
ni más amor, ni más cariño exceso,
que el amor de mi madre que me diera
el ultimo consejo con un beso.

Las rosas de mi amor se marchitaron;
la flor de la esperanza con mi gloria,
cual aves agoreras se alejaron . . .
¡solo quedó una tumba por memoria!

Allí, donde mis flores bendecidas,
de mi madre al recuerdo, cada noche,
con lágrimas de amor humedecidas,
bajo el ojo de Dios abren su broche.

¡Una tumba! Donde muere mi gemido
mezclado con el lúgubre y doliente
llorar de algún ciprés entristecido,
que arrulla los sepulcros tristemente . . .

¡Pobre madre! Mis labios no lograron
unirse con los tuyos, cuando, yertos,
al mundo de los vivos se cerraron
para abrirse a la sombra de los muertos.

Mas . . . oye mi canción entristecida,
que suena, al extenderse en lontananza,
lo mismo que una estrofa desprendida
del arpa del dolor sin esperanza.

Y verás, madre mía, que rompiendo
mi alma entonces las sombras de la ausencia,
en alas del recuerdo fue gimiendo
a escuchar tu postrera confidencia.

Y hoy ante el recuerdo de esa hora
que surgió de una noche entre lo espeso,
mientras que mi alma tras la ausencia llora,
te manda sus caricias con un beso.

Y siempre en la morada del olvido
y sobre el mármol que tu tumba sella,
mi canto será un rezo bendecido
y mi alma alumbrará como una estrella.

Then I believed that I could reach
no higher love nor more excess of care,
than the love of my mother who would give
her last kind counsel with a kiss.

The roses of my love withered there;
the flower of present hope and future glory,
like ill-omened birds that at their parting . . .
left as their only trace a lonely tomb.

There, where my blessed flowers,
remembering my mother, every night,
dewed with the tears of my love,
open their brooch under the watchful eye of God.

A tomb! Where my tears die,
amidst with the gloomy and susurrant
moans of a mournful cypress,
that sadly sings the sepulchers to sleep . . .

Poor mother! My lips did not manage
to find yours, when, rigid,
they closed to the world of the living
and opened themselves to the shadows of the dead.

Yet . . . may you hear still my mournful song
as it resounds into the distance,
resembling a stanza that falls
from a harp made of pain without hope.

And you will see, mother mine, that my soul,
breaking through the shadows of absence,
on the wings of memory went whispering
to listen to your final confidence.

And today, before the memory of that hour
which rose up amidst the darkness of a night,
though my soul cries after your absence,
it sends you its caresses with a kiss.

And forever in the house of forgetting
and over the marble that seals your tomb,
my song will be a blessed prayer,
and my soul will shine there like a star.

¡Mentira!

Yo no sé con qué fin se me ha tildado
de ofensor de mi madre y mi bandera,
porque en versos de amor el alma entera
a mi enseña y mi madre les he dado.

La humildad de mi nombre han insultado
con audacia falaz y traicionera,
alegando ¡traidor! el que lo hiciera
que a un amigo mis versos he robado.

¡Mentira!—sin orgullo le contesto.
La mentira por siempre yo detesto
del horror en el colmo del exceso.

A mi enseña y mi madre idolatrada
yo les di mi canción enamorada,
como el hijo a la madre le da un beso.

Lie!

    I know not to what end I have been branded
an offense to my mother and my flag,
because I have given in verses of love
to my standard and my mother all my soul.

    The humility of my name insulted
with an audacity false and traitorous,
he alleged, that traitor who would not balk at theft,
that I have stolen my verses from a friend.

    A lie!—without pride I answer him.
For lies I detest forever
with a horror at the height of excess.

    To my standard and my idolized mother
I gave my loving song,
like a child to his mother gives a kiss.

La jauría

¡Cuánta baba se vierte en la obra mía
por cerebros enfermos, corrompidos!
¡Con qué saña prorrumpe en alaridos
de los viles la fétida jauría!

Siempre baba engendró la cobardía,
y cobardes lo son envilecidos
los hombres que, en reptiles convertidos,
no dan cara jamás a la hidalguía.

Yo, surcando de baba un Océano,
huyendo del cobarde y del villano,
de la paz llevo rumbo a las regiones:

A través de ese mar de baba inmunda
que con olas de envidia me circunda,
boga firme el bajel de mis canciones.

The Pack of Hounds

 How much drool is poured on my work[18]
by corrupted and infirm brains!
With such cruelty those vile ones
break out in howls: a fetid pack of hounds!

 Cowardice has always engendered drool,
and cowards they are, the debased
men who, converted into reptiles,
never turn their faces to noble sentiments.

 I, plowing through an ocean of drool,
fleeing from the coward and the villain,
carry on toward the regions of peace:

 Through that sea of nasty drool and drivel
that surrounds me with waves of envy,
I row firm the little ship of my songs.

¿Por qué callas?

Me insultaste con pérfida insolencia,
como insulta el espíritu cobarde;
de baboso reptil hiciste alarde
¡Y ahora callas vilmente en tu impotencia!

¿Por qué callas? ¿Te acusa la conciencia?
Es muy justo que el reo se acobarde,
cuando escucha, temprano o bien más tarde,
la justa acusación de la inocencia.

No derrames ya más tu inmunda baba,
que no infiltra al espíritu sereno,
ni hace a un alma que vuela ser esclava.

Me arrojaste tu baba y tu veneno . . .
enmudeces cuando hablo y te condeno . . .
¿en qué, entonces, tu saña se cebaba?

Why Do You Hold Your Tongue?

    You insulted me with perfidious insolence,
like a cowardly spirit spits insults;
you made a show as a drooling reptile
and now you fall quiet in your impotence!

    Why so quiet? Does your conscience accuse you?
It is just that the convict should become a coward
when he hears, early or yet later
the justified accusation of innocence.

    Don't let fly with any more of your filthy drivel,
that does not infiltrate the serene spirit,
nor make a soul that can fly into a slave.

    You threw your spittle and your venom at me . . .
yet you become mute when I speak and condemn you . . .
on what, then, did your viciousness sup?

El hombre que infama

  Del hombre que infama no quieras ni el oro,
que puede aquel oro tornarse en traición;
rehúye su afecto, si tienes decoro,
pues brota veneno de su corazón.

  Y puede el veneno del vil infamante
en tu alma su germen nocivo verter;
no escuches tampoco su voz denigrante;
la voz que denigra te puede perder.

  Si acaso te obstruye con necia porfía,
procura no logre su absurda falsía
mancharte tus obras con el deshonor.

  El hombre que infama, que siempre es el necio,
inspira desdenes y horror y desprecio,
porque es muy cobarde, muy vil y traidor.

The Man Who Defames

    Of the defamer, do not covet even his gold,
for that gold can turn itself into betrayal;
refuse his affection, if you have decency,
for venom pours out from his heart.

    And the venom of the vile slanderer can
slip its sickening seed into your soul;
don't listen to his denigrating voice;
the voice that speaks ill can ruin you.

    If he should obstruct you with stubborn foolishness,
ensure that his absurd deceit does not attain
the slightest stain of dishonor on your works.

    The man who defames, who is always a fool,
inspires but disdain, horror and slights,
for he is but a coward, both vile and traitorous.

Es un iris tu voz

*Al poeta F. Domínguez Pérez
con afecto de hermano.*

He escuchado tu voz de visionario,
y el vibrar de sus ecos peregrino,
en el duro bregar de mi camino,
resonó de mi pecho en el santuario.

Convertido mi sol en tenebrario
yo no sé si por leyes del destino,
como un iris de luz, de amor divino,
me da aliento tu voz en mi calvario.

Es un iris tu voz, y en la remota
soledad de la ausencia, en cada nota
sabe unir de amistad con tierno lazo.

Poeta: yo no tengo voz vibrante,
pero en cambio, de mi alma sollozante
te doy la gratitud con un abrazo.

Your Voice Is an Iris[19]

To the poet F. Domínguez Pérez
with the affection of a brother.[20]

    I have heard your visionary voice,
and the vibration of its peregrine echoes,
in the hard drudgery of my path,
it resounded from my heart in the sanctuary.

    With my sun converted to a candelabra,[21]
I do not know if by the laws of destiny,
like an iris of light, of divine love,
your voice gives me strength in my Calvary.[22]

    Your voice is an iris, in the remote
solitude of absence, in each note it
knows to unite friends with tender bonds.

    Poet: I do not have a vibrant voice
but in exchange, from out my sobbing soul
I give you my gratitude with an embrace.

A mi padre

    Ya recorres los últimos peldaños
de la escala azarosa de la vida;
al mirar tu cabeza encanecida,
yo maldigo quizá los desengaños.

    Esa nieve que al hombre dan los años
al final de la senda recorrida,
deja mi alma perpleja, entristecida:
¡placeres e ilusiones son engaños! . . .

    No agigantes tu paso, peregrino;
poco a poco concluye tu camino,
que al final es la senda muy obscura.

    Vas delante: no olvides que venimos
los hijos tras de ti. Ciegos seguimos . . .
¡no nos dejes sin luz en la negrura!

To My Father

    You traverse now the final steps
of the perilous ladder of life;
on seeing your head gone white,
I curse perhaps its disappointments.

    That snow that the years give to man
at the end of his traversed path,
leaves my soul perplexed and saddened:
all pleasures and all daydreams but a ruse! . . .

    Don't lengthen so and rush your stride, pilgrim;
little by little your walk will end,
for at its last the path is ever dark.

    You go ahead: don't forget that we come,
your children after you. Blindly we follow . . .
don't leave us without a light in the darkness!

Una patria azul

Para el culto cronista R. Miqueli.

Yo he pensado en el misterio de una noche silenciosa,
contemplando las estrellas desde el buque en alta mar,
que los mares son la patria de la vida venturosa,
donde embriáganse las almas del romántico soñar.

Una patria azul, muy bella con sus brisas y su bruma,
esa bruma que parece de los cielos regio tul;
una patria donde flotan, cual partículas de espuma
los ensueños, las quimeras, embriagándose de azul.

Porque azules son los mares y los cielos y las olas,
y al correr veloz la nave todo azul se ve cruzar;
los ensueños, como espuma, fingen tiernas barcarolas,
y las brisas los suspiros de la amada al despertar.

Esas olas siempre errantes con que sueñan los poetas,
abstraídos por la dicha de lo azul en su redor,
cuando llegan a la playa, sollozando siempre inquietas,
traen sueños y esperanzas en sus ósculos de amor.

El Océano es la patria del amor y del misterio,
de las dúlcidas nostalgias, es un sueño de embriaguez;[23]
los acentos de los mares son edénico salterio,
y una urdimbre de ilusiones su azulada redondez.

En su inmensa superficie yo he soñado con mi amada
y escuché sutil su acento sobre lo infinito azul,
y soñando sentí el beso de su boca apasionada,
entre el mar y el cielo inmenso, bajo su azulado tul.

Yo no temo de los mares tristes horas de agonía,
ni las olas encrespadas de fatídico clamor;
si en los mares hay a veces ronca tempestad bravía,
hay también las horas gratas del ensueño y del amor.

El mar tiene sus quejidos, su gemir y sus ciclones,
sus tormentas, sus misterios y su tétrico bramar;
sus abismos y sus brumas y sus férvidas pasiones,
pero embriaga de dulzura su divino sollozar.

A Blue Patria

For the learned chronicler R. Miqueli.[24]

I have thought about the mystery of a night that's wreathed in silence,
gazing upward at the stars from aboard a ship on the high seas,
for the seas are the patria of a life full of adventure
where the spirit gets itself drunk on the most romantic of dreams.

A blue patria, oh so lovely with her breezes and her brume,
her fog that is like a splendid royal tulle that veils the heavens;
a patria where float, like so many particles of seafoam,
every daydream, every fantasy, getting themselves drunk on blue.

Because the seas are blue, the skies are blue, and the waves they are blue,
and as the ship runs on swiftly, all of blue it seems in crossing;
daydreams born there, like the seafoam, conjure up tender barcarolles,[25]
and the breezes seem the sighs of a beloved upon waking.

Those errant waves, ever roaming, about which all the poets dream,
themselves engrossed by the blissful blueness that is all around them,
when they make their way to the beach, sobbing and forever restless,
they bring with them dreams and hopes in every osculation of love.

The wide Ocean is the patria of great love and mystery,
of the sweetest of nostalgias, it is a dream of drunkenness;
the sweet accents of the sea are as an Edenic psaltery,
and a warp of intrigue, wishful thinking, its azure curvature.

On the vastness of its surface, I have dreamed of my beloved
and I heard, subtly, her accent across the blue infinity,
and in dreaming, I felt the kiss, the heated ardor of her lips,
between the sea and the vast sky, beneath the azure woven tulle.

I do not fear from the sea sad hours full of deepest anguish,
nor do I fear the choppy waves with their ominous groaning knell;
if sometimes on the sea there is a roaring tempest, unbroken,
there are also pleasing hours made only for dreaming and for love.

The sea it has its moans and whimpers, its groaning, and its cyclones,
it has its storms, its mysteries, and its plaintive, dismal roaring;
its abysses, shrouding fogs, and its boiling fire of passion,
but it wraps in intoxicating sweetness its divine sobbing.

En sus bravos remolinos, cuando ruge la tormenta,
en los rayos de sus iras, de sus odios y rencor,
hay instantes en que el alma la amargura experimenta,
mas, después de aquel momento ¿no es el mar todo dulzor?

Hay momentos indecisos y las olas se agigantan,
y el relámpago se enciende por la obscura inmensidad:
son las horas silenciosas de amor que se quebrantan;
en la noche de un minuto nos faltó la claridad.

Que después nuevas auroras con sus esperanzas bellas
se desatan placenteras con bendito resplandor;
surgen noches con urdimbre toda azul llena de estrellas,
y las naves fingen sueños en los mares del amor.

Yo quisiera allá, en los mares apagar mi sed de amores,
y embriagarme de placeres de unos labios todo miel;
allí a solas con la amada no pensar en mis dolores,
olvidando las tristezas que me abruman en tropel.

Que es muy bello en la azulada superficie misteriosa
de los astros diamantinos el divino reflejar,
y los mares son la patria de la vida venturosa,
donde embriáganse las almas del romántico soñar.

In the fierceness of its maelstroms, when the storm gives voice to its roar,
in the lightnings of its rages, of its hatreds and resentment,
there are instants in which the soul experiences bitterness,
but, after such a moment, is not the sea then all of sweetness?

There are uncertain moments when waves build themselves ever higher,
and the lightning catches fire all across the dark immensity;
they are the silent hours of love that crash and break all around us;
in the night when for one moment we lost our hold on clarity.

That afterward, new dawnings with their lovely hopefulness intact
burst forth, ever delightful, with the shine of blessed radiance,
and then fall nights too with their warp all of blue and filled up with stars,
and passing ships are pretend dreams sailing the seas of love itself.

I should like, there, on those same seas, to slake at once my thirst for love,
and get drunk on the pleasures of a pair of lips of pure honey;
there alone with my beloved I would not think once of life's pains,
letting go of all the sorrows that overwhelm me with their weight.

Because it is so lovely, on that mysterious azure surface
the divine reflection of the diamantine astral bodies,
and the seas are the patria of a life full of adventure
where the spirit gets itself drunk on the most romantic of dreams.

Yo tengo aquí en mi cuarto...

    Yo tengo aquí en mi cuarto dos fieles compañeros,
que son mis confidentes en horas de dolor,
y se hablan y se besan y cantan placenteros...
parece que me piden un verso por su amor.

    Dos pájaros muy bellos que se aman y se quieren,
igual a dos amantes en alas del amor;
y son mis compañeros tan buenos, que prefieren
vivir aquí conmigo sin una triste flor.

    Los vi cuando de amores hablaban con ternura,
después cuando se amaban también los contemplé,
y todas las mañanas, henchidos de dulzura,
al despuntar la aurora, sus trinos escuché.

    Se amaron mucho, mucho, forjaron un ensueño,
lo mismo que dos novios ardiendo de pasión,
y viven sus dos almas unidas por un sueño;
su canto es un idilio, su vida una ilusión.

    Los vi cuando se dieron de amor su primer beso,
y cuando se juraron eternamente amor,
y ¡qué de cosas tiernas, de dúlcido embeleso
decíanse en lenguaje de acento encantador!

    Los vi tejer su nido y entonces yo pensaba
que fueron más felices de lo que he sido yo;
pensando en sus amores quizá los envidiaba,
porque hasta un dulce nido la suerte me negó.

    El pájaro cantaba, rimando una quimera,
porque un amor tenía cerrado en su prisión,
y ¡cómo le adoraba su dulce compañera,
al par que ambos tejían su nido de ilusión!

    Por eso yo añoraba su dicha y sus amores,
y al ver cómo se amaban crecía mi dolor,
que siempre se acentúan del alma los dolores
viviendo sin un nido, sin dicha y sin amor.

I Have Here in My Room . . .

    I have here in my room two faithful companions,
who are my confidants in long hours of pain,
and they speak together, kiss each other, and sing pleasingly . . .
it seems that they beg of me a verse for their love.

    Two very lovely birds who love and hold each other dear,
just like two lovers on the very wings of love;
they are such good companions to me, for they prefer
to live here with me without even the saddest flower.

    I saw them as they spoke of love with tenderness,
and later, seeing their affection, I watched them there,
and every morning, ripe with sweetness,
at the break of dawn, I heard their trills.

    They loved each other well, so well, they forged a fantasy
just like two newlyweds, burning in their fresh passion,
and they live with their two souls joined by a dream;
their song is an idyll, their life is a daydream.

    I saw them when they gave their love's first kiss,
and when they swore its everlasting strength,
and what sweet things, of dulcet fascination
they would say in words and tones enchanting!

    I saw them weave their nest and then I thought
that they were more happy than I had ever been;
thinking on their loves, perhaps I envied them,
for luck has denied me even the sweetness of a nest.

    The one sang on, rhyming, chimeric,
because he had a love closed in its prison,[26]
and how she loved him, his sweet companion,
as they wove both together their nest of dreams!

    And so I yearned for their good fortune and their love,
and seeing how they loved, my pain yet grew,
for the pains of the soul are always sharpened
by living without a nest, without good fortune, without love.

Después de amarse mucho, de amores en su nido,
nacieron sus hijitos que endulzan su vivir,
y ahora los contemplo, los miro enternecido,
y envídioles su vida sin llantos ni sufrir.
. . . .

¡Si yo tuviese un nido y un ser que comprendiera
los sueños que he forjado con férvida pasión,
en vez de mis tristezas bendita paz sintiera
y en vez de un llanto fuera mi vida una ilusión.

After loving each other so well, from their loves in their nest,
their little ones were born, who make life so much sweeter,
and now I see them there, I watch them, with my heart gone soft,
and I envy them their life free from tears and suffering.
. . . .

    If only I had a nest and someone who could understand
the dreams that I have forged with fervent passion,
instead of my sadness I would feel a blessed peace
and instead of tears, my life too would be a daydream.

Las palmas

    Yo no sé lo que tienen sus gemidos;
los rumores y el eco de las palmas
unas veces antójanse quejidos
y otras veces suspiros de las almas.

    Ora son como arrullos sus rumores,
ora fingen verter intenso llanto;
unas veces avivan los dolores
y otras veces alegran con su canto.

    Oyéndolas, las creo hermanas mías,
porque dicen de penas y alegrías,
porque dicen de amor y de aflicciones.

    Palmas bellas igual a vuestro canto,
de alegría, de amores y de llanto,
son los ecos que dejan mis canciones.

The Palms

    I don't know what to read in the groans,
the murmurings and the echo of the palms
sometimes they seem to be moans,
and other times the sighing of souls.

    Now their sounds are like a lullaby,
now they seem to overflow with tears;
sometimes they stoke the fires of pains
and other times they bring joy with their song.

    Hearing them, I see them as my sisters,
because they speak of sorrows and of joys,
because they speak of love and of affliction.

    Beautiful palms, just like your singing
of joy, of loves, and of tears,
are the echoes that my songs leave behind.

El tiempo

*Para el eximio poeta y publicista
hondureño D. Salvador Turcios R.*

Es un átomo perdido, más sutil que una añoranza
desprendida de las rosas del jardín de la esperanza,
donde ansioso forja el hombre las quimeras del vivir;
es un hálito de vida que, al nacer, sutil nos besa;
es lo mismo que la estela que dejara una promesa
que en los cielos del ensueño se lograra percibir.

Ese arcano que es un algo sin dejar de ser la nada,
sobre el ala de misterio, siempre en marcha agigantada,
relegando va los siglos al abismo del no ser;
a su paso jamás queda ni una página de historia,
pues tan solo el hombre guarda de los tiempos la memoria,
porque sabe que los tiempos le besaron al nacer.

Y fue un día que los hombres a un Filósofo llamaron,
y anhelantes y curiosos ¿qué es el tiempo —preguntaron—
esos días y esas noches en continua sucesión?
y aquel Sabio contestóles: "cuando nadie preguntaba
yo sabía qué era el tiempo, fácilmente lo explicaba,
pero cuando me preguntan no sé dar explicación."

Porque el tiempo, cual los mares, tiene abismos insondables
y los días, cual las olas en vaivén, interminables,
de la vida van rompiéndose en las rocas del dolor;
y los años y los siglos en su marcha agigantada
son revuelto torbellino que del ser hacia la nada
va lanzando las edades con indómito furor.

Cual las águilas caudales, remontado a las alturas,
majestuoso mide el hombre del espacio las anchuras,
y con mágica destreza surca intrépido la mar;
descubriendo de la tierra los secretos misteriosos,
acortando las distancias, los caminos azarosos,
en su anhelo de victoria quiere todo conquistar.

Pero el hombre que divaga, travesando las esferas,
errabundo que persigue la ilusión de sus quimeras
y que busca sin espinas un camino al corazón,

Time[27]

> *For the illustrious Honduran poet and publicist*
> *Don Salvador Turcios R.*[28]

It is a single missing atom, subtler than the faint longing
given off by each rose grown in the garden of hope
where man anxiously forges his chimeric, illusory life;
it is the wafting breath of life, which at birth kisses us subtly;
it is the same as the wake left behind by a passing promise
which, in the sky of a daydream, hovers at the edge of perception.

That enigma which is some thing, without ceasing to be nothing,
riding the wings of mystery, always made giant on its way;
it relegates the centuries to the abyss of not being,
its passing never leaving a mark in the pages of history,
for it is only man who keeps a memory of time's passing
because he knows that time gave that kiss to him at birth.

And one day the men called to them a philosopher,
and eagerly and curious they brought the question: "What is time,
all of those days and of those nights in continuous succession?"
and the sage came to his answer: "in the time when no one asked me,
I used to know well what time was, and I explained it easily,
but now that you come and ask me, I have no ready words."

Because time, like unto the seas, has unfathomable chasms
and a life's days, like the sea's waves that rise and fall, unendingly,
go on breaking themselves over and against the rocks of sorrow;
and the years and the centuries in their exaggerated march
are a topsy-turvy whirlwind which from being into nothing
goes on launching off the ages with indomitable fury.

Like the royal golden eagles, carried up to the greatest heights,
majestic, man takes the measure of space in all of its spanned breadth,
and with a magic knowledge he sails, intrepid, across the seas;
dredging out of every land the mysterious secrets that it holds,
making shorter the distances, the fateful peril of the way;
with his eagerness for triumph, he wants to conquer all.

But the man whose way is rambling, in his traversing of the spheres,
the wandering one who pursues the illusion of his fantasies
and who seeks without a single thorn a pathway to the heart

ante el soplo de los tiempos abrumado se detiene,
sin saber de los arcanos en que gira y se sostiene
esa órbita ignorada de continua sucesión.

Pues la rueda de los tiempos silenciosa va girando,
y el reloj intransigente de la vida va marcando
paso a paso de los hombres las etapas de dolor:
les la rueda abrumadora que en olímpica carrera,
no se aparta de la ruta que trazada apareciera
en el libro del destino por el dedo creador!

Y el propósito del hombre de triunfar sobre la vida
es tan solo un ansia loca por la dicha apetecida,
que en titánicos esfuerzos cree, necio, conquistar;
pero triste y errabundo, como eterno peregrino,
cuando apenas, altanero, va empezando su camino,
sus anhelos tras la tumba ve por siempre sepultar . . .

before the blowing breeze of time weighted down he must come to pause,
without knowing the enigmas in which he spins and holds himself
that disregarded orbit in its never-ending surge.

    Well, the wheel of all the ages goes on, silent, in its spinning,
and the uncompromising clock of life keeps on marking,
step by step, for all mankind the stages of pain and sorrow:
it is the devastating wheel that in its Olympian race,
does not move aside from the route that has been traced
in the book of destiny by the finger of the creator!

    And man's single-minded purpose to triumph over life itself
is but a crazy yearning for the fortune that he fancies,
such that by titanic effort he thinks, foolish, that he'll conquer;
but unhappy and wandering, like an eternal pilgrim,
when just barely, in his swagger, he is beginning on his way,
he sees his yearnings in a grave forever laid to rest . . .

La eterna queja

Para "Kubelik," mi desconocido amigo.

Yo adivino la pena que devora
al que ha perdido una ilusión querida;
yo también, como tú tengo una herida
aquí, en el corazón desgarradora.

Yo adivino la angustia del que llora
sin un beso de amor que le dé vida,
que es muy triste una senda recorrida
sin la luz del amor consoladora.

Lo adivino y lo sé, porque mi lira,
al hablar del amor siempre se inspira,
y al sentir el dolor nunca se calla.

Voy regando la senda con mi llanto;
doy a las penas y al amor mi canto,
¡pero mi queja la respuesta no halla!

The Eternal Complaint

For "Kubelik," my unknown friend.[29]

    I divine the sorrow that devours
him who has lost a beloved dream;
I as well, like you, have a wound
here, unbearable in my heart.

    I divine the anguish of him who cries
bereft of any kiss of love granted him by life,
for it is a very sad path to travel
without the light of a consoling love.

    I divine it and I know it, for my lyre,
on speaking of love is always inspired
and on feeling pain never quiets.

    I go on now, watering the path with my tears;
I give to sorrows and to loves my songs,
but my complaint finds no response.

La escuela

   Es faro luminoso, el áncora sublime
que ampáranos en medio del recio vendaval:
el áncora divina que salva y que redime
al mundo de un horrible naufragio universal.

   Se crean a su amparo, con santa dulcedumbre,
espíritus sencillos, bañados de candor,
y aquella de la escuela la bienhechora lumbre
los trueca en los robustos contenes del dolor.

   Lo mismo que los cuerpos el pan del alimento
exígennos en lucha del acendrado afán,
las almas nos recaban el pan del sentimiento,
el pan de las escuelas que es el divino pan.

   El niño no divisa lumínicas auroras
que habrán de darle luces en medio del vivir,
sino cuando se eleva con alas voladoras
por medio de la escuela que enséñale a sentir.

   El padre que a sus hijos legara solamente
las horas de colegio por toda religión,
hubiérales legado un casi omnipotente
factor de inmensa dicha: la santa educación.

   Por eso los maestros que afrontan el desvelo
de darnos su caricia con verbo bienhechor,
son casi nuestros padres que encauzan nuestro anhelo
por bellos derroteros, con ansia y con amor.

   Aquella de maestro tarea educativa
que tiene su bendita simiente en el hogar,
despierta en nuestras almas la bella perspectiva
de que sin las escuelas podemos naufragar.

   Son vida las escuelas, son pan santificado
que brota de la entraña de un santo manantial,
que brota de la entraña del libro en que han libado
las almas de los niños su férvido ideal.

School

It is a luminous lighthouse, the sublime anchor
that shelters us in the midst of a fierce gale:
the divine anchor that saves and that redeems
the world from a horrific and universal wreck.

They create this shelter, with sainted sweetness
simple spirits, bathed in candor,
and the benefactor hearth of the school
makes them into robust curbs to pain.

Just as our bodies the bread of nourishment
demand of us in the fight of untarnished eagerness,
the souls demand of us the bread of sentiment,
the daily bread of the schools that is divine.

The child cannot make out the luminous dawns
that will give him light in the midst of his life,
save for when he rises on flying wings
by means of the school that teaches him to feel.

The father who to his sons bequeaths only
hours of instruction as a lone religion,
would bequeath to them an almost omnipotent
factor of immense good fortune: a sainted education.

And so, the teachers who confront a lack of sleep
by giving us their caress with a kind-hearted word
are almost our parents, who channel our yearning
by lovely paths, with eagerness and love.

That educative toil of the teacher
that has its blessed seed in the home,
awakens in our souls the dear perspective
that without schools our ship can wreck.

The schools are life, they are the sanctified bread
that pours forth from the depths of a sainted spring,
that pours forth from the depths of the book from which
the souls of the boys have sipped fervid ideals.

Sagrario inmaculado que guarda de ilusiones
un célico tesoro de grata esplendidez;
que encierra los latidos de tiernos corazones,
que alberga el sentimiento feliz de la niñez.

Sin esos de la escuela benditos valladares
en que de las pasiones estréllase el rugir,
¿qué fuera de los hombres en medio de los mares
que en bruscos remolinos agitan el vivir? . . .

La escuela es de los hombres el áncora sublime
queампáralos en medio del recio vendaval,
el áncora divina que salva y que redime
al mundo de un horrible naufragio universal.

Immaculate sanctuary that keeps of daydreams
a heavenly treasure of pleasing splendor;
that encloses the beatings of tender hearts,
that harbors the happy feeling of childhood.

Without those blessed ramparts of the schools
against which the roar of passions crashes,
what would become of the men in the wide sea
which in abrupt eddies agitates life? . . .

School is for men the sublime anchor
that shelters them in the midst of a fierce gale:
the divine anchor that saves and that redeems
the world from a horrific and universal wreck.

Página gris

Para O. J. Monteresy.

La tarde en Occidente se apagaba;
el velo de la noche se extendía;
y allá, tras la casucha tosca y fría
una luz moribunda se asomaba.

La brisa sus canciones modulaba
de la tarde a la plácida agonía,
en tanto aquel lucero se extinguía,
fingiendo una ilusión que se acababa.

Yo también a la tarde agonizante,
con el alma de ensueños embriagada,
fui tejiendo un cantar acariciante.

Y aquella mi canción enamorada
fue una estrofa de ensueño delirante,
que con besos tejí para la amada . . .

Gray Page

For O. J. Monteresy.[30]

    The gloaming went, quenching itself in the West;
the shadows of night beginning to unfurl;
and there, just behind the cabin, rough and cold
a moribund light flickeringly peeked out.

    The breeze was modulating the key of its song,
from the afternoon to placid agony,
as that half hidden light winked out again,
as if it were a mirage that found its end.

    I too, to the dying fading afternoon,
with my soul made drunk on flighty fantasies,
went weaving thread by thread a caressing song.

    And that song of mine, itself wrapped up in love
was a stanza of delirious desires,
which with kisses I wove for my beloved . . .

El derrumbe universal

Para Santiago García.

Sigue el hombre desatando sus pasiones furibundas,
siguen roncos los cañones por sus bocas tremebundas
vomitando la metralla con fatídico clamor;
cada día silba el plomo, se agigantan los horrores,
surge el humo en espirales, como nubes de Dolores,
y una mole ensangrentada finge el campo en derredor.

Cada día se levantan de cadáveres montañas,
diariamente beben sangre de la tierra las entrañas,
y atraviesa corazones de mil madres el puñal;
cada día, como espectros que reflejan los pesares,
sin hogar y sin cariño surgen niños a millares,
contemplando los escombros del derrumbe universal.

Es el rayo que fulminan los torrentes de guerreros
que, en fatídico alboroto y al chocar de los aceros,
hacen moles de granito, cuando pasan, conmover;
son las balas silbadoras, la mortífera metralla,
el intenso remolino que refleja la batalla...
¡es la noche de los lutos que no tiene amanecer!

Ruge el mundo y se estremece, centellean sus entrañas,
sus llanuras son sepulcros y son tumbas sus montañas,
y ¡cuán lúgubre en las tumbas suena el eco del clarín!
gime el viento, llora el aura del dolor en lo infinito;
derribáronse los pueblos y los montes de granito,
y los ríos sangre arrastran de un confín a otro confín.

Llora el Arte como lloran desgarrándose las Ciencias,
el Progreso y las Industrias, la Fe misma y las Creencias,
peregrinos de la muerte, de venganza van en pos;
¡bajo escombros los Poderes, los Imperios y cuidados
y esos Códices y Leyes que alumbraban las edades!...
Tal parece que los hombres ciegos luchan contra Dios.

Dios eterno: si eres justo, como el orbe te proclama,
¿por qué niegas a los hombres un destello de tu llama,
que a esta noche de los lutos trueque en bella claridad?
¿por qué inmenso no les mandas desde el solio de tu cumbre

The Universal Collapse

For Santiago García.[31]

    Man lets loose his frenzied passions without end,
from out their savage mouths the hoarse cannons
keep on vomiting shrapnel with an ominous clamor;
every day the lead whistles, the horrors grow giant,
the smoke rises in spirals like clouds of pains,
and the countryside seems a bloody mass.

    Every day, mountains of cadavers pile up,
daily the entrails of the earth drink blood,
and a dagger pierces the heart of a thousand mothers;
every day, like ghosts that reflect their sorrows,
without a home and without care thousands of children rise,
contemplating the debris of the universal collapse.

    It is the lightning that strikes down the torrents of warriors
who, in ominous uproar and on the clashing of blades,
manage to shift masses of granite on their passing;
it is the whistling bullets, the lethal shrapnel,
the intense whirlwind that reflects the battle . . .
it is a night of mourning that has no dawn!

    The world roars and trembles, its entrails flash with light,
its plains are sepulchers and tombs are its mountains,
and how mournful sounds the echo of the bugle in a tomb!
The wind whines, the ripples of pain cry out to the end of limitless space;
the towns and the mountains of granite all collapsed,
and the rivers drown in blood from one bank to the other.

    Art cries just as the Sciences cry at being ripped apart,
Progress and Industry, Faith itself and all Belief,
pilgrims of death, of vengeance, follow behind;
beneath the debris of Power, Empires and cities
and those Codes and Laws that illuminated the ages! . . .
So it seems that blind men fight against God.

    Eternal God: if you are just, as the globe proclaims you,
why do you deny to men the merest glimmer of your flame,
that could turn this night of mourning into lovely clarity?
Why, immense, do you not send forth from your throne on the peak

un relámpago siquiera de los rayos de tu lumbre
a estas ciegas multitudes, a esta pobre humanidad?

¿Por qué lloran esos niños que caer vieron sus padres?
¿por qué gimen enlutadas a millones esas madres?
las hermanas, las esposas ¿por qué tienen que llorar?
oye allá entre los zumbidos y el roncar de los cañones
apagarse de inocentes tantas quejas, a millones...
¡Pobres madres! nadie escucha vuestro triste sollozar.

Yo he pensado que los hombres son más fieras que las fieras,
y sus odios más odiosos que el rugir de las panteras,
y su instinto sanguinario más temible que el león;
si las fieras contemplasen el montón de los caídos,
ante el llanto de una madre y el clamor de sus gemidos,
más que el hombre embrutecido, sentirían compasión...

Madres buenas que les disteis de alimento a los cañones
con la fe del deber patrio, vuestros santos corazones,
y la tierra fecundasteis con la sangre maternal:
enlutadas acercaos con la mente visionaria,
penetrad hasta las tumbas y reunid vuestra plegaria
con los ecos doloridos de mi canto funeral...

Madres buenas: En las hoscas soledades de misterio
¡qué resuenen nuestros ecos en el vasto cementerio,
formulando una plegaria porque cese ya el cañón!
¡qué se arríen los pendones del rencor y la avaricia!
¡flote ya gallardo y puro de la paz y la justicia
en las crestas de los montes el heráldico pendón!

even a single bolt of lightning from the rays of your flame
to these blind multitudes, this pitiable humanity?

    Why do those children cry who saw their fathers fall?
Why do those mothers moan grief-stricken in their millions?
The sisters, the wives, why must they cry?
Hear there among the whirring and the roar of the cannons
the complaints of so many innocents extinguish themselves in their millions . . .
Poor mothers! no one hears your sobbing.

    I have thought that men are more ferocious than the beasts,
and their hatred more hateful than the roar of the panthers,
and their bloody instincts more fearsome than the lion;
if the beasts should contemplate the heap of the fallen,
before the tears of a mother and the clamor of her sighs,
more than brutish man, they at least would feel compassion . . .

    Good mothers who gave as fodder for the cannons,
with the faith of patriotic duty, your sainted hearts,
and the land you made fecund with maternal blood:
all in mourning come near with visionary mind,
make your way to the tombs and reunite your prayers
with the pained echoes of my funereal song . . .

    Good mothers: in the gloomy solitude of mystery,
let our echoes resound in the vast cemetery,
formulating a prayer that the cannon may cease!
That the flags of rancor and avarice may be struck down!
That may float, gallant and pure, on the crests of the mountains
the heraldic banner of peace and of justice!

La barquilla y el alma

    Rompiendo las olas velera barquilla
graciosa entre brumas se pierde en el mar;
galante a su paso toda onda se humilla
y trueca en arrullo su ronco cantar.

    Parece un ensueño que boga perdido
en pos del recuerdo bendito que fue . . .
semeja la sombra que sigue al olvido
si aún vive en el alma radiosa la fe.

    Tras densas neblinas perdióse ligera;
no sabe el piloto si habrá de tornar;
tal vez de las olas la voz plañidera
pregone un sepulcro en el fondo del mar.

    Acaso quebranten su mástil gallardo
las furias y el brío del recio huracán;
tal vez el Destino le clave su dardo
que obstruya su ruta y apague su afán . . .

    La barca es el alma con sus ilusiones;
el hombre el piloto; la vida es el mar.
Rugiendo cual rugen las recias pasiones
barquilla velera ¿tú habrás de tornar?

    ¡Quién sabe! . . . Mejor, no abandones la orilla,
que el mar de la vida es furioso y traidor.
¿No sientes bramando, ligera barquilla,
fatídicas olas de horrendo clamor? . . .

    Ya ves . . . de la mar en la noche brumosa
tras lucha enconada cedió el timonel . . .
¡Oh! pobre barquilla! semeja angustiosa
la sombra callada de hundido bajel . . .

The Little Boat and the Soul

    Breaking through the waves, the little boat
delightful amid the mists, loses herself in the sea;
gallant at her passing each wave bows down
and makes a lullaby of its hoarse song.

    She seems a fantasy that rows on, lost
in pursuit of a blessed memory that went . . .
similar to the shadow that follows forgetting
if yet lives in a soul a radiant with faith.

    Amidst a dense fog she lost herself lightly:
the pilot doesn't know if he'll have to turn back;
perhaps the plaintive voice of the waves
announces a tomb in the depths of the sea.

    Maybe they will break her gallant mast
those furies and the spirit of the fierce hurricane;
perhaps Destiny will pin her with his dart
that will obstruct her way, and quench her eagerness . . .

    The little boat is the soul with all its wishing;
man is the pilot; life is the sea,
roaring as fierce passions roar.
Light little boat, will you have to turn back?

    Who knows! Better to not abandon the shore,
for the sea of life is furious and a traitor.
Don't you feel them howling, light little boat,
those ominous waves with their horrendous clamor? . . .

    Now you see . . . out to sea in the foggy night,
after a peaked battle the helmsman gave in . . .
Oh, poor little boat! she seems now in her anguish
the quiet shadow of a sunken wreck . . .

Mis versos

    Mis versos nacidos
en horas de ensueño, de amor y de fe,
    son versos henchidos
de férvido anhelo de dicha y placer.
    Cadencias sentidas
en noches felices de grata ilusión,
    cual flores nacidas
al beso querido de un rayo de sol.
    Son vivos fulgores
del claro reflejo de luz matinal,
    son puros amores
que nacen del alma con vívido afán.
    Son voz de arroyuelo
que dulce murmura, cantando a una flor,
    suspiros del cielo
que brotan sutiles cual rayos de sol.
    La música sana
que canta de amores la dicha que fue...
    son voz de campana
que en alas del viento propaga la fe.
    Un canto de aromas
más dulce y más tierno que un beso de amor,
    cantar de palomas
más suave y más puro que aliento de flor.
    Recuerdo adorado
de días que el alma se siente feliz,
    recuerdo sagrado
del beso que en sueños un día sentí...
    Pedazos del alma,
—suspiros acaso de nítido amor—
    canciones de calma
que encierra misterios lo mismo que Dios...
    Yo vivo soñando
las tiernas caricias de un fiel corazón,
    yo vivo esperando
un ser que comprenda mis sueños de amor...
    Por eso nacidos
mis versos en horas de amor y de fe,
    son versos henchidos
de férvido anhelo de dicha y placer.

My Verses[32]

    My verses, born
in hours of fantasy, of love, and of faith,
    are ever ripe
with fervent longings for fortune and pleasure.
    Cadences felt
on happy nights arrayed with pleasant daydreams,
    like flowers born
to the dear kiss of the sun's rays. They are the
    living brilliance,
a clear reflection of matutinal light,
    they are pure loves
that are born from the soul with bright affection.
    They are the voice
of a brook that murmurs sweet, singing to a flower;
    heaven's own sighs
that break through subtle as the rays of the sun.
    The wholesome sound
of love's music that fortune past sings still . . .
    They voice a bell
that on the wings of the wind propagates faith.
    A song of scents
more sweet and more tender than a kiss of love,
    the song of doves
more gentle than a flower's exhalation.
    Adored record
of days with a soul happy and fulfilled;
    sacred record
of the kiss that in dreaming one day I felt . . .
    Shards of the soul,
—sighs, perhaps of the sharpest clearest of loves—
    songs made of calm
that enclose mysteries as God himself does . . .
    I live dreaming
of tender caresses from a faithful heart,
    I live wishing
for someone to understand my dreams of love . . .
    And for all that,
my verses, born in hours of love and of faith,
    are verses ripe
with fervent longings for fortune and pleasure.

Mis ilusiones

A mi madre.

Madre: soy la golondrina
que, en las brumas invernales
y en los ásperos breñales,
vierte notas de dolor;
vi alejarse mi esperanza,
de nostalgia llena el alma,
sin un instante de calma,
sin una ilusión de amor.

La fatal melancolía
por eterna compañera,
sin que ni una vez siquiera
goce mi alma una ilusión,
mis cantares son la queja
que jamás la respuesta halla,
son dolor triste que acalla
mi oprimido corazón.

Ya no escuchas mis acentos
ni a llorar vienes conmigo;
ya en tus brazos un abrigo
jamás puedo yo encontrar;
ya no acudes cariñosa
esa lágrima que rueda,
ni la que en mis ojos queda
con tus besos a enjugar.

No hay un beso de ternura,
ni quien vele satisfecho,
al pie de mi blando lecho,
mi tranquilo adormecer;
quien mis lágrimas recoja
en mi derredor sombrío,
que consuele al pecho mío
en su eterno padecer.

My Daydreams

To my mother.

Mother: I am the swallow
that, in the mists of winter
and in the rough and rocky scrub
pours forth notes of pain;
I saw my hope become distant,
my soul full of nostalgia,
without an instant of calm,
without a daydream of love.

With a fatal melancholy
my eternal companion,
without even a single time when
my soul could rejoice in a daydream,
my songs are the complaint
that never finds response,
they are the sad pain that quiets
my oppressed heart.

Now you do not hear my voice
nor come you to cry with me;
now in your arms sweet safety
never can I find;
now you do not come all caring
to that tear that falls,
nor to the one that stays in my eye,
to dry them with your kisses.

There is no touch of sweetness,
nor anyone to watch with satisfaction
from the foot of my soft bed
my tranquil drifting off;
who would catch up my tears
in my somber surrounds,
who could console my heart
in its eternal suffering.

Esas lágrimas que ruedan
cuando se sufre y se siente,
resbalando locamente
entre hieles de pesar,
esas son . . . ¡mis ilusiones!
¡sin que pueda al ser querido
de la tumba del olvido
con mis besos despertar!!

Those tears that roll down
when one suffers, when one feels,
running madly
between the bitternesses of suffering,
those are . . . my daydreams!
And from the tomb of oblivion,
I cannot with my kisses
that dear woman call to wake!!

¡Cuba y mi amada!

A bordo del "Barcelona," 1917.

 Ante el recuerdo querido
de esa tierra idolatrada,
florida siempre, encantada
de dichas y amores nido,
de una ilusión al latido
brota mi canción sincera
que, cruzando mensajera
la azul curva de los mares,
va decirle mis pesares
a mi amada que me espera . . .

 Yo siento nacer las flores
del huerto de mi ternura,
temblando entre su espesura
la canción de mis amores;
yo siento que mis dolores
son la ausencia que me abruma,
y mi cantar, cual la espuma
que consumiéndose va,
a mi amada llegará
como una canción de bruma . . .

 Siento que de mi alma brota
algo que mi pecho agita:
una promesa bendita,
un suspiro en cada nota;
un raudal que no se agota
de esperanzas y de anhelos,
de dulcísimos consuelos
para el alma que suspira,
pulsando triste la lira
entre la mar y los cielos . . .

 Bajo la niebla indecisa
que sobre la mar se extiende,
y el humo que se desprende
del buque, al cruzar la brisa,
grata asoma una sonrisa

Cuba and My Beloved![33]

On board the "Barcelona," 1917.

 Before the beloved memory
of that idolized land,
flowery always, enchanted
by good fortune and the nest of loves,
of a dream upon the heartbeat
springs forth my sincere song
which, crossing as a messenger
the blue curve of the seas
is going to tell my woes
to my beloved who awaits me ...

 I feel the birth of the flowers
in the orchard of my affection,
trembling amongst the vegetation
the song of my loves;
I feel that my sorrows
are the absence that overwhelms me
and my singing, like the seafoam
that goes along consuming itself,
to my beloved will arrive
like a song of fog ...

 I feel that from my soul springs forth
something that my chest agitates:
a blessed promise,
a sigh in every note;
a torrent that does not run dry
of hopes or of longing,
of the sweetest of solaces
for the soul that sighs
plucking sadly the lyre
between the sea and the skies ...

 Beneath the indecisive mist
that extends across the sea
and the smoke that pours forth
from the ship when the breeze crosses it,
pleasing appears a smile

a mis labios cariñosa,
y una canción amorosa
fluye entonces dulcemente,
como el suspiro inocente
de alguna mujer hermosa...

    No puedo olvidarme ¡no!
de esa tierra tan florida,
que una ilusión muy querida
en mi pecho despertó;
y esa ilusión que brotó
en torno del alma mía,
con invisible armonía
la canto en lánguido giro,
como un tímido suspiro
perdido en la noche umbría...

    En esa patria que encierra
tantos recuerdos de gloria;
en ese "Altar de la Historia";
en ese "Edén de la tierra";
bajo sus palmas quisiera
dar al viento mis cantares
y, olvidando los pesares
con que me abruma la ausencia,
gozar de alegre existencia
allá en sus benditos lares...

    Y sobre su virgen suelo,
do se querellan sin penas
la brisa y las azucenas
bajo un purísimo cielo,
en la embriaguez de mi anhelo
por la caricia soñada,
lograr la dicha anhelada
de unos divinos amores,
tejiendo un nido con flores...
y con besos de la amada.

on my affectionate lips,
and an amorous song
flows then sweetly,
like the innocent sigh
of some lovely woman . . .

   I cannot ever forget, no!
that land so decked in flowers
that caused a much beloved dream
to awaken in my breast;
and that dream that sprang forth
around my soul,
with invisible harmony
I sing in languid turns,
like a timid sigh
lost in the shadowy night . . .

   In that patria that encloses
so many memories of glory
in that "Altar of History";
in that "Eden on Earth";[34]
under her palms I would like
to give my songs over to the wind
and, forgetting all the sorrows
with which my absence burdens me,
delight in the joyful existence
there in her blessed hearths . . .

   And over her virgin soil
where lament without shame
the breeze and the lilies
beneath the purest sky,
in the euphoric intoxication of my yearning
for the long-dreamt-of caress,
to achieve the longed-for happiness
of some divine love,
weaving a nest with flowers . . .
and with the kisses of my beloved.

El pescador

Para Paco Pineda.

I

Como el astro feliz de la esperanza,
    la aurora transparente
desátase sutil. En lontananza
    la brisa suavemente
en sentidas canciones de añoranza
    escúchase doliente.
    Ligera la barquilla,
como un sueño de amor sobre la espuma
    se aleja de la orilla,
cruzando placentera aquella bruma
    flotante que se orilla
o se interna en los mares y se esfuma.

II

    De allá la mar rugiente
sufrido el pescador una mirada
    como un deseo ardiente,
tendió hacia la casita idolatrada,
    aquel nido caliente,
albergue de sus hijos y su amada.
    Por entre aquella bruma que surgía,
tejida con lágrimas del cielo,
    su rústica morada distinguía,
    el nido de su anhelo,
desde donde la amada le decía
    ¡adios! con el pañuelo . . .
    Despues . . . allá en los mares,
tras la curva azulada, en lontananza,
    sin quejas ni pesares,
flotaba la barquilla en la bonanza,
    igual que los cantares
sobre el ala sutil de la esperanza.
Tejía el pescador gratas canciones
    al ritmo de las olas,
y en su torno, lo mismo que oraciones,
    las tiernas barcarolas

The Fisherman

For Paco Pineda.[35]

I

Like the happy star of hope,
    the transparent dawn
stretches forth subtly. In the far distance
    the breeze softly
in heartfelt songs of longing
    can be heard in its pain.
    Lightly the little boat,
like a dream of love upon the foam
    pulls away from the sand,
crossing pleasantly that floating
    mist that rolls ashore
or that advances on the sea and vanishes.

II

    From there off the roaring sea
the long-suffering fisherman cast a look
    like a most ardent desire
toward the little house of his idolatry,
    that warm nest,
safe harbor of his children and beloved.
    There amidst the mist that was rising,
woven from the tears of heaven itself,
    he made out his rustic dwelling,
    the nest of his longing,
from where his beloved said to him
    goodbye! with fluttering kerchief . . .
    Thereafter . . . there off on the sea,
beyond the blued curve, in the very distance,
    without complaints nor sorrows,
floated the little boat in fair weather,
    just like his songs
on the subtle wings of hope.
The fisherman was weaving pleasing songs,
    to the rhythm of the waves,
and in their turn, the same as prayers,
    the tender barcarolles

fingían las dorados ilusiones
    del alma que está a solas . . .
La cántiga divina en la faena
    del hombre por la vida,
ligera como el viento en la serena
    mañana bendecida,
llegó hasta la casita que está llena
    del ansia más querida.
    Llegó como un latido
en el ala del aura susurrante
    al santo hogar querido,
como llega el rumor acariciante
    de un beso enternecido
en la paz de la tarde agonizante.
Y fue que el pescador en un exceso
    de dicha idolatrada
tejiera una canción toda embeleso,
    de amor una balada
que llevase a sus hijos dulce beso
y otro beso de amor para la amada.

III

    El hombre peregrino
al partir en las horas de bonanza,
    se olvida del destino,
que, a veces, al amor y la esperanza,
    los trueca en el camino
por la triste y cruel desventuranza.
    Al día placentero
sigue negra la noche tormentosa,
    al plácido sendero
signe acaso la senda peligrosa
    y al fúlgido lucero
le obscurece una nube maliciosa . . .
Mientras forja un hogar sus ilusiones,
    sintiéndose en la orilla
el rítmico sonar de las canciones,
    acaso la barquilla
finge en medio del mar y sus pasiones
    un astro que no brilla.

pretended to be the golden daydreams
    of the soul that is alone . . .
The divine canticle in the task
    of man about his life,
light like the wind on a serene
    and blessed morning,
made it all the way to the little house that is full
    of his most desired yearning.
    It arrived like a heartbeat
on the wings of the whispering dawn,
    to the sacred and beloved home,
as arrives the caressing touch
    of a moving, heartfelt kiss
in the peace of a dying afternoon.
And so it was that the fisherman in an excess
    of idolatrized good fortune
should weave a song all of sweetness,
    a very ballad of love
that would carry to his children a sweet kiss
and another kiss of love for his beloved.

III

    The man on his pilgrimage,
leaving in the hours of good weather,
    forgets the destination,
that, sometimes, changes love and hope
    in the middle of their way
to a sad and most cruel misfortune.
    On the heels of the pleasant day
follows black the stormy night,
    on the placid path
the cross of the dangerous way
    and the fulgent light
is obscured by a malicious cloud . . .
As he forges for his daydreams a home,
    hearing off on the shore
the rhythmic sounding of the songs,
    perhaps the little boat
feigns in the middle of the sea and its passions
    a star that does not shine.

IV

La mar se enfurecía,
el cielo semejaba estar llorando,
   el trueno ensordecía,
los vientos se agitaban sollozando,
   y todo predecía
la noche del dolor que está llegando.
   Las nubes que lloraban,
el cárdeno relámpago corriendo,
   los vientos que silbaban
y el tétrico huracán que iba rugiendo
   lo mismo semajaban
que la mar y los cielos combatiendo.
   La barca por los vientos
furiosos que silbaban azotada,
   allá en los elementos
era una alma que sufre acongojada,
   o, en medio de tormentos,
el hombre en la pasión que se anonada.
Y el pobre pescador en su impotencia,
en contra de las leyes inmutables
   que Dios en su conciencia
escribiera con letras imborrables
   ¿qué finge en la inclemencia
de la mar y sus leyes insondables?
   Buscando bendecido
un padazo de pan, una esperanza
   para el hogar querido,
¡cuántos hombres despues de la bonanza
hallaron la cruel desventuranza
   del pescador sufrido!

V

   La mar ya no rugía
ni el cielo semajaba estar llorando,
   el trueno no se oía,
ni el viento se agitaba sollozando,
   y todo predecía
el día del amor que está llegando.
   Lo mismo que un latido,
en alas de la brisa susurrante

IV

The sea began to rage,
the sky appeared to be weeping,
    the thunder deafened,
the winds whipped up sobbing,
    and everything presaged
the night of pain that came on apace.
    The clouds that were crying,
the bruised lightning running,
    the winds in their whistling
and the dismal hurricane with growls grown long
    looked as if
the sea and the skies were locked in combat.
    The boat struck by winds
both furious and whistling,
    there off amidst the elements
it was a soul that anguished suffers,
    or, in the middle of the torment,
a man gripped by passions that astonish.
And the poor fisherman in his impotence,
up against the immutable laws
that God in his care
wrote with unerasable letters,
what can he do in the inclemency
of the sea and its unfathomable laws?
    Searching for a blessed
piece of bread, a single hope
    for his beloved home,
how many men after fair weather
have found the cruel misfortune
    of the long-suffering fisherman!

V

Then the sea no longer roared
nor did the heavens seem to weep,
    the thunder could not be heard,
nor the winds whipped up to sobbing,
    and everything was a presage
to the day of love that is arriving.
    Just like a heartbeat,
on the wings of the whispering wind

voló un cantar querido,
como vuela el rumor acariciante
de un beso enternecido
en la paz de la tarde agonizante.
Y fue que de amor en un exceso,
con ansia idolatrada,
dos hijitos, henchidos de embeleso,
los de alma sosegada,
mandaron hacia el mar un dulce beso
y otro beso de amor mandó la amada.
Mas... pronto y sollozando,
yo no sé si de angustia o de pesares,
las olas suspirando,
a aquel beso de amor y los cantares
responden, vomitando
un cadáver que arrancan a los mares.

. . . .

Las brisas se quejaban,
al Rey astro una nube obscurecía,
los vientos se agitaban,
y hasta el cielo parece que gemía,
contemplando a dos hijos que lloraban
y a una madre infeliz en la agonía...

flew a beloved song,
as flies the caressing sound
    of a moving, heartfelt kiss
in the peace of a dying afternoon.
And it was that in an excess of love,
    with idolatrized yearning,
two little children, filled with enchantment,
    those with a tranquil soul,
sent toward the sea a sweet kiss
and the beloved sent another kiss of love.
    But . . . soon and sobbingly
I know not if in anguish or in sorrow
    the waves sighing,
to that kiss and those songs
    respond, vomiting forth
a cadaver to be pulled from the seas.

    . . . .

    The breezes were complaining,
the King star was obscured by a cloud,
    the winds stirred themselves up
and even the sky it seems was moaning,
contemplating the two children who were crying
and an unhappy mother in agony . . .

Paisaje nocturno

Para la excelente escritora Sra. A. de P. Rolo.

Ayer y cuando todo reposaba,
y las flores cerraran ya su broche,
asomado al balcón yo contemplaba
un muy bello paisaje de la noche:

En el denso celaje, allá muy lejos,
mil cárdenos relámpagos corrían,
y, al partir de la nube, sus reflejos
sobre el mar azulado diluían.

En la augusta grandeza de la noche,
cuando ya toda flor cerró su broche,
mirando aquel paisaje, me detuve.

Y de un verso encontré la grata esencia,
inspirado en la bella transparencia
del claro centelleo de una nube . . .

Nocturnal Landscape

For the excellent writer Mrs. A. P. Rolo.[36]

    Yesterday and when all was at rest
and the flowers closing already their brooch,
leaning on the balcony I was contemplating
a very lovely landscape in the night:

    In the dense cloudscape, there far off,
a thousand opalescent lightnings were running,
and, on leaving a cloud, their reflections
dissolved into the blue of the sea.

    In the august greatness of the night,
when already each flower had closed its brooch,
watching that landscape, I stood.

    And of a verse I found the pleasing essence,
inspired by the lovely transparency
of the clear flashing of a cloud . . .

En la ausencia

En la ausencia,—tú lo dices—
en lares de extraña tierra
cual la gota que se encierra
en el cáliz de una flor,
oigo el eco del pasado
resonar como un lamento
que, arrastrado por el viento
me habla de un perdido amor . . .
    Del amor que fue muriendo
entre sombras y dolores,
que era puro cual las flores,
pero ¡ingrato! lo olvidé,
cuando loco y ambicioso
y cantando barcarolas
con el ritmo de las olas,
de mi patria me alejé . . .
    Cuando, pobre marinero,
que abandona los hogares
y en las rocas de los mares
va lanzando su canción,
fui, traidor a tus caricias,
tras de ensueños y quimeras
a las playas extranjeras,
persiguiendo otra ilusión . . .
    Hoy lo pienso arrepentido
y, al oir triste al acento
que en sus alas trae el viento
recordando aquel amor . . .
yo, cantando, sufro y siento,
y el recuerdo del pasado,
porque, ¡ingrato! te he olvidado,
acrecienta mi dolor.
    Y detrás de inmensos mares
de las nevadas espumas
y de las espesas brumas,
que me separan de tí,
con acento dolorido,
en la ausencia y sus pesares,
voy llorando en mis cantares
esa dicha que perdí . . .

In Absence

    In this absence,—as you say—
at a hearth in a strange land
like a dewdrop enclosed
by the chalice of a flower,
I hear the echo of the past
resonate like a lament
that, dragged there by the wind
speaks to me of a lost love . . .
    Of the love that was dying
between shadows and pains,
that was pure like the flowers,
but, ungrateful, I forgot it,
when mad and ambitious
and singing barcarolles
with the rhythm of the waves,
from my patria I pulled away . . .
    When, poor mariner,
who abandons the hearth
and to the rocks of the seas
goes flinging his song,
I was a traitor to your caresses,
and after fantasies and chimeras
to foreign shores,
went chasing a different daydream . . .
    Today I think repentant
and on hearing the sad sound
that on its wings the wind brings
to remind me of that love . . .
I, singing, suffer and am sorry,
and the remembrance of the past,
because, ungrateful!, I abandoned you
only increases my pain.
    And across immense seas
over snowy foam
and through the thick fogs,
that separate me from you,
with a pained sound,
in absence and its sorrows,
I go on lamenting in my songs
that good fortune that I lost . . .

¿Por qué despertarla?...

Para J. M. Subirats.

I

"Bajaron los ángeles
a donde ella estaba;
le hicieron un lecho
con plácidas alas,
y lleváronla lejos, muy lejos,
en noche callada . . .
Del alba al reflejo
sonó la campana,
allá en la alta torre
de iglesia lejana;
los ángeles mismos,
plegando sus alas,
exclaman al verla dormida:
¿por qué despertarla"? . . .

II

Sus notas al aire
la alondra lanzaba,
cantando a una niña
muy dulce alborada:
cantábale amores nacidos
en noche callada . . .
El suave murmurio
de arroyo que pasa,
tranquilo lamiendo
con ondas rizadas
la fértil ribera
que encauza sus aguas,
muy quedo en sus notas decía:
¿por qué despertarla? . . .

III

Y el mar que solloza,
y el ave que canta,

Why Wake Her? . . .[37]

For J. M. Subirats.[38]

I

"The angels came down
to where she was;
they made her a bed
with their tranquil wings,
and they carried her far, very far,
in the silent night . . .
At the glimmer of the dawn
the bell tolled,
there off in the tall tower
of the distant church;
the angels themselves
folding their wings,
exclaim on seeing her sleeping:
why wake her?" . . .[39]

II

Her notes to the air
the lark was launching,
singing to a young
and very sweet dawn:
she sang of loves that were born
in the quiet of the night . . .
The smooth murmur
of the brook that passes,
tranquilly lapping
with rippling waves
the fertile bank
that channels its waters,
so softly her notes were saying:
why wake her? . . .

III

And the sea that sobs
and the bird that sings,

y el viento que gime
meciendo las ramas,
arrullan el sueño tranquilo
de aquella que tú amas . . .
Y el mar y las aves,
y el viento y las auras,
y el dulce arroyuelo
que límpido pasa,
igual que la alondra
amores le cantan,
y al verla soñando repiten:
¿por qué despertarla? . . .

and the wind that whines
shaking the branches;
they lull the tranquil dreams
of her that you love . . .
And the sea and the birds,
and the wind and the air,
and the sweet little brook
that limpid passes by,
just like the lark
they sing to her of love,
and seeing her dreaming repeat:
why wake her? . . .

El Angelus

   Era un día feliz de primavera;
la tarde iba cediendo en sus fulgores;
cerraban ya sus pétalos las flores,
cubriéndose de luto la pradera.

   Ya Febo de su rubia cabellera
no esparcía los pálidos colores;
de la luna los tibios resplandores
titilando vagaban por doquiera.

   Un labriego feliz que contemplaba
de la tarde la plácida agonía
ferviente un plegaria murmuraba:

   Al oír la campana que plañía
de hinojos humilde se postraba
fervoroso exclamando: ¡Ave, María!

The Angelus[40]

    It was a happy day in spring;
the afternoon was fading in its brilliance;
the flowers were already closing up their petals,
covering the meadow in mourning.

    Already Phoebus from his golden tresses
was no longer scattering the pale colors;
the cooler radiance of the moon
wandered flickeringly about.

    A happy farmer who was contemplating
the placid dying of the afternoon
fervently murmured a prayer:

    On hearing the bell that was keening,
on his knees humbly he made his obeisance
devoutly he exclaimed: Ave Maria!

Soñaba

Para Arturo Doreste, fraternalmente.

En un nido que el aire columpiaba
con el vaivén arrullador del viento,
he visto a una hermosa que soñaba
con un blanco, muy blanco pensamiento.

Y a la niña inocente que dormía
radiante como el fuego de la aurora,
el beso de las auras la mecía
con su tierna caricia arrulladora.

Dichosa con la dulce indiferencia
del que al amor da su callado asilo,
mirábase a la luz de su inocencia
bajo el fúlgido azul siempre tranquilo.

De su vida en el dulce relicario
no soñaba tristezas sino gloria,
del pasado evocando la memoria
por camino de rosas sin calvario.

¿Qué será, como alondra mañanera,
—soñaba—lo que escucho en dulce idioma,
"que canta como canta la paloma,
y gime como gime la palmera"? . . .

Dormitaba feliz en grata calma
—esa calma que falta al alma mía—
y sus sienes inspirábanle a su alma
los fulgores de luz de un nuevo día.

. . . Despertó y ya la alondra mañanera
no se oía en aquel tan dulce idioma,
"que canta como canta la paloma
y gime como gime la palmera."

De su vida en el dulce relicario
la hermosa no vislumbra ya la gloria,
del pasado evocando la memoria . . .
¡encontró las espinas de un calvario!

I Used to Dream[41]

For Arturo Doreste, fraternally.[42]

In a nest that the air used to rock
with the lullaby swaying of the wind,
I have seen a beauty who would dream
with a pure, very pure thought.[43]

And to the innocent girl who was sleeping,
radiant like the fires of the dawn,
the kiss of the gentle breeze would rock
with its tender and lullaby caress.

Lucky her with the sweet indifference
that gives to love its quiet sanctuary
she saw herself in the light of her innocence
under the glowing, ever tranquil blue.

Of her life in the sweet reliquary
she did not dream of sadness but of glory,
evoking the memory of the past
on a path of roses with no Calvary to brave.

What could it be that, like the lark of the morning
—she dreamed—that which I hear in sweet language,
"that sings like the dove sings,
and moans like the palm moans?" . . .[44]

She was dozing happy in pleasing calm
—that calm that is missing from my own soul—
and her temples were inspiring in her soul
the flaming light of a new day.

She awoke and already the morning lark
could not be heard with that such sweet language
"that sings like the dove sings,
and moans like the palm moans."

Of her life in the sweet shrine
the lovely one could no longer see the glory,
of the past evoking memory . . .
she found instead the thorns of a Calvary!

    Y en la noche raudales ya no siente
ni en la aurora al despertar el día,
que es la vida la llama indiferente
que las horas del vivir torna agonía,

    Entonces exclamaba: ¡Que tormento
son aquellas del vivir las horas!
¡Oh, vida! ¡qué de llantos atesoras!
¡Oh, sueño de mi blanco pensamiento!

    Y tornóse al ensueño idolatrado
en su nido que el aire columpiaba,
aquella niña hermosa que soñaba . . .
recibir las caricias del amado.

And in the night she does not feel the torrents
nor in the dawn at the waking of the day,
the indifferent flame that is life
that the hours of living make an agony,

    And she used to exclaim: What a torment
are these the hours of living!
Oh, life! How you amass tears!
Oh, I dream now of my pure thought!

    And she turned to the idolized fantasy
in her nest that the air used to rock,
that beautiful girl who used to dream . . .
of receiving the caresses of a lover.

La mano del amigo

Para Leandro de Torres.

Del cariño la esencia perfumada
siempre lejos estuvo de mi vida;
he corrido una senda obscurecida;
con mi llanto quizás queda regada.

De la ausencia en la noche despiadada
mi ilusión va quedando adormecida:
va muriendo, cual muere entristecida
mi canción en la noche de la nada.

En la senda sin luz en que batallo
busco amores y paz, y no los hallo . . .
peregrino de amor, no lo consigo.

Pero siempre diviso en lontananza
una luz que refleja una esperanza,
cuando estrecho la mano de un amigo.

The Hand of a Friend

For Leandro de Torres.[45]

 From the perfumed essence of care
my life was always far off;
I have run a darkened path;
perhaps still well-watered by my tears.

 Wearied by absence in the heartless night
my hopes and dreams go slipping into numbness
dying out, just as dies all saddened
my song in the night of nothingness.

 On the path with no light on which I battle
I seek loves and peace, and never find them . . .
peregrine of love, I cannot reach it.

 But I can always make out in the distance
a light that reflects to me a hope
when I hold tight to the hand of a friend.

¿Te acuerdas?

   Muy hermosa te he soñado
en mis instantes de amor,
y en mi sueño idolatrado
viví siempre enamorado
de tu desdén seductor.

   Hice versos para tí
sin que tú mi acento oyeras
y tus desprecios sufrí,
mas nunca te maldecí
¡aunque tú lo merecieras!

   He buscado por qué odiarte;
quise loco no quererte,
mas, no pude, y, al amarte,
tuvo mi alma que adorarte,
sin poder aborrecerte.

   Nunca mi dicha soñada
se trocó en desventuranza,
porque el alma enamorada,
aunque viva despreciada,
vive siempre en la esperanza.

   En mis sueños te seguí
sin saber cómo y por qué;
por tus desdenes te dí
las lágrimas que vertí,
siempre en alas de mi fé.

   Así para mi pasaron
los tiempos en cruel dualismo:
mis ansias no se acabaron
ni tus desdenes lograron
poner fin a mi optimismo,

   ¿Iba yo tras lo imposible
en alas de algún ensueño?
No. Sufriendo lo indecible,
añoraba lo apacible,
lo bendito de mi sueño.

Do You Remember?

    I have dreamed you so lovely
in my instants of love
and in my idolatrous dreams
I lived always enamored
by your seductive disdain.

    I made verses for you
without your ever hearing my voice
and I suffered your disregard,
but I never spoke you ill
even if you deserved it!

    I have sought a reason to hate you,
I wished madly to not love you
but I could not, and on loving you
my soul had to adore you,
unable to forsake you.

    Never did my dreamed-of happiness
turn itself into misfortune
because a soul in love,
though it live despised,
lives always in hope.

    In my dreams I followed you
without knowing how or why;
for your disdain I gave you
the tears that I spilled,
always on the wings of my faith.

    And so time passed for me
in this cruel duality:
my longing did not end,
nor did your disdain manage
to put an end to my optimism.

    Was I after the impossible
on the wings of some fantasy?
No. Suffering the unspeakable,
I yearned for gentleness,
the blessing of my dream.

Iba rimando a la vida
el cantar de mi añoranza,
tras de la imagen querida,
y con el alma prendida
del ala de mi esperanza.

Porque la fe me inspiraba,
tras la esperanza amorosa
que en mis suspiros brotaba,
una lámpara radiosa
en el mar que yo surcaba . . .

¿Te acuerdas? . . . Arrepentida
de tu perfidia y traición
dijiste, mujer querida:
"poeta: sigue, a la vida
cantando, con tu ilusión."

Olvida las crueles horas,
y de amor en el exceso,
bajo las nuevas auroras,
toma las dichas que añoras:
toda mi alma . . . en este beso.

    I went on rhyming to life
the song of my longing,
following the beloved image,
with my soul aflame
on the wings of my hope.

    Because faith inspired me,
following that amorous hope
that burst forth in my sighs,
a radiant lamp
in the sea through which I ploughed . . .

    Do you remember? . . . Repentant
of your perfidy and betrayal
you said, beloved:
"Poet, carry on singing
to life and to your dream."

    Forget the cruel hours,
and take in love,
under fresh auroras,
the excess of joys that you long for:
all of my soul . . . in this kiss.

Yo

He vivido hasta aquí de vagabundo,
despreciando el saber de la experiencia;
consumióse mi rauda adolescencia
como el triste vivir del errabundo.

Aún hoy vivo creyendo que es el mundo
una cárcel muy cruel de mi conciencia;
sus fronteras comprimen mi existencia
y su ambiente de luz me es infecundo.

A pesar de las brumas del destino,
mil escollos tocando en el camino,
aún aliento mi espíritu recobra.

En medio del sendero tan obscuro
siento un algo auroral para el futuro . . .
que me da fuerza para seguir mi obra.

Self

    I have lived my life to here, to now, roving,
discounting the wisdom of experience
burning up my too-fleeting adolescence
like the sad life that's born of endless wandering.

    Even now, the world is, by my figuring,
a cruel prison constructed by my conscience;
its borders press in on my existence
and its glaring environs yield me nothing.

    In spite of the dark mists that shroud destiny,
the thousand jagged reefs that mark the journey,
still my spirit renews its inspiration.

    Following this trail of darkness and of dread
I can sense something like dawn ahead . . .
that gives me strength for my work of creation.

En la playa

Fue en la paz del crepúsculo doliente;
daba el viento a los mares su canción;
el poeta y la amada dulcemente
hablaban en feliz conversación.

La Amada:— ¿Por qué la mar sollozando
  va las arenas besando
    con pasión?
  El Poeta:— Porque las olas errantes
  tienen de amor sus instantes,
  lo mismo que los amantes
    su ilusión...
La Amada:— ¿Por qué la hermosa barquilla
  deja tan lejos la orilla
    sin temor?
  El Poeta:— Porque es cual alma dichosa
  que cruza alegre y graciosa
  sobre la mar silenciosa
    del amor...
La Amada:— ¿Por qué se escucha distante
  una canción susurrante
    y un gemir?
  El Poeta:— Porque es la brisa una amada
  que canta y gime angustiada
  por la caricia soñada
    del vivir...
La Amada:— ¿Por qué se extiende esa bruma
  y eclipsa la blanca espuma
    de la mar?
  El Poeta:— Porque la mar es la vida,
  y aquella bruma perdida
  finge, en la mar extendida,
    el pesar...
La Amada:— ¿Por qué en el cielo esos astros
  dejan lumínicos rastros
    al correr?
  El Poeta:— Porque es un astro en el cielo
  lo que en un pecho el anhelo
  que va esparciendo el consuelo
    y el placer...

On the Beach

    In the peace of a sorrowful twilight;
    with the wind giving its song to the sea;
    the poet and the beloved all in sweetness
    conversed together happily.

The Beloved:— Why does the sobbing sea
  go on kissing the sands
    with such passion?
The Poet:— Because the errant waves
  have their moments of love
    just like lovers have
      their dreams . . .
The Beloved:— Why does the lovely little boat
  leave the shore so far behind
    without fear?
The Poet:— Because it is like the happy soul
  that crosses joyous and delighting
    over the silent sea
      of love . . .
The Beloved:— Why is there in the distance
  a murmuring and moaning
    and a song?
The Poet:— Because the breeze is a beloved
  who sings and moans, anxious
    for the long-dreamed-of caress
      of life . . .
The Beloved:— Why does that haze extend
  and eclipse the white spray
    of the sea?
The Poet:— Because the sea is life,
  and that lost haze
    imitates, in the wide sea
      all sorrow . . .
The Beloved:— Why do those stars in the sky
  leave luminous traces
    at their passing?
The Poet:— Because a star in the sky is
  the yearning in a heart
    that goes scattering solace
      and pleasure . . .

La Amada:— ¿Por qué las olas que besan
la playa, es que nunca cesan
    de besar?
El Poeta:— Porque es su caricia amable
de un amor inacabable,
y es tan grande e interminable
    como el mar...
La Amada:— ¿Si nuestro amor aquí a solas
es más grande que las olas
    y que el mar?...
El Poeta:— Amada: escucha distantes
dulces canciones errantes,
que hablan de amor susurrantes
    al pasar...
. . . .

Las canciones que se oían...
nuestros labios que se unían...
    y los dos...
Fue aquel beso inacabable,
cual los mares fue insondable,
fue tan grande e interminable
como Dios...

The Beloved:— Why do the waves that kiss
 the beach, why do they never cease
  their kissing?
 The Poet:— Because it is the kind caress
  of an everlasting love,
   that is as great and unending
    as the sea . . .
The Beloved:— And if our love, here all alone,
  is even greater than the waves
   and than the sea? . . .
 The Poet:— Beloved: listen to the distant
  and sweet errant songs,
   that speak murmuring of love
    at their passing . . .
. . . .

The songs that could be heard . . .
our lips that came together . . .
 and the two . . .
It was that unending kiss,
unfathomable as the seas,
It was as great and interminable
as God himself . . .

F. Domínguez Pérez

   Cerebro de luces, de rayos divinos,
que en rápidos vuelos se arriesga a volar;
poeta sincero, va abriendo caminos,
portando este lema: ¡luchar y luchar!

   Y tiene en la senda de espinas, que escruta,
dejando a su paso regueros de bien,
por trono sus libros que alumbran su ruta,
por cetro una pluma que alumbra también.

   Volando, volando soñó la victoria;
constante, en la cumbre mirando la gloria,
llegar a la cumbre por lema escogió . . .

   Poeta: prosigue tu rápido vuelo;
tu sién—no lo dudes—de gloria en su anhelo,
tendrá los laurels que siempre soñó.

F. Domínguez Pérez[46]

    Mind of lights, of divine rays,
that in swift flights takes the risk of flying;
sincere poet, he goes charting new paths,
bearing this motto: to fight and to fight!

    And he has on the path of thorns that he pores over
leaving in his wake traces of goodness,
as a throne his books, which illumine the route,
as his scepter a pen, which illumines as well.

    Flying, flying he sounded the victory;
constant, on the peak looking toward glory
to arrive at the peak he chose as a motto . . .

    Poet: follow your swift flight;
your temples—never doubt it—will be crowned
by glory's ever-dreamed-of laurels.

El dos de noviembre

    Fecha que, cual denso velo,
con sus fúnebres crespones,
cubre nuestros corazones
y nos causa amargo duelo;
por eso con desconsuelo
lanzo al espacio mi acento,
y en alas del sentimiento
y en lugar de alegre nota,
de mi lira solo brota
un tristísimo lamento.

    Un cantar entristecido
que ofrenda mi alma a los muertos,
y allá en los sepulcros yertos,
finge un lúgubre quejido;
un cantar adolorido
una estrofa funeraria;
una nítida plegaria
por el alma del que fue:
un cantar de amor y fe
en su tumba solitaria . . .

    Allí, donde de la vida
las pompas y vanidades
se estrellan con las verdades
de la tumba entristecida;
allí, donde, prometida
la verdad eternal y pura,
sin ambiciones perdura,
proclamando hora tras hora
la igualdad aterradora
en la negra sepultura.

The Second of November[47]

    A date which, like a dense veil,
of funereal crepe
covers over our hearts
and causes us bitter pain;
because of that, all disconsolate,
I launch my voice into space
and on the wings of sentiment
and instead of a joyous note
from my lyre only bursts forth
a most sad lamentation.

    A saddened song
that my soul offers to the dead
and there, in their unyielding tombs
it feigns a lugubrious moan;
a pained song,
a funereal stanza;
a sharply drawn prayer
for the soul departed:
a song of love and faith
in his solitary tomb,

    There, where the pomp
and vanities of life
crash into the truths
of the sepulchral sadness;
there, where, promised
the truth eternal and pure,
without ambitions it persists,
proclaiming hour after hour
the terrifying equalizer
that is the black tomb.

En esta fecha luctuosa,
recordemos los que fueron,
y por siempre se perdieron
en lo oscuro de una fosa;
en su tumba silenciosa
que no tiene ni una flor,
con lágrimas de dolor
depositemos fervientes
la oración de los creyentes,
la plegaria del amor.

On this tragic date,
let us remember those who've gone
and forever lost themselves
in the darkness of a grave;
in a silent tomb
that has not even one flower,
with tears of pain
let us leave fervently
the prayer of the believers,
the supplication of love.

¿ . . . . ?

 No hay un hombre tan dichoso
que viva siempre en la calma
sin que las flores del alma
se lleguen a marchitar;
aún llevando por delante
las luces de la experiencia,
nublan siempre la existencia
las tinieblas del pesar.

 Apenas la luz miramos
del sol que nos dió la vida,
ya alguna ilusión perdida
enluta nuestro vivir;
aquellas dichas que el hombre
eternas gozar pensó
¡cuán pronto trocarlas vió
en doloroso gemir!

 Aquellas tardes serenas,
risueñas, tíbias, hermosas
que al alma cubren de rosas,
de flores al corazón
¿qué dejaron al pasar? . . .
Sus recuerdos son ruinas
y sus flores son espinas
y es mentira su ilusión.

 Y ¡qué rápidas se han ido
en el carro de los años!
¡qué pronto los desengaños
nos abruman en tropel!
Brilla la luz que nos guía
porque vivimos soñando;
vamos quimeras forjando,
mas . . . éstas nos dan su hiel.

 Preguntádselo a mi lira
que en sus cantos de tristura,
finge un eco que murmura
desde un abismo sin luz:

¿ . . . . ?

 There is no man so lucky
that he lives forever in calm,
without the flowers of his soul
coming to wither;
even carrying before him
the lights of experience,
existence is forever shadowed,
by the darkness of suffering.

 We hardly see the light
from the sun that gave us life,
already some lost daydream
drapes our life in mourning;
those joys that man thought
eternally to enjoy,
how quickly he saw them turn
into a painful moaning!

 Those serene afternoons
smiling, warm, beautiful
that cover the soul in roses,
that cover the heart in flowers,
what did they leave on their passing? . . .
Their memories are ruins,
their flowers thorns,
and their daydream is a lie.

 And how fast they have gone
in the course of the years!
How soon the disappointments
overwhelm us in their droves!
The light that guides us shines out
because we live by dreaming;
we go on forging chimeras,
and yet . . . they give us only bile.

 Ask it of my lyre
that in its songs of sadness,
it feign an echo that murmurs
from an abyss without light:

es que el alma del poeta
al cumplir veinticinco años
lleva ya de desengaños
sobre sí una dura cruz.

Lo que fugaz huyó un día
el tiempo no lo renueva,
y el tiempo ¡ingrato! se lleva
las flores de la ilusión;
y al morir aquellas flores
de los amores divinos
¡por cuán obscuros caminos
vamos a la decepción!

Y después, como el espectro,
en pos vamos del destino,
sin más luz en el camino,
sin más vida en derredor,
que las horas de nostalgia
que reflejan el pasado,
y las sombras que ha dejado
sobre el camino el dolor.

Y hasta que la traicionera
Parca impía, aterradora
rompe el velo abrumadora
de la horrible eternidad,
ciegos somos y no oímos
resonar aquel acento,
que al vivir llama lamento
y a la tumba la verdad.

for the soul of the poet
on turning twenty-five
bears already, above his head
a hard cross built of disenchantments.

   That which fleeting fled one day
the passing of time does not renew,
and time, ungrateful! carries off
the flowers of a daydream;
and at the dying of those flowers
of divine love,
by what obscure paths
do we go toward disappointment!

   And after, like mere specters,
we go on following destiny,
without more light on the way forward,
without more life all around,
than the hours of nostalgia
that reflect the past,
and the shadows left
upon the path by pain.

   And until the traitorous
Parca, impious, terrifying[48]
breaks the oppressive veil
of horrible eternity,
we are blind and do not hear
that voice resonate,
that names living a lamentation
and names the tomb the truth.

España: ¡Salve, bandera mía!

¡Salve, noble enseña que en tus pliegues atesoras
las grandezas de mi España con su santa redención!
a través del fuego sacro que destellan tus auroras
yo descubro las dos almas de mi patria redentoras:
a Pelayo en Covadonga y en América a Colón.

De la España recruzando la extension de sus llanuras
van prendidas de tus pliegues mis estrofas por tu amor;
si no vibran, por lo menos son romances de ternura,
pero cantan las hazañas de tu intrépida bravura
cuando róncos resonaban los clarines del dolor.

Sangre noble representa de tus hijos la arrogancia,
y el hispano su arrogancia de Pelayo la heredó;
nunca el yugo del romano render pudo la Numancia,
como nunca mi bandera se humillara ante la Francia,
cuando el "Déspota del Sena" contra España se lanzó.

Mil poemas todo fuego se tejieron por tu gloria
cuando el eco se apagara del fatídico clarín;
aún hoy vibran majestuosas las trompetas de tu historia
las montañas pirenáicas aún repiten tu Victoria
que en la Francia resonara de un confín a otro confín.

Es de gloria tu horizonte, patria mía, muy fecundo
en victorias que nimbaron tus pendones de splendor;
mi bandera es una madre de cariño muy profoundo:
aún hoy vuelve sus miradas a través del Nuevo Mundo,
entre lágrimas y besos, por los hijos de su amor . . .

Noble enseña de Castilla que en tus pliegues atesoras
la fe santa, patriotismo, libertad y redención:
no hay artista que no admire tus magníficas auroras,
unas veces porque sufres, porque gimes, porque lloras,
y otras veces porque finges bello manto de ilusión.

Eres vida y eres alma y eres sol, bandera mía,
de una patria que al abismo nuevos mundos arrancó;
de una patria que es la cuna del valor y la hidalguía,
generosa con los suyos, con el invasor bravía,
y por eso su bandera de los nobles se llamó.

Spain: Hail, Flag of Mine![49]

    Hail, noble standard who in your folds amass
the greatnesses of my Spain with her sainted redemption!
Through the sacred fire with which your dawning flashes
I discover the two souls, redeemers of my patria:
Pelayo at Covadonga and in America, Columbus.[50]

    Crossing and recrossing the expanse of the plains of Spain,
my stanzas hang from your folds, pinned there by your love;
if they do not ring out, they are at least ballads full of tenderness,
though they sing the hazards of your intrepid ferocity
when hoarse resounded the clarions of pain.

    Noble blood represents the arrogance of your sons,
and your children inherited their arrogance from Pelayo;
the Roman yoke could never break Numancia,[51]
just as my flag would never humble itself before France,
when the "Despot of the Seine" launched himself against Spain.[52]

    A thousand poems all of fire were woven to your glory
when the echo did abate of that fateful clarion;
still today they ring forth majestic the trumpets of your history;
the Pyrenean mountains still echo with your Victory
which in France resonated from one border to the other.

    Your horizon, oh my patria is with glory very fertile
with victories that drew a nimbus of splendour round your standard;
my flag is a mother of a very profound affection:
still today she turns her looks across all the New World,
between tears and kisses, for of the children of her love . . .

    Noble ensign of Castille who in your folds amass
the sainted Faith, patriotism, liberty and redemption:
there is no artist who would not admire your magnificent shine,
sometimes because you suffer, because you moan, because you cry,
and other times because you assume the lovely mantle of a dream.

    You are life and you are soul and you are sun, flag of mine,
of a patria that new worlds ripped forth from the abyss,
of a patria that is the cradle of valor and nobility,
generous with her own, with the invader fierce,
and for that the noble call you their flag.

Yo he pensado, tras la ausencia, y al mirarte majestuosa
tremolando en los navíos con mirífico splendor,
que me traes de la patria los mensajes, cariñosa,
pues tambien al hijo ausente sabes tierna y amorosa
prodigarle una caricia de la ausencia en el dolor.

Y por eso, cuando miro a esas naves que se alejan
hacia el nido de mi infancia, peregrinas de la mar,
sobre el ala de los vientos que ora ríen o se quejan,
yo te mando mis canciones y mis besos que reflejan
cuanto sufro si te alejas sin poderte contemplar.

    I have thought, after my absence, and seeing you majestic
waving on the ships with marvelous splendor,
that you bring me messages from my patria, affectionate,
for you also know, tender and loving, on your absent son
to bestow a caress in the pain of his absence.

    And because of this, when I see those ships that pull away
toward the nest of my childhood, pilgrims of the sea,
on the wings of the wind that now laugh or complain,
I send you my songs and my kisses that reflect
how much I suffer if you depart without my seeing.

Año viejo

    Un átomo que rueda, cual hoja desprendida
del árbol de los años, del roble de la vida,
que en medio de los tiempos tronchara el huracán . . .
Y ¡cuántas las del alma benditas ilusiones,
fingiendo hojas que arrancan los recios aquilones
al terminarse el año los hombres perderán . . .

Año nuevo

    Un átomo que surge, fingiendo en lontananza
alguna ilusión nueva, quizá alguna esperanza,
que alienta de los hombres con ansia el corazón . . .
En tanto que unos lloran perdidas ilusiones,
De amor entonan otros quiméricas canciones . . .
¡Los llantos son la vida, y el canto la ilusión!

Old Year[53]

 An atom that spins, like a leaf torn off
from the tree of years, from the oak of life,
that in the midst of all the hurricane may shear . . .
And how many of a soul's most blessed dreams,
as leaves ripped free by the strong north winds
on ending the year, all men shall lose . . .

New Year

 An atom that surges, pretending in the distance
to be some new dream, perhaps some hope,
that spurs on the heart of man with fresh longing . . .
While some weep for hopeful dreams now lost,
others intone chimeric songs of love . . .
Those tears are life, the song is but a dream!

Cuba

¡Salve, bandera amada!

¡Salve, espléndida bandera de la estrella solitaria,
bella imagen luminosa, cual fantástico rubí!
De una patria toda flores sacra enseña visionaria:
tú me inspiras las estrofas que se truecan en plegaria
en las tumbas silenciosas de Agramonte y de Martí.

En las cumbres de los montes y en las fértiles praderas
de una tierra toda ensueños, toda amores e ilusión;
en sus valles y campiñas y en sus vírgenes riberas,
cuando el rio sollozaba, suspirando las palmeras,
te formó libre y gallarda de tus hijos la legion.

Yo no sé si te formaron del amor de sus legiones,
o del rayo fulguroso de algún cuerpo luminar;
pero sé que eres emblema de sus blancas ilusiones,
y el latido fervoroso de sus grandes corazones,
y la imagen bendecida que se adora en el hogar.

Eres alma en los hogares y en los pueblos eres vida,
eres fuego en las conciencias y en los pechos un altar;
en la guerra fuiste aliento de una patria enardecida,
y en la paz la madre amante por sus hijos elegida,
para unir tiernos cariños que se cruzan sobre el mar.

Hoy se cruzan los cariños del hermano con su hermano,
los amores de la madre con los hijos de su amor:
la bandera de mi España con la enseña del cubano,
enlazadas se confunden a través del Oceano,
olvidados ya los odios y las guerras y el rencor . . .

Noble enseña toda amores con tu estrella solitaria
esplendente y luminosa, cual fantástico rubí;
de una patria toda flores bella imagen visionaria:
por ti brotan mis canciones que se truecan en plegaria
en las tumbas silenciosas de Agramonte y de Martí.

Fue mi cuna por las brisas del Cantábrico mecida,
y, al mirar la luz mis ojos, vieron luz de hispano sol;
pero un día, yo muy niño, una tarde entristecida,

Cuba

¡Hail, Beloved Flag![54]

Hail, splendid flag with your solitary star,
lovely and luminous image, like a fantastical ruby!
Of a patria all of flowers the sacred visionary standard:
you inspire in me the stanzas that become a prayer
at the silent tombs of Agramonte and Martí.[55]

At the peaks of the mountains and in the fertile valleys
of a land made all of fantasy, all of love and hope;
in her valleys and countryside and on her virgin shores,
when the river sobbed and the palms sighed,
the free and gallant legion of your children made you.

I know not if they made you from the love of their legions
or from the shining ray of some luminous body;
but I know you are the emblem of their purest dreams,
and the fervid beating of their great hearts,
and the blessed image adored in every home.

You are the soul of the home and in the towns you are life,
you are the fire in a conscience and an altar in the heart;
in the war you were the spirit of a roused and fiery patria,
and in peace are the loving mother chosen by her children,
to unite tender affections that cross over the sea.

Today sees joined the affections of a brother for his brother,
the love of a mother with the children of her love:
the flag of my Spain with the ensign of the Cuban,
intertwined they blur across the ocean,
hate and rancor forgotten like the war . . .

Noble standard all of love, with your solitary star
splendid and luminous, like some fantastical ruby;
of a patria all aflower the lovely visionary image:
My songs spill out for you now, that soon become a prayer
at the silent tombs of Agramonte and Martí.

My cradle was rocked by the breezes of the Cantabrian,
and, on looking to the light my eyes the saw the light of a Spanish sun;
but one day, very young, one sad and gloomy afternoon,

me lancé, cual ave tierna que, en sus vuelos atrevida,
en pos vaga de un ensueño, de una patria de arrebol.

    Desprendido de los brazos de mi España idolatrada,
con los ojos de la mente ví otra patria toda amor;
y al impulso de las olas de una mar que ruge airada,
fui bogando . . . y en los brazos de una madre enamorada
encontréme, cual la gota del rocío en una flor.

    Era Cuba aquella patria que caricias me brindaba;
era Cuba y sus caricias los rumores del palmar.
¡Otra patria, cual la mía, que en sus brazos me estrechaba!
¡Al dejar, quizá por siempre, a una madre que adoraba,
en los brazos de otra madre noble abrigo fui a encontrar!!

I launched myself, like a tender bird who, daring in his flights,
roams in pursuit of a fantasy, of a patria in roseate glow.

    Ripped from the arms of my idolatrized Spain,
with my mind's eye I saw another patria all of love;
and propelled by the waves of a sea that roars in anger,
I went on paddling . . . and in the arms of an enamored mother
I found myself, like a drop of dew on a flower.

    Cuba was that patria that welcomed me with caresses;
Cuba and her caresses were the murmur of the palms.
Another patria, just like mine, to hold me close in her arms!
On leaving, perhaps forever, a mother who adored me,
in the arms of another mother, kind shelter I came to find!!

El grito de Yara

Poesía leída en "San Carlos" en la Fiesta del 10 de Octubre.

Un grito resonó un día
y sobre el ala del viento,
fue llevando el sentimiento
a un pueblo que sucumbía;
brotó de un alma bravía,
y en las crestas y cimeras
y del río en las riberas
por mil ecos repetido,
fue el estigma de ¡vencido!
en las turbas extranjeras.

Un grito en ruedas aladas,
que el espacio recruzó,
y en los valles resonó
y en las abruptas cañadas;
por los montes y ensenadas
y recodos del camino,
fue aquel grito peregrino
resonando, a las ciudades
y a las huecas soledades
sobre el soplo vespertino.

Fue que un Genio sin segundo,
en el ardor de su anhelo,
a través del patrio suelo
lanzaba un reto profundo:
lanzaba a la faz del mundo
que ardor santo le encendía,
y aquel pueblo que le oía
no era de cobardes gentes,
sino un pueblo de valientes
que bravo luchar sabía.

Rompiéronse las cadenas
al son del clarín sonoro;
brotó de la patria un lloro
el grito sonara apenas;

The Cry of Yara

Poem read at the "San Carlos" at the Celebration of the 10th of October.[56]

A cry rang roundly out one day
and upon the wings of the wind,
it went carrying a feeling
to a people near succumbing;
it burst forth from an untamed soul,
and on the crests and the summits,
and of the river on the banks
by a thousand echoes repeated
it was a shadow of defeat
upon the foreign multitudes.

A cry on winged wheels
that crossed and recrossed space
and that resonated through the valleys
and in the steep ravines;
across the mountains and the inlets
and every bend in the path,
it was that pilgrim cry,
resonating to the cities
and to the resonant solitudes
on the evening breeze.

And so a genius without peer,
in the fire of his yearning
across the land of his patria
launched a most profound challenge:
he threw it in the face of the world
that a sainted ardor burned him,
and that people who heeded him
were the farthest thing from cowards
rather a nation of the brave
who knew well how to fiercely fight.

They broke through iron chains
at the sound of the ringing bugle;
a sob burst forth from the patria,
then the crying was barely heard;

roncas voces de sirenas
hicieron temblar la tierra,
y las trompetas de guerra
más allá del horizonte,
retumbaron en el monte,
en el valle y la pradera.

    El león ensangrentado
sacudiendo su melena,
sintió quebrar la cadena
de aquel pueblo esclavizado;
rugiendo encolerizado,
abrirse vio la frontera
y dar paso a la extranjera
turba loca enrojecida
con la sangre que dio vida
a la cubana bandera.

    La bandera que soñara
Céspedes al pronunciar,
de la patria ante el altar,
el raudo grito de Yara:
la bandera que forjara
con su mente soñadora:
la misma que flota ahora
en el Morro de la Habana,
que dio a la patria cubana
su libertad redentora.

    La que surgió como el velo
de los filiales amores,
nimbada con los colores
divinos del patrio cielo:
la que en su ardiente desvelo
concibiera enardecido
el cubano embravecido,
y con la sangre tiñera
al tiempo que se rompiera
el dogal envilecido.

    Para la enseña bendita
de la fe y de los amores,
de las rosas y las flores

the rough voices of the sirens
made the very ground start to shake,
and the trumpets of war
beyond the horizon,
echoed across the mountain,
and in the valley and the meadow.

   The bloodied lion
shaking his mane,
felt the chain break
of that enslaved people;
roaring in his rage,
he watched the border open
and make way for the foreign
mob, wild and red hot
with the blood that gave life
to the Cuban flag.

   The flag that he would dream of,
Céspedes, upon pronouncing,
for his patria before the altar
the swift cry of Yara:
the flag that he would forge
with his visionary mind:
the same one that floats now
at the Morro in Havana,
that gave to the Cuban nation
her redemptive liberty.

   That rose up like the veil
of filial love,
nimbused with the colors
divine of the native sky;
the one that in his burning insomnia
the Cuban, full of passion,
should conceive, all bravery,
and with blood should dye
at the moment that should break
the debased noose.

   For the blessed standard
of faith and of our love,
of the roses and the flowers

y la esperanza inmarchita;
para el pendón que hoy se agita
entre los libres pendones,
dio Martí sus ilusiones,
y Agramonte y Aguilera
su añoranza postrimera
y sus grandes corazones.

   Bandera amada, por ti
dio su aliento soberano
otro valiente cubano
de apellido Sanguily;
el corazón de Martí
lleva prendido tu estrella,
por eso luces tan bella,
flotando libre a los vientos,
y el clamor de mis acentos
tu eternal victoria sella.

   La palma de sus deberes
lograron por ti los hombres,
ellos te dieron sus nombres...
y sus besos las mujeres;
fuiste de aguerridos seres
que te brindaron el alma,
la que les diste la palma,
al verte surgir radiante
con tu estrella rutilante,
que es sol de la augusta calma.

   Después, cuando libre fueras,
y un himno de paz y gloria
cantaban y de Victoria
dulcemente las palmeras,
oyeron las extranjeras
huestes bélicas un canto
que las llenara de espanto:
el pueblo gritó estridente:
¡viva Cuba independiente!
¡ya no más gotas de llanto!!

   Y fue aquel grito estridente
el mismo que resonara

and of hope unwithered;
for the banner that today waves
among the free flags,
Martí gave his dreams,
and Agramonte and Aguilera[57]
their last longing
and their great hearts.

   Beloved flag, for you
another valiant Cuban
by the name of Sanguily[58]
gave his sovereign breath;
the heart of Martí
your star will wear forever,
and so you give a lovely showing,
floating freely on the winds,
and the clamor of my words
seals your eternal victory.

   The final glory of their duty
your men achieved for you;
they gave you their names . . .
and the women their kisses.
You were, for those battle-hardened,
who offered you their souls,
the one who gave them glory,
on seeing you rise up, radiant,
with your rutilant star,
itself the sun of august calm.[59]

   Later, when you were free,
And a hymn of peace and glory
the palm trees sang,
sweetly, to Victory,
the foreign warlike hosts,
could perceive a song
that filled them with fright:
the people shouted, strident:
Long live Cuba, independent!
The time for tears is done!

   And it was that strident cry,
the same one that resonated

en los confines de Yara
el diez de Octubre, doliente:
el grito de "independiente"
que Céspedes pronunció
y Agramonte recogió,
para legar a Martí,
logrando secar así
el llanto que se vertió.

Ahora, Cuba querida,
ya no sufres, ya no lloras,
y las trompetas sonoras
te proclaman redimida:
no brota sangre la herida
que tu corazón partiera;
ya tienes una bandera
gallarda, libre y triunfante,
que te legara vibrante,
en Yara una voz guerrera . . .

Lleva ramos inmarchitos,
rocíalos con ternura,
a la fría sepultura
de tus mártires benditos;
de tus rezos infinitos,
sobre el sacrosanto osario,
vierte el eco funerario,
lo mismo que mis acentos
yo mando sobre los vientos
al boscaje solitario.

Del jardín de su candor
lleve el niño tiernas flores;
del huerto de sus dolores
lleve el anciano una flor . . .
cubana: lleva tu amor
y tus besos de mujer,
que el diez de Octubre ha de ser
para que en las tumbas vibre
el sentir de un pueblo libre
que cumple con su deber.

in the pained confines of Yara
on the tenth of October:
the cry of "Independence!"
that Céspedes pronounced
and Agramonte gathered up
to bequeath it to Martí,
so managing to staunch
the flow of tears that were spilled.

   Now, beloved Cuba,
now you don't suffer, now you don't cry,
and the sonorous trumpets
proclaim you redeemed:
blood does not well up from the wound
that would break your heart;
now you have a flag
gallant, free, and triumphant,
that was bequeathed to you, vibrant,
in Yara by a warrior's voice . . .

   Take now unwithered bouquets,
and strew them with tenderness,
at the cold tomb
of your blessed martyrs;
of your infinite prayers
over the sacrosanct ossuary,
let fall the funerary echo,
just as here my words
I send upon the winds
to the solitary grove.

   From the garden of your candor
let the child carry tender flowers;
from the orchard of your pains
let the old man take a bloom . . .
Cubana: carry your love
and your woman's kisses,
for it must be the tenth of October,
that in the tombs there should vibrate
the feeling of a free people
who fulfill their duty.

Y vosotros de lealtad,
mártires que sucumbisteis,
ya que hermosa brillar visteis
la estrella de libertad,
en la tumba descansad,
y tendedle vuestra mano
al libre pueblo cubano,
llevándolo por la senda
que le diera como ofrenda
vuestro aliento soberano.

Y al valiente que hoy dirige
la nave ya rescatada
de la patria libertada,
a que otra guerra hoy aflige,
dadle el aliento que rige
con las leyes oportunas;
si las huestes importunas
intentan campear allí
¡qué encuentren otro Martí
en el héroe de las Tunas!

¡Qué brille siempre radioso
el sol de la patria libre!
¡Qué el santo entusiasmo vibre
de ese pueblo generoso!
¡Qué Cuba grabe glorioso,
en su pecho, como en lienzo,
de libertad el comienzo,
que inspira el deber bendito,
proclamado por el grito
del Mártir de San Lorenzo!!

Y a mí, si otra vez retumba
el cañón, Cuba, en tu suelo,
y quiere quizás el Cielo
que allí también yo sucumba,
no me niegues una tumba
debajo de una palmera,
y en mi morada postrera,
como bendito sudario
¡qué cubra mi triste osario
tu libertada bandera!

And you, all made of loyalty,
martyrs who succumbed,
now that you see shining lovely
the star of liberty,
rest easy in your tombs,
and reach out your hands
to the free Cuban people,
guiding them along the path
that like an offered blessing
your sovereign encouragement should give.

And to the valiant who today directs
the ship now rescued
of the liberated patria,
which another war afflicts today,
give him the inspiration to govern
with the appropriate laws;
and if inopportune armies
attempt to campaign there,
let them find another Martí
in the hero of Tunas![60]

Let shine forever radiant
the sun of our free patria!
let the sacred enthusiasm vibrate
of that generous nation!
Let Cuba engrave, glorious,
on her breast, as on a canvas,
the beginning of liberty,
that inspires the blessed duty,
proclaimed by the cry
of the martyr of San Lorenzo![61]

As for me, if again the cannon
should resound, Cuba, on your shores,
and the Heavens should desire
that there I too should succumb,
don't deny me a tomb
beneath a palm tree,
and in my final abode,
like a blessed shroud,
let cover my sad ossuary
your liberated flag!

LA SOCIEDAD "CUBA" Y SU EDIFICIO

La Voz de un Poeta

Nuestro particular y distinguido amigo, el culto e inspirado poeta F. Castro, ha escrito expresamente, el hermoso himno que publicamos en lugar de honor de esta Crónica, la cual consideramos honrada con tan hermosa producción.

El joven poeta, dedica sus vibrantes estrofas a la juventud en general; a la cual se une en la valiente cruzada que tendrá por seguro resultado, el edificio de la Sociedad "Cuba."

He aquí el hermoso himno:

¡Cubanos, proseguid!

Cubanas juventudes: ¡salvad vuestra bandera!
¡Qué arraigue entre vosotros valiente el ideal!
¡Qué surja el bello templo! ¡Qué pronto en su cimera
ondee de los nobles aquel pendón leal!

Si fuere así preciso, corred duro calvario,
luchando hasta que logre la planta descansar
encima, allá en la cumbre del patrio santuario.
¡Qué surja de las sombras gigante vuestro altar!

No importan los escombros de una obra derruida;
no importa que en cenizas trocaran la ilusión;
la juventud cubana, de aliento noble henchida,
yo sé que por su patria se arranca el corazón.

Yo sé que de valientes hereda su entereza,
de aquellos que supieron morir de cara al sol;
de aquellos que a la patria legaron su nobleza,
tiñéndola de sangre, después con arrebol . . .

Cubanas juventudes: llamad vuestra conciencia
por ver qué os insinúa, y al corazón oíd;
oíd lo que la patria reclama tras la ausencia,
y oiréis un solo grito: *¡Cubanos, proseguid!*

Lo mismo a que os alienta la voz de un extranjero
que sabe que es muy triste vivir sin un hogar;

THE "CUBA" SOCIETY AND ITS BUILDING

The Voice of a Poet

Our particular and distinguished friend, the cultured and inspired poet F. Castro has written this lovely hymn which we publish in pride of place, expressly for our Chronicle, which we consider to be honored by such a lovely production.

The young poet dedicates his vibrant stanzas to the youth in general; to which he joins himself in the valiant crusade that will surely have a result, the building of the Society "Cuba."[62]

Here follows the lovely hymn:

Cubans, Carry On!

Youth of Cuba: hail your flag!
Let the valiant ideal take root amongst you!
Let there spring up a lovely temple, on whose crest
shall soon wave the loyal pendant of the most noble!

And if it should so be needful, run the harsh Calvary,
fighting until you come your foot to rest
atop it, there on the summit of the national shrine.
May your altar spring forth gigantic from the shadows!

The debris from a destroyed work do not matter;
it does not matter that to ashes those dreams are turned;
the youth of Cuba, swollen with noble breath,
I know that for their patria will rip out their very heart.

I know that from the valiant they inherit their integrity,
from those who knew how to die with their face to the sun;
from those who to the patria bequeathed their nobility,
staining it with blood, later with a roseate glow . . .

Youth of Cuba: call your conscience
to see how it pricks you, and listen to your heart;
hear what the patria demands after this absence,
and you will hear only one cry: *Cubans, carry on!*

Just as you can be strengthened by the voice of a foreigner
who knows how sad it is to live without a home;

vosotros lo perdisteis: perdisteis el primero,
y para tener otro debéis saber luchar.

Unidos y luchando, ¡qué broten de ilusiones
las rosas de la patria de vuestro corazón!
Allí donde se aúnan valientes corazones,
revive en sus cenizas un templo de ilusión.

¡Qué surja la gloriosa pirámide que ostente
de vuestro afecto patrio el resurgir leal;
un Centro que os recoja, grandioso, y represente
la patria y su bandera: sublime el ideal!

¡Revivan los escombros! ¡Levántese sublime
el "Templo de la patria"! ¡Reviva el patrio amor!!
Cubanas juventudes: Es algo que redime
vencer con sacrificios, triunfar sobre el dolor . . .

Prosiga su camino la juventud cubana,
que andando el movimiento precisa demostrar;
recoja el noble aliento que de mi voz emana,
que yo también mi ofrenda sabré depositar.

¡Aliento! que emprendisteis la senda visionaria,
que acaba en horizontes divinos de arrebol.
¡Qué ondee sobre el "Centro" la estrella solitaria!
¡Aliento! que os alumbra la patria con su sol.

F. CASTRO

Las listas de donantes que semanalmente publicamos, serán motivo de satisfacción para el distinguido poeta, pues ellas demuestran que la juventud cubana se he dado cuenta de lo mucho que vale y significa la Sociedad "Cuba," la cual, en vez de desaparecer, resurgirá más gallarda y prepotente,

R. MIQUELI.
Key West, 1917.
Del Semanario "Florida"

so you who lost it, who lost the first chance at one,
for another you ought to know to fight.

    United and fighting, may they burst from idle dreams
the roses of the patria of your hearts!
There where valiant hearts become one,
from its ashes that temple of a daydream may arise.

    Let surge up the glorious pyramid that can boast
the loyal resurgence of your national affection;
a Center that gathers you, magnificent, and that may
represent the patria and her flag: that sublime ideal!

    Raise up the debris! May the "Temple of the patria"
rise up sublime! Bring new life to that love of nation!!
Youth of Cuba: It is a road to redemption
to win with sacrifices, to triumph over pain . . .

    May the youth of Cuba proceed upon their path,
that by their passage they may show the way;
and let them take noble encouragement from my voice,
that I too may know how to leave a proper offering.

    Take heart! for you set out upon the visionary path,
that ends in divine horizons of roseate glow.
May the solitary star one day wave over the Center!!
Take heart! And may Cuba's sun bathe you in its light.

F. CASTRO

    The lists of donors that we publish weekly will be the cause of satisfaction for the distinguished poet, for they demonstrate that the Cuban youth has realized the full grade of the value and significance of the Society "Cuba," which, instead of disappearing, will resurge more gallant and powerful.

R. MIQUELI.
Key West, 1917.
From the weekly "Florida"

Bodas de plata del Centro Español de Tampa
Honor a sus Fundadores

    Honor al que ha vencido en lid honrada
y que surge del mundo en el proscenio,
como estrella en la bóveda azulada,
dando luz con las alas de su genio.

    Honor para los nobles caballeros,
que dieron a la patria honor no escaso,
trazando con su heroico y firme paso
de amistad fraternal anchos senderos.

    Aquellos que cifraron sus blasones
en derramar la luz hora tras hora,
uniendo los hispanos corazones
bajo un cielo de paz encantadora.

    Ramírez y los Vega y Bustamante:
no fueron lumbre fatua vuestras glorias;
surgisteis como el astro fulgurante
que alumbra eternamente las victorias.

    Los Méndez y Pendás, Ramón Carreño,
Alonso y otros más, egregios hombres,
lograsteis realizar el noble sueño
de erigir un altar a vuestros nombres.

    Ese Centro Español, obra grandiosa,
himno eterno de amor y sentimiento,
alzóse cual pirámide gloriosa
por vuestro augusto y paternal aliento.

    Esa obra a la que el arte luz imprime
dignifica una causa y una idea:
de la patria al amor grande y sublime
altar de unión para sus hijos crea.

    Fue escabrosa la senda que seguisteis
limpiándola de sombras y de abrojos,
pero la senda donde ayer sufristeis
es hoy toda fulgor a vuestros ojos.

The Silver Anniversary of the Spanish Center in Tampa[63]
In Honor of Its Founders

   Honor to him who has won in honorable battle
and who rises up on the proscenium of the world
like a star in the blued vault,
giving light with the wings of his genius.

   Honor to the noble gentleman,
who gave to the patria no few honors,
tracing with his heroic and firm step
wide paths of brotherly friendship.

   Those who distill the value of their glory
to the spilling forth of light hour after hour
uniting all Hispanic hearts
under a sky of enchanting peace.

   Ramírez and the Vegas and Bustamante:
your glories were no fleeting fancy;
you rose up like the glowing star
that illumines victory forever.

   The Méndezes and the Pendás, Ramón Carreño,
Alonso and yet others, illustrious men,
you managed to make real the noble dream
of erecting an altar to your names.

   That Spanish Center, a great work,
eternal hymn to love and sentiment,
was raised up like a glorious pyramid
by your august and paternal breath.

   That work to which art imprints light
dignifies a cause and an idea:
from the great, sublime love of the patria
it created an altar of union for its sons.

   Rough was the path that you followed
cleaning it of shadows and of thistles,
but that trail where yesterday you suffered
is today all brilliance to your eyes.

Ya en cinco lustros se olvidó la guerra,
yo no marca el terror vuestras conquistas,
ni hay un solo español en esta tierra
que no os dedique adoración de artistas.

El pueblo os ama con amor profundo
y vuestros nombres guarda en sus anales,
y anhela proclamaros ante el mundo
"españoles heroicos e inmortales."

"Héroes" que disteis perdurable ejemplo
a los que aman el suelo en que han nacido;
"inmortales," que, alzando un bello templo,
lo habéis glorificado y redimido.

España que os proclama hijos amantes
y os bendice en su espíritu sereno,
os busca con sus ojos anhelantes
como busca la madre hijo bueno.
. . . .

¡Qué esa patria que amáis tierna recoja
en vuestras obras el filial tribute,
y los vientos no arranquen a la hoja
hasta que caiga sazonado el fruto!

Y la gloria con bellos arreboles
ilumine enlazadas vuestras manos,
"aquí" donde a tantos españoles
les habéis enseñado a ser hermanos.

Already in five times five years the war is forgotten,
And terror does not mark your conquests,
nor is there a single Spaniard in this land
who does not offer you the adoration of an artist.

The people love you with a deep love
and keep your names in their annals,
and they yearn to proclaim you before the world
"heroic and immortal Spaniards."

"Heroes" who gave a lasting example
to those who love the land on which they were born;
"immortal," who, erecting a lovely temple,
have glorified and redeemed it.

Spain who proclaims you loving sons
and blesses you in your serene spirit,
seeks you with her yearning eyes
like a mother seeks out her dear child.

. . . .

May the patria that you love tenderly gather
from your workings a filial tribute,
and may the winds not tear free a single leaf
until the ripened fruit should fall!

And may glory, with its lovely afterglow
illuminate your interlaced hands,
here, where you have taught
so many Spaniards to be brothers.

Mensaje de lágrimas

Para el culto R. M. Alzay.

Muchas veces parécenos que canta
el triste pajarillo que se queja,
y es que gime y su mágica garganta
entre las ramas la amargura deja

Es lo mismo que el bardo que, cantando,
en tristezas muy hondas se debate,
porque el bardo es un pájaro dejando
en sus versos la angustia que le abate.

Errante, yo cruzaba por el mundo
sin saber de las quejas y pesares,
cuando un surco muy hondo, muy profundo
dejó abierto el dolor en mis cantares:

A la rosa de amor: la madre mía
que aromaba el jardín de mis amores,
despiadado huracán la tronchó un día
y de luto dejó todas mis flores.

¿A quién he de decirle de mis quejas?
¿a quién podré acudir en mis pesares?
¡Oh, muerte, qué vacío mi hogar dejas!
¡cómo anegas en llanto mis cantares!

Tengo miedo a vivir, deshecho el nido
donde alegre gocé el amor primero;
mientras bebo las hieles del olvido
¡qué enlutado ha de estar todo el sendero!

¡Si volviese a gozar de aquel abrigo
que he dejado lanzándome a la ausencia!
pero, no, que ensañóse así conmigo
del destino fatídica inclemencia.

¡Si pudiese de pena en mis excesos
acercarme a la tumba entristecida,
y con notas de amor y con mis besos
despertar a mi madre, darle vida!

Message of Tears

For the learned R. M. Alzay.[64]

    Many times we hear as a seeming song
the complaint of the sad little bird,
when in truth he moans, and his magical throat
leaves the bitterness amongst the branches.

    It is the same for the bard, who, singing,
speaks on the deepest of sorrows,
because the bard is a bird, leaving
in his verses the anguish that crushes him.

    Errant, I crossed the world over
without knowing of complaints or sorrows,
when a furrow very deep, very profound
made apparent the pain in my songs:

    To the rose of love: oh mother mine,
who perfumed the garden of my loves,
a merciless hurricane cut short one day
and left all of my flowers in mourning.

    To whom should I tell my complaints?
to whom can I go with my sorrows?
Oh death, who leaves my home so empty!
How you inundate with tears my every song!

    I fear living, with the nest all undone
where happy I enjoyed the first blush of love;
while I drink the bile of forgetting,
how mournful lies the path ahead entire!

    If only I could once more enjoy that shelter
that I've long since left on leaping into absence!
but no, so merciless has been for me
the fateful inclemency of destiny.

    If only I could, in my excess of sorrow
draw near to that tomb wreathed in sadness,
and with notes of love and with my kisses
awaken my mother, give her life!

Aquella golondrina voladora
que llevaba a mi hogar grato mensaje,
¿qué dirá, cuando llegue, desde ahora,
encontrando tan solo aquel paraje? . . .

Golondrina gentil: tú de mis penas
no les digas jamás a mis hermanas,
que mis pobres hermanas son muy buenas,
y no deben llorar penas tempranas.

No les quieras decir que también lloro
la desdicha infinita que presiento,
ni que suena a dolor la lira de oro
en estrofas de inmenso sentimiento.

Cuando llegues, que finja tu garganta
no más que expresión leve de una queja:
sabe ser como el pájaro que canta,
aunque en las ramas su amargura deja.

Que no sepan mis llantos y mis penas
esas niñas que gimen angustiadas;
aunque sufren, no dejan de ser buenas,
y no deben llorar abandonadas.

Toma y lleva y déjalos impresos
sobre el mármol de aquella tumba fría,
los mensajes de lágrimas y besos,
que esperando estará la madre mía.

Y después que allí dejes el mensaje
tejido de mis ojos con rocío,
huye rauda, abandona aquel paraje
de caricias y amores tan vacío.

Retorna; yo te espero a que me digas
de mis pobres hermanas enlutadas,
tras la sima sin fondo de fatigas,
en la eterna orfandad abandonadas.

Golondrina gentil: ven, que te espera
un mensaje de amores nuevamente;
tú por siempre has de ser mi mensajera,
mientras duerme mi madre eternamente.

That far flying swallow
who was bearing to my home a sweet message,
what will he say, when on arriving there, and ever more,
he finds but an empty wilderness? . . .

Courteous swallow: of my sorrows
you must never tell my sisters,
for my poor sisters are so good,
and ought not cry for future pains.

Do not wish to tell them that I also cry
for the infinite misfortune that I feel coming,
nor that a lyre of gold sounds like pain
in stanzas of immense sentiment.

When you arrive, may your throat pretend
to bear no more than a mild expression of complaint:
may you know how to be like the bird who sings,
and leaves all his bitterness amidst the branches.

May they not know my tears and my sorrows,
those girls who weep in their own anguish;
though they suffer, they do not cease their goodness,
and they should not cry abandoned.

Take and carry and leave imprinted
on the marble of that cold tomb,
the messages of tears and kisses
that my mother will be awaiting.

And after you leave the message there
woven with the dew from my eyes,
flee swiftly, abandon that place
so empty of caresses and of love.

Return then, I will await, for you to tell me
of my poor sisters in their mourning,
across the chasm of fatigue with no bottom,
in eternal orphanhood abandoned.

Courteous swallow: come, for here awaits
a new message of love;
you forever must be my messenger,
while my mother sleeps eternally.

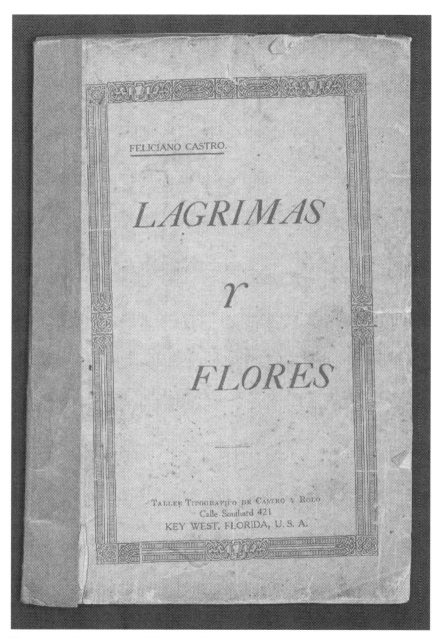

Illustration 1. Front cover of *Lágrimas y flores*.

Illustration 2. Feliciano Castro circa 1918. Photo included in *Lágrimas y flores*.

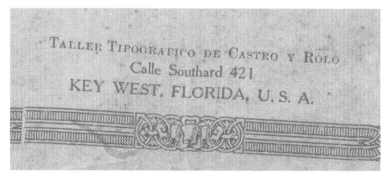

Illustration 3. Enlargement of printing press information.

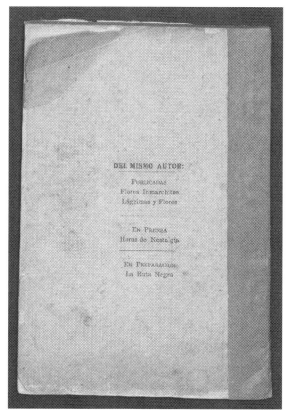

Illustration 4. Back cover of *Lágrimas y flores*.

Illustration 5. Section-dividing page of *Lágrimas y flores*.

FLORES

Mi ofrenda

A Dulce María Bravo, devotamente.

 Rendir quiero mi ofrenda de honor a tu belleza,
tejer con mis estrofas muy bello un pedestal:
en versos muy divinos rimar por tu grandeza
un poema todo efluvios de néctar celestial.

 Yo quiero orlar mis rimas con besos y con flores,
dorarlas con esencias de nítida ilusión,
y en medio de mis versos de mágicos colores
lo mismo que una rosa prender el corazón.

 Verter aquí infinitos raudales de armonía,
de arrullos y caricias tu imagen circundar;
por eso es que semeja, por ti, la lira mía
un eco rumoroso de célico arrullar.

 Fingir quiero el concierto de miles de querubes
que armónicos viniesen en coro angelical,
traerte su homenaje, por entre blancas nubes
vertiendo sus cadencias en cántico triunfal.

 Como ellos ofrendarte mi cántiga de amores
con una suave lira de heráldico sonar;
hablarte de los sueños de regios trovadores
que el trono de su reina se acercan a besar.

 Tener el sentimiento de miles de violines,
el dúlcido suspiro del arpa del amor,
y así fingir un coro de alados serafines,
y así verter mis notas, soñando, en tu redor.

 Mis notas y mis versos tejidos con sonrisas;
decirte en mis cadencias con lira de marfil:
"Tus ojos son dos soles, tu aliento cual las brisas
que alumbran y eternizan las flores del Abril."

 Ungir de grata esencia mi voz y mi lenguaje,
fingiendo la balada divina del amor;
mandarte en estos versos de dichas un mensaje,
tejido con destellos de luz y resplandor.

My Offering

To Dulce María Bravo, devotedly.

To render I desire my offering in honor of your beauty,
to weave you with my stanzas a lovely pedestal:
in divine verses rhyme by means of your greatness
a poem all outpourings of celestial nectar.

I want to trim my rhymes with kisses and with flowers,
gild them with the essence of crystalline illusions,
and amidst my verses all of magical colors,
just like a rose to fasten my heart.

To pour out here infinite torrents of harmony,
with cooings and caresses your image to surround;
and for all this my lyre will resemble, for you
a murmuring echo of heavenly lullaby.

To feign I want the concert of thousands of cherubs
that in harmony should come in angelical choir,
to bring you their homage, among white clouds
pouring forth their cadences in triumphal canticle.

Like them to offer you my cantiga of love[65]
with a soft lyre of heraldic sound;
to speak to you of the dreams of royal troubadours,
who the throne of their queen approach to kiss.

To have the feeling of a thousand violins,
the dulcet sigh of the harp of love,
and thereby to feign a chorus of winged seraphs,
and so pour forth my notes, dreamlike, all around you.

My notes and my verses woven with smiles;
to tell you in my cadences with a marble lyre:
"Your eyes are two suns, your breath like the breezes
that illumine and eternalize the flowers of April."

To anoint with pleasing essence my voice and
my language, feigning the divine ballad of love;
To send you in these verses of good tidings a message,
woven with sparkles of light and of radiance.

Traer hasta tu senda las sílfides y ondinas
con liras de oro y plata de célico tañer,
con ellas acercarme; mis cántigas divinas
también a tus hechizos poderlas ofrecer.

Mis cántigas y, acaso, de amor una romanza,
que todos tus hechizos reflejan el amor;
y nunca puede el bardo trazar una semblanza
sin luz de los amores que préstanle esplendor . . .

Después que te cantara, después que mis loores
llegasen a tu oído, cual mágica canción,
igual que ante su reina los regios trovadores,
poner como una rosa también mi corazón.
. . . .

Yo quise un homenaje rendir a tu belleza,
mas nunca tu belleza quizás logre copiar;
circúndante aureolas inmensas de grandeza
que alejan al poeta de tu glorioso altar.

En cambio al homenaje, en cambio de la ofrenda
y aquel que yo forjara divino pedestal,
arrojo entre las flores que viven en tu senda
mi lira y una rosa, mujer toda ideal.

To bring to your path the sylphs and undines
with lyres of gold and silver that ring out heavenly,
and with them approach you, that my divine cantigas
also to your enchantments I can offer.

My cantigas, and perhaps some ballad of love,
for all of your enchantments reflect love;
and never can the bard trace a semblance
without the light of the loves that lend him splendor . . .

After singing to you, after my praises
should arrive to your ear, like a magic song,
just like before their queen the royal troubadours,
to lay like a rose before you also my heart.
. . . .

I wanted to render homage unto your beauty,
but your beauty perhaps I could never hope to copy;
immense aureoles of greatness surround you
that distance a poet from your glorious altar.

Instead of the homage, instead of the offering
and that with which I would forge a new pedestal,
I throw down amidst the flowers that fill your path
my lyre and a rose, for you lady, all ideal.

A mis hermanas

   Hermanas: en mis horas de amargura,
mientras bebo las hieles de la ausencia,
en pedazos divide mi existencia
y os la mando en estrofas de ternura.

   Otra ofrenda no tengo, y os doy pura
de mis versos de amor la grata esencia:
vuestra senda de amor y de inocencia
yo la riego con notas de dulzura.

   ¡Loco!—me llamasteis—porque, errante,
de arideces seguí por el sendero,
escudado en mi lira sollozante . . .

   Hermanas: reprocharos yo no quiero;
si soy loco, de un loco así, sangrante
partid el corazón que os mando entero.

To My Sisters

    Sisters: in my hours of bitterness,
while I drink the bile of absence,
my existence splits into pieces
and I send it to you in stanzas of fondness.

    I have no other offering, and I give you, pure,
of my verses of love the pleasing essence:
your path of love and of innocence
I water with notes of sweetness.

    Mad!—you called me because, roaming,
I followed a track wracked by drought
shielded by my sobbing lyre . . .

    Sisters: I have no wish to reproach you;
if I am mad, then of a madman, still bleeding
break the heart that I send you whole.

A las obreritas

    Bellas mujeres trabajadoras
que en los talleres pasáis las horas,
y allí encerrasteis vuestra ilusión:
al contemplaros, como la palma
gentiles siempre, brota de mi alma
para vosotras una canción.

    Cuando sumisas cruzar os veo,
como esperanzas, como un deseo,
buscando vida para el hogar,
quisiera amante cambiar la vida,
para que os fuese siempre florida,
y no supierais lo que es llorar.

    Cruzáis los mares de la quimera,
y, cuando lejos de la ribera,
halláis las olas en tempestad,
a esa mar triste de los hogares
tórnanla alegre vuestros cantares:
trueca humilde vuestra humildad.

    Es el trabajo amor que sublima,
y en los hogares un canto rima
frente por frente de la virtud:
es la diadema de vuestra frente,
ante quien pongo yo reverente
el tosco canto de mi laúd.

    Y si mi canto tuviese flores,
la grata esencia de los amores
o tiernas rosas que deshojar,
a vuestras plantas las deshojara:
amor y flores os ofrendara
sobre las gradas de vuestro altar.

    Si yo tuviese gratos consuelos
para cambiaros vuestros desvelos
por la ventura como broquel,
nunca lloraran, ¡no! vuestros ojos,
ni de la vida, de sus abrojos
probarais nunca la amarga hiel . . .

To the Factory Girls

    Lovely women workers
who in the workshops pass your hours,
and there shut in your dreams:
on seeing you, like the palm,
always courteous, a song bursts forth
from my soul for you.

    When all obedient I see you cross,
like hopes, like a desire,
seeking a living for the home,
I should like, lovingly, to change your lives,
so that it should be for you always in bloom,
and that you should know not what it is to cry.

    You cross the chimeric seas,
and, when far from the shore,
you find the waves tossed by a storm,
that sad sea of home and hearth
is made joyful by your songs,
is made humble by your humility.

    Labor is a love that ennobles,
and rhymes a song at home
face to face with virtue:
It is the diadem on your brow,
before which I offer, reverent,
a rough song of my praises.

    And if my song were to have flowers,
the pleasing essence of love,
or delicate roses to pluck petal by petal,
I would strew them at your feet:
love and flowers I would offer
on the steps of your altar.

    If I had pleasing consolations
to change your sleepless nights
for good fortune like a shield,
your eyes, no, they would never cry,
nor of life, nor of its thorns,
would you ever taste the bitter bile.

Aunque las busco, no encuentro notas
y en vano quiero con alas rotas
llegar al trono de vuestro altar;
siempre mis versos son de tristeza,
y por lo mismo vuestra grandeza
solo muy triste puedo cantar.

Mas, aunque canto por el acaso,
igual que el ave que va de paso
rimando al viento triste canción,
al dejar estos queridos lares,
pondré mi lira en vuestros altares
como una ofrenda del corazón.

Y cuando lejos de vuestros ojos,
vaya cruzando por entre abrojos
hacia otros climas, os mandaré
con la paloma de mis cantares
canción hermosa que en estos lares
venga deciros que os recordé.

Though I seek them, I find not the notes
and in vain I want, with broken wings
to arrive to the throne of your altar;
always my verses are of sorrow,
and by the same your greatness
only very sadly can I sing.

But though I sing by chance,
just like the bird who passes by,
rhyming with the sad wind his song,
on leaving these dear hearths,
I will put my lyre on your altar
as an offering from my heart.

And when far off from your eyes,
I should go crossing amidst the thorns
toward other climes, I will send you
with the dove of my songs
a beautiful poem that to your hearths
shall come to say that I remember you.

Quisiera...

A Elvira Salazar.

Quisiera ser el sol de tu ventura,
el ángel admirando tus hechizos,
el pájaro cantando tu hermosura
y el céfiro jugando con tus rizos.

Quisiera darte dicha en mis cantares,
—si mi canto tal vez la dicha encierra—
tener todos los cetros de la tierra
y ponerlos por gala en tus altares.

Arrancar un laurel a mi destino,
y arrojarlo a tu paso en el camino,
como lírica alfombra de ternura.

Que eres todo un portento de belleza,
pues que guardas de lirio la pureza
que es fuente inagotable de hermosura.

I Should Like . . .

To Elvira Salazar.

 I should like to shine sun-like on your fortune,
be the angel that admires your every charm,
the bird that sings of nothing but your beauty
and the zephyr playing sweetly with your curls.

 I should like to give you joy with my singing,
—if it should chance that my verses contain joy—
to gather all the scepters from across the earth
and lay them as regalia on your altar;

 To uproot a laurel that's destined for me,
and to throw it at your passing in your path,
as a lyrical carpet of tenderness.

 Because you are a prodigy of beauty,
because you keep the lily's purity,
which is the endless fountain of loveliness.

¿Por qué te escribo?

Para "Lolita" Toledo.

Mujer divina: son tus amores
la fiel imagen de tu belleza;
eres fragrante como las flores;
son tus perfumes embriagadores;
eres un lirio todo pureza.

Son tus miradas angelicales
las que me inspiran sueños y amores;
son tus caricias sentimentales;
todas tus formas son ideales;
fingen tus rizos hermosas flores.

Hay en tus labios la miel divina
de los panales del grato amor;
eres la bella gentil ondina
que cuando pasa hiere y fascina;
tienes un alma toda candor.

Eres la fuente de la ambrosia
que brinda al alma dulce ilusión;
eres la imagen de la alegría
y eres el astro de hermoso día
que enciende el fuego de la pasión.

Por eso quiero, bella sultana,
también un verso rimar por ti;
es tu belleza tan soberana,
que si te fijas, mujer galana,
te dirá el verso "por qué escribí".

Why Do I Write to You?

For "Lolita" Toledo.

 Heavenly woman: the love you give is
the faithful image of your own beauty;
you are fragrant like the very flowers;
your perfumes each are intoxicating;
you are a lily all of purity.

 It is your angelical glances
that ever inspire in me dreams and loves;
your merest caress is sentimental;
every inch of your figure is ideal;
your curls imitate lovely flowers.

 There is on your lips the divine honey
of the honeycombs of a most pleasant love;
you are the lovely, courteous undine
that when she passes wounds and fascinates;
you have a soul all made of innocence.

 You are the fountain of the ambrosia
that affords to the soul these sweet daydreams;
you are the picture of joyfulness
and you are the star of the lovely day
that sets alight the fire of passion.

 And so I want, beautiful sultana,
also a verse to rhyme in your honor;
your beauty is so sovereign to itself
that if you pay heed here, stylish lady,
the verse will tell you "why it is I wrote."

Rimas

A Adelaida Fueyo.

I

Suenan voces soñadoras,
dulces músicas sonoras
en redor:
son suspiros de la amada
que gimiendo enamorada,
va tejiendo la balada
del amor...

II

Trina el ave con ternura,
y la brisa en la espesura
deja oír:
el arrullo acariciante
que semeja del amante
el ensueño delirante
del vivir...

III

Los rumores de los vientos
simbolizan los lamentos
y el dolor:
son la queja misteriosa
de la amada quejumbrosa,
en la noche silenciosa
del amor...

IV

Cuando lleguen a tu oído
de mis versos el gemido
y el llorar:
en mis ansias anhelante,
yo semejo aquel amate
que sentiste acariciante
suspirar...

Rhymes

To Adelaida Fueyo.

I

Dreaming voices sound,
sweet sonorous music
all around:
they are the sighs of the beloved
that moaning besotted,
goes weaving the ballad
of her love . . .

II

The bird trills with tenderness,
and the breeze in the thicket
lets one hear:
the caressing murmur
like that of a lover
the delirious fantasy
of living . . .

III

The sounds of the winds
symbolize laments
and pain:
they are the mysterious complaint
of the plaintive beloved,
in the silent night
of love . . .

IV

When arrives to your hearing
the moan of my verses
and its tears:
in my eager longing
I am like that lover
Whose breath you felt as a
caress . . .

V

    Y es entonces cuando un beso
todo amor, todo embeleso
brotará:
de mis labios ardoroso,
y en los tuyos amoroso,
un idilio venturoso
buscará . . .

V

And it is then that a kiss
all love, all enchantment
will burst forth:
from my burning lips
and on your amorous ones
a fortunate idyll
will seek . . .

A Dulce María Bravo

—en su álbum—

    Cuando asoma la pálida alborada
allá entre los celajes del Oriente,
el beso de sus rayos dulcemente
te acaricia con ansia apasionada.

    Cuando llega al final de la jornada
el sol y va a morir solemnemente,
cada un rayo que parte de Occidente
nimba de oro tu senda perfumada,

    La alborada en sus besos placentera
y el sol en su mirada postrimera,
acarician en ti todas las flores,

    Pues saben que son ellas tus hermanas,
y ellas mismas sonrientes y lozanas,
te proclaman la flor de sus amores.

To Dulce María Bravo

—In her album—

    When appears the pallid dawn
off there among the cloudscapes in the Orient,
the kiss of her rays sweetly
caresses you with passionate thirst.

    When at labor's end the sun comes
and then goes solemnly to die,
each of the rays that departs from the Occident
nimbuses in gold your perfumed path,

    The dawn, in her kisses pleasing
and the sun in his final glance,
caress in you all of the flowers,

    For they know that they are your sisters,
and they themselves, smiling and in good health,
proclaim you the flower of their loves.

A Antonia Martínez

   A la par que tus ojos divinales
alumbran suavemente tu camino,
un río de ambrosia cristalino
efluye de tus labios virginales.

   Exquisito perfume de rosales
de intensa dulcedumbre, muy divino,
emana de tu cutis terso y fino,
en efluvios que arroban, celestiales.

   Eres bella y seduces como el hada;
dichoso el que te logre para amada,
vertiendo al pasar tú, de amor sus flores.

   Deben ser tus caricias de ternura,
y tus besos, henchidos de dulzura,
como chispas de amor abrasadores.

To Antonia Martínez

    Together with your divine eyes
that illuminate softly your path,
a river of crystalline ambrosia
pours out of your virginal lips.

    An exquisite perfume of roses
of intense sweetness so divine,
emanates from your skin so smooth and fine,
in outpourings that enchant, celestial.

    You are beautiful and you seduce like a fairy;
lucky he who wins you for his lover,
spilling out, at your passing, all love's flowers.

    Your caresses must be all tenderness,
and your kisses swollen with sweetness,
like sparks of burning love.

A "Conchita" Saenz

Que aceptes quiero, bella "Conchita",
la humilde ofrenda de mi canción,
como una rosa siempre inmarchita
de los jardines de la ilusión.

A tus encantos fascinadores
justo homenaje quiero ofrendar:
con mis estrofas, con mis loores
vengo mi ofrenda depositar.

Es tu belleza deslumbradora,
y es tu semblante como la aurora,
y hay en tus ojos luz divinal.

Y eres hermosa y eres fragrante
y eres la imagen acariciante
de los amores, del ideal . . .

To "Conchita" Saenz[66]

    I wish you'd accept, lovely "Conchita,"
the humble offering of this my song,
like a rose that's forever unfading
from the gardens of wishful thinking.

    To your enchanting charms, my dear,
a just homage I want to offer up:
with these my stanzas, with these my praises
I come, my offering to leave.

    It is, your beauty, so wholly dazzling,
your countenance, radiant like the dawn,
and there is in your eyes a divine light.

    And you are lovely and you are fragrant
and you are the image that caresses
with the promise of love, of the ideal . . .

Tu debieras tener . . .

Para Adolfina Salgado.

Tú debieras tener lleno de flores
y de nardos y rosas el camino;
una sonrisa de ángel por destino,
y por trono el altar de los amores.

Las auroras de bellos resplandores
por hermanas de rostro purpurino,
y los astros de rayo diamantino
por espejos de mágicos colores . . .

El arpa del amor que te ensalzara;
la lira de marfil que te cantara,
y un bardo soñador por elegido

Porque es tu alma de luz como la aurora,
y tienes no sé qué de arrulladora
en tu cuerpo de amores bello nido.

You Ought to Have . . .

For Adolfina Salgado.

You ought to have, filled with flowers,
with polianthes and roses your path;[67]
the smile of an angel for your destination,
and for your throne an altar made of love.

The dawns with their bright radiances
for sisters with their rosy fingers
and the stars of that diamantine shine
as mirrors of magical colors.

The harp of the love that should sing your praises;
the lyre of marble that would sing to you.
and a visionary bard of your choosing.

Because your soul is made of light like the dawn,
and you have I know not what lulling cooing
in your body of loves a lovely nest.

A Graciela Corbett

Los astros con su luz y sus fulgores
envidian tus destellos virginales:
tú robaste a los mundos siderales
dos estrellas: tus ojos seductores.

Del cielo de ensueño y los amores
son tus ojos dos astros divinales,
que esparcen, al abrirse celestiales,
de tu amor los divinos resplandores.

Y es un cielo tu cara, y esos astros
que dejan al mirar divinos rastros,
fingen soles de eterna bienandanza.

¡Bien quisiera algún bardo peregrino
que alumbraran tus ojos su camino
lo mismo que dos astros de esperanza!

To Graciela Corbett

    The stars with their light and their shinings
envy your virgin sparkles;
you stole from the sidereal worlds
two stars: your seductive eyes.

    From the heaven of fantasies and of lovers
your eyes are two divine stars
that scatter, upon their celestial opening,
the divine radiance of your love.

    And your face is a heaven, and those celestial bodies
that leave with their looking divine traces,
seem suns of eternal good fortune.

    Well might a peregrine bard desire
that your eyes should light his way
the same as could two stars of hope.

A "Teresita" Colón

Yo pienso en las rosas divinas y amadas,
mirándote siempre tan bella cruzar;
yo pienso en las flores de besos nimbadas,
pues ellas parecen tu imagen copiar.

Las flores que se abren al beso querido
que imprime en sus broches el rayo del sol,
vertiendo su aroma de néctar henchido,
muy puras reflejan tu bella ilusión.

Por eso las mimo, quien sabe las beso
y dejo en su cáliz un ósculo impreso,
porque ellas parecen tu imagen copiar.

¡Que nunca esas flores marchitas se vean!
¡Que sean eternas, tu dicha que sean,
y en ellas por siempre te pueda admirar!

To "Teresita" Colón

    I think about roses, divine and beloved,
seeing you, always so lovely as you pass;
I think about the flowers nimbused by kisses,
because they seem to copy your image.

    The flowers that unfurl at the desired kiss
that the ray of the sun imprints on their brooches,
spilling their aroma bursting with nectar,
very pure, they reflect your lovely eagerness.

    And so I indulge them, perhaps I kiss them
and leave in their chalice the imprint of an osculation,
because they seem to copy your image.

    Let those flowers never be seen faded
let them be eternal, your joy let them be,
and in them forever I will be able to admire you.

A Célida Bravo

—en su álbum—

    Una estrofa la escribo por tu gloria;
tiene dulce sabor de sentimiento,
porque lleva prendido un pensamiento
con hojas perfumadas, de victoria.

    Otra escribo de honor para tu historia,
cuyas páginas bellas leo y siento,
de flores impregnadas con aliento,
perpetuando en tu álbum mi memoria.

    Porque dejo yo en él flor más bella
y un ramo de ilusión prendido de ella
como dulce sonrisa del destino.

    A esa flor de perfumes y de galas,
cuando fiero huracán tronche mis alas,
dale un beso al hallarla en tu camino.

To Célida Bravo

—In her album—

 One stanza I write to your renowned glory;
it holds such a sweet flavor of sentiment,
because it carries, held fast, a thought
of victory, of petals full of perfume.

 Another I write to honor your story,
whose so lovely pages I read and I see
as being made flowers impregnated with breath,
sustaining in your album a memory of me.

 Because I leave in it my most lovely bloom
and pinned to it a posy of eager dreams,
like the persistent sweet smile of destiny.

 To that flower of perfumes and elegance give,
if a fierce hurricane should chance to clip my wings,
a kiss, on finding it fallen there in your path.

A Josefina López

 Hizo Dios con la luz tu pensamiento,
tu semblante del sol con los fulgores,
con la noche tus ojos, y tu aliento
con el suave perfume de las flores.

 Te formó para amar y ser amada,
y le dio, como emblema de victoria,
un poder infinito a tu mirada,
que es blasón indeleble de tu gloria.

 Hizo tu alma, que finge una añoranza,
con estrofas sutiles de esperanza,
lo mismo que las almas de las flores.

 Y después que te dio su luz intensa,
en tu pecho encerró la dicha inmensa
de un tierno corazón brindando amores.

To Josefina López

    God himself made, with his holy light, your mind,
your countenance with the sun's own radiance;
with the dark night he made your eyes, and your breath
with the most gentle perfume of his flowers.

    He created you to love and to be loved,
and he gave—as an ensign of victory—
an immeasurable power to your gaze:
the indelible blazon of your glory.

    He wrought your soul, in its seeming nostalgia,
with delicate stanzas each woven of hope,
just the same as he made souls for the flowers.

    And after he gave you of that intense light,
in your breast he enclosed the immense fortune
of a tender heart brimming over with love.

A Rosa María López

Empezando a escribir un verso triste,
embriagóme un efluvio de esperanza,
y prendida de aquel, como añoranza,
tú también, de repente apareciste.

Mujer bella: ¿de dónde tú surgiste,
que así cambias la triste remembranza,
y así truecas en horas de bonanza
las horas de nostalgia? . . . ¿Por qué existe

En tu ser esa llama bienhechora
que, vertiendo su luz consoladora,
da a mis versos la dúlcida armonía? . . .

Empezaba escribiendo sollozante . . .
¡tu me diste un efluvio acariciante
cual si fueras la dulce amada mía!

To Rosa María López

    As I was beginning to write a sad verse,
a sudden outflowing of hope made me reel,
and pinned to those new hopes, like a sweet longing,
you also appeared to me, quite suddenly.

    Lovely woman: from what place did you appear,
that in this way you can so change a sad remembrance,
and so turn to hours of fertile bounty
my hours of nostalgia? . . . Why does it exist,

    central to your being, that philanthropic
flame, which on pouring forth its comforting light
gives to my verses a dulcet harmony?

    I set out upon my writing wracked by sobs . . .
you gifted me this caressing inspiration,
as if you were yourself my sweet beloved!

A Sofía Pérez Rolo

   Con citas, con ensueños con flores,
para ti quiero hacer un canto bello
como un rayo de luz, como un destello
del iris de la dicha y los amores.

   Con versos muy divinos, de colores
inocentes y puros, cual ninguno,
una rosa engarzando en cado uno,
mis estrofas orlando con loores.

   Eres bella y gentil como la palma;
y llevas tantos sueños en el alma
como estrellas de luz la clara noche.

   Es tu cuerpo gentil nido de amores,
y tu cara seméjase a las flores
cuando al beso del sol abren su broche.

To Sofía Pérez Rolo[68]

    With sweet words, with fantasies, and with flowers,
I want to compose for you a lovely song
like a ray of light, like a flash, a glimmer
of the iris of good fortune and of love.

    With verses so divine and all of colors
innocent and pure, like unto none other,
a rose, set gemlike into each one of them,
my stanzas decorating with your praises.

    You are lovely and pleasing like the palm tree;
and you carry as many dreams in your soul
as the clearest of nights does in flashing stars.

    Your body is a pleasing nest for lovers,
and your face is so like those of the flowers
when at the kiss of the sun, petals unfurl.

En el baile

Las Mujeres

Parecían ensueños desprendidos
de un cielo tachonado de esperanza;
cada rostro fingía una añoranza
que alumbraran dos astros encendidos.

Pasaban como seres que, embebidos
en un dulce arrullar de bienandanza,
se perdieran allá en la lontananza
de una noche de amor, adormecidos.

Apartado del baile, concebía
mil ensueños de amor mi fantasía
que surcaba un Edén en ansia loca.

Era el ansia febril del alma inquieta,
que, avivando los sueños del poeta,
manda un beso de amor a cada boca . . .

At the Dance

The Women

    They seemed to be fantasies detached
from a sky studded with hope;
each face evinced a longing
that two burning stars should illumine.

    They passed like beings who, absorbed
in a sweet murmur of happiness,
should lose themselves there in the distance
of a night of languid love.

    Away from the dance, my fevered mind
conceived a thousand fantasies of love
that ploughed through an Eden of wild yearning.

    It was the febrile yearning of an unquiet soul,
which, rekindling the dreams of the poet,
sends a kiss of love to every mouth.

A Graciela Avalo

   Como el rayo de luz de la alborada
o las brisas que gimen rumorosas,
tú me inspiras estrofas cadenciosas
que semejan de amor una balada.

   Como el ave que canta en la enramada,
desgranando mis rimas como rosas,
a tu paso las vierto melodiosas,
en tu senda de amores, perfumada.

   Son estrofas que tú me has inspirado,
no son versos de amor interesado,
pero brotan del mismo corazón.

   Un soneto, quizás sin armonía,
que te ofrenda sincera el alma mía,
como el beso feliz de la ilusión . . .

To Graciela Avalo

   Like the first ray of the day's breaking
or the breezes that moan murmuringly,
you inspire in me rhythmical stanzas
that approximate a ballad of love.

   Like the bird that sings in the brush,
pulling the seeds form my rhymes like roses,
at your passing I pour them out, melodious,
in your loving path, full of perfume.

   They are stanzas that you have inspired in me;
they are not the verses of an opportunist love,
but rather spring forth from my very heart.

   A sonnet, perhaps without harmony,
that my soul sincerely offers to you,
like a happy kiss of wishful thinking . . .

Tu boca

Para Georgina López.

Quiero un canto tejer, un canto de esos
que inspiran al nacer las ilusiones:
quiero orlar hoy mis dúlcidas canciones
con la esencia divina de los besos.

De los besos ardientes que provoca,
circundada de perlas y diamantes,
una boca de mieles embriagantes,
una boca de amor, como tu boca.

Ardorosa los besos pide tanto,
que al orlar yo con ellos este canto
parece que me inspiro en algún beso . . .

Los que brinda tu boca indefinible,
deben ser una chispa inextinguible,
que desprenden tus labios de embeleso.

Your Mouth

For Georgina López.

    I want a song to weave, a song of those
who inspire, on being born, fantasies;
I want to trim today my dulcet songs
with the divine essence of kisses.

    Of those ardent kisses provoked by,
encircled by pearls and by diamonds,
a mouth of intoxicating honey,
a mouth of love, like your mouth.

    Ardent, it asks for so many kisses,
that on my trimming with them this song
it seems that I become inspired now to kiss . . .

    Those that your undefinable mouth affords,
must be an inextinguishable spark
of enchantment given off by your lips.

A Delia López

    Tienes ojos de amor, fuego y ternura,
son tus labios de miel ricos panales,
y a tu boca cedieron los rosales
su aliento embriagador, todo dulzura.

    Como el hada gentil de la hermosura,
la que engendra benditos ideales,
viertes tú los de amor bellos raudales,
y en mis versos candor, porque eres pura.

    En tu faz brilla siempre seductora
la sonrisa que finge, soñadora,
cuando se abre su cáliz, una flor.

    Tu semblante refleja irisaciones,
como el iris divino de ilusiones
que ilumina los cielos del amor.

To Delia López

    You have eyes of love, of fire and tenderness,
your lips are rich combs of honey,
and to those lips the roses ceded
their intoxicating breath, all of sweetness.

    Like the genteel fairy of beauty,
the one who engenders blessed ideals,
you pour out torrents of love,
and in my verses candor, because you are pure.

    In your face shines always, dreamer,
the seductive smile that imitates,
the opening of the chalice of a flower.

    Your countenance reflects iridescences,
like the divine iris of daydreams
that illuminates the skies of love.

A Celia Avalo

   Si un rico pedestal todo grandeza
tejiese con mi voz serena y pura,
orlado con mil besos de ternura,
lo ofrendara, mujer, a tu belleza.

   Sobre un trono de amor y gentileza
y en estrofas de regia galanura,
rindiérale homenaje a tu hermosura:
un himno le cantara a tu pureza.

   A la luz de los bellos resplandores
del sol abrasador de tus amores,
te ofreciera mi cántico, de hinojos.

   El cántico de inmensa dulcedumbre,
que inspiran los destellos y la lumbre
del fuego misterioso de tus ojos.

To Celia Avalo

    If a rich pedestal all of grandeur
I should weave with my voice serene and pure,
bordered with a thousand kisses of tenderness,
I would offer it, lady, to your beauty.

    Upon a throne of love and graciousness
and in stanzas of regal elegance,
I would render homage to your loveliness:
I would sing a hymn there to your purity.

    In the light of the lovely radiances
of the burning sun of your loves,
I would offer you my canticle, on my knees.

    The canticle of immense sweetness,
inspired by the flashes and the heat
of the mysterious fire of your eyes.

Tu caricia

Para Celeste Pintado.

Debe ser toda ensueños y poesía,
como un soplo de amor arrulladora:
debe ser tu caricia embriagadora
como néctar divino de ambrosia.

Como rayo de sol abrasadora,
lo mismo que las flores perfumada:
debe ser tu caricia idolatrada,
como un beso de virgen seductora.

Prodigada por ti, debe ser fuego;
temerosa quizá, atrevida luego . . .
lo mismo que la dicha ambicionada.

Debe ser de emociones tu caricia,
debe ser un arrullo de delicia,
como el beso primero de la amada.

Your Caress

For Celeste Pintado.

It ought to be all fantasies and poetry,
like a breath of love that coos sweet nothings:
your caress ought to be intoxicating
like the divine nectar from ambrosial blooms.

Like a ray from the blazing sun,
equal to the flowers in their perfume:
it ought to be, your caress, idolized,
like the kiss of a seductive virgin.

Bestowed by you, it should be fire;
timid perhaps, daring later . . .
like the most coveted of fortunes.

Your caress ought to be made of emotion,
it ought to be a murmur of delight,
like the first kiss from a beloved.

A "Consuelito" Rivero

 Yo quisiera en estrofas melodiosas
y a despecho de Venus arrogante,
la reina sobre un trono de diamante
proclamarte de todas las hermosas.

 Acercarme con flores y con rosas
al Solio de tu amor acariciante;
yo después aclamárate triunfante
sobre todas las reinas y las diosas,

 Bien merece llamarse reina bella
la mujer toda luz como la Estrella
que en la noche, mirífica fulgura.

 La que tiene cual tú, negros ojazos,
que divinos parecen dos pedazos
de una noche infinita de dulzura.

To "Consuelito" Rivero[69]

    I should like, in melodious stanzas
and to spite arrogant Venus,
the queen on a throne of diamonds
to proclaim you amongst all beauties.

    To draw near with flowers and with roses
to the throne of your caressing love;
then to hail you triumphant
over all the queens and the goddesses,

    for she should call herself the queen of beauty,
that woman all of light, who like a star
in the night, shines marvelous;

    the one who has, like you, big black eyes,
that divine seem to be two pieces
of a night infinite in its sweetness.

Estela Rodríguez

   No hay un astro de luz como tus ojos
en su dulce brillar inconfundible;
no hay un astro de luz inextinguible
que al mirar no le inundes tú de enojos.

   No hay clavel que no sufra entre sonrojos,
contemplando la grana indefinible
que abandona su broche inmarcesible,
esmaltando a la par tus labios rojos.

   No produce el jardín de la esperanza
una flor más divina en su semblanza,
con pétalos de amor, ni más preciosa,

   Que tu rostro de virgen hechicera,
pues semejas, sonriendo placentera,
al abrirse su cáliz, una rosa.

Estela Rodríguez

    There is no star with light like your eyes,
in their sweet shining unmistakable;
there is no star with a light unextinguishable
that your glances do not flood with resentment.

    There is no carnation that does not suffer in its blushing,
contemplating the deep indefinable red
that abandons its unwithered brooch,
to adorn instead your red lips.

    The garden of hope cannot produce
a flower more lovely than your semblance,
with petals of love, nor more precious,

    than your bewitching, virgin face,
for you look, on smiling pleasingly,
as does, on opening its chalice, a rose.

La amada mía

    Como un sueño forjado en dulce calma,
o un efluvio divino de una estrella,
lleva en su cara retratada su alma:
humilde siempre, pero siempre bella.

    Y a través de su fúlgida mirada
y en torno de su boca centellea
la expresión de una dicha idolatrada,
que seduce, que encanta, que recrea…

    Como el hada gentil, arrobadora,
sutilísima ráfaga de encantos;
armónicos bendícenla en sus cantos
los pájaros que trinan en la aurora.

    Parece que le cuentan sus amores,
yo no sé con qué plácida armonía;
son sus cantos cantares de alegría,
lo mismo que un suspiro de las flores.

    La brisa que susurra quedamente,
sus notas diviniza al ensalzarle,
y los vientos que gimen suavemente
endulzan su canción para arrullarle.

    "Porque es ángel con alas rutilantes,
que irradia con variados arreboles,
un iris de riquísimos cambiantes,
más bellos que los iris de los soles"

    Porque de ángel posee la ternura,
y del cielo las noches estrelladas;
del ensueño la nítida dulzura,
del poema los cantos y alboradas.

    Y es su voz un arrullo de paloma,
entonando el cantar de los amores;
se parece al rumor de aquel idioma
con que el aura acaricia tiernas flores.

My Beloved

    Like a dream forged in sweet calm,
or a divine outpouring from a star,
she carries her soul drawn on her face :
humble always, always lovely.

    And through her shining gaze
and around her mouth sparkles
the expression of an idolized joy
that seduces, that enchants, that entertains . . .

    Like the kind fairy, entrancing
as a subtle gust of charms;
in harmony they bless her in their songs
those birds who trill at the dawn.

    It seems that they tell her of their loves,
with I know not what placid harmony;
their singings are signs of joy,
the same as the sigh of the flowers.

    The breeze that whispers quietly,
deifies its notes on lauding her,
and the winds that softly whine
sweeten their song to lull her to sleep.

    "Because she is an angel with sparkling wings
who radiates with a roseate glow
a rainbow of rich reflections,
more lovely than the irises of all the suns"[70]

    Because she possesses the tenderness of an angel,
and of the sky its starry nights;
of a fantasy its crisp sweetness,
of a poem its cantos and dawn chorus.

    And her voice is the murmur of a dove,
intoning the song of loves;
it seems like the sound of that language
with which the air caresses tender flowers.

Marchítase la rosa en su presencia,
y el clavel encendido está en agravios,
que es su boca un rosal de pura esencia
y el color del clavel llevan sus labios.

Sus labios de coral, labios tan bellos
que jamás han dejado de ser puros,
¿No palpitan—parece—en torno de ellos
ardientes los de amor besos "futuros"?

Cuando ríe, de indefinible encanto
escúchase el acento de su risa;
si llora, son las gotas de su llanto
las lágrimas del cielo o de la brisa...

Inmortal es un trono de esplendores,
de donde brota de fulgor un cielo,
y su alma soñadora es toda anhelo,
y su cuerpo gentil nido de amores.
. . . .

Quisiera, de mi vida el postrer día,
sobre mi pecho su cabeza amante,
y yo cariñoso, al inclinar la mía,
su cabeza cubrir con mi semblante.

Y al morir, en dulcísimo embeleso
con lágrimas de amor regar su frente,
y apagando mis ecos, balbuciente...
sellar su eterna dicha con un beso.

The rose withers in her presence,
and the fiery carnation is injured,
for her mouth is the pure essence of the rose,
and her lips bear the color of the carnation.

Her lips of coral, lips so lovely
that they have never stopped being pure,
Does it not seem that around them pulse
burning those kisses of loves "yet to come"?

When she laughs, the indefinable enchantment
of the accent of her mirth is made plain;
if she cries, the drops of her crying are
the tears of the heavens or of the breeze . . .

She is an immortal throne of splendors,
from whence bursts out the brilliance of a sky,
and her dreamer's soul is all longing
and her body a kind nest for loves.

. . . .

I should like, on the final day of my life,
to have on my chest her loving head,
and I, affectionate, on inclining,
to cover her head with my countenance.

And on dying, in the sweetest enchantment,
with tears of love to water her face,
and my echoes extinguishing themselves, stuttering . . .
to seal her eternal good fortune with a kiss.

Ofrenda póstuma

A Ofelia Pita.

    Paloma de los besos y las flores
que dejas sin tu amor un nido yerto;
golondrina gentil de los amores:
al marcharte, un hogar quedó desierto.

    Mas… no mires siquiera hacia este mundo
donde todo es mentira, engaño todo,
que es la tierra un fangal, el más inmundo,
y es un mito el amor; la vida es lodo.

    Si vuelves tu mirar desde la cumbre
a este valle de vicio y podredumbre,
todo engaño, mentiras y dolor,

    Mira solo al hogar que abandonaste,
piensa solo en el nido que dejaste
sin la dulce caricia de tu amor.

Posthumous Offering

To Ofelia Pita.

    Dove of kisses and of flowers
who leaves without your love a lifeless nest;
courteous swallow of loves;
on your departure, a home was left deserted.

    But . . . don't so much as look to this world
where all is a lie, deceit all,
for the earth is a quagmire, the most filthy,
and love is a myth; life is but mud.

    If you turn your gaze from the peak
to this valley of vice and degradation,
all deceit, lies and pain,

    look only to the home that you abandoned,
think only on the nest that you have left
without the sweet caress of your love.

A Ofelia Rivero

   Yo he aprendido del ave el dulce idioma,
que embriaga con suavísima armonía,
y por eso, al sonar, la lira mía
finge el blando arrullar de la paloma

   Suena dulce por ti, flor toda aroma,
con pétalos divinos de ambrosía,
orlada con los besos de alegría
que da el sol del amor, cuando se asoma . . .

   La paloma gentil me dio sus notas,
y aunque tengo—lo sé—mis alas rotas,
aún quisiera emprender un raudo vuelo . . .
¡Ojalá que no pueda detenerme! . . . . .
yo quisiera volar hasta perderme
en la sima infinita de tu anhelo.

To Ofelia Rivero

    I have learned from the birds the sweet language
that intoxicates with the most subtle harmony,
and because of that, on its sounding, my lyre
feigns the soft cooing of the dove.

    It sounds sweet for you, a flower all scent,
with divine petals of ambrosia,
garlanded with the kisses of joy
that the sun of love gives when it rises . . .

    The courteous dove gave me his notes,
and though I have—I know—broken wings,
I should still like to attempt a swift flight . . .

    God will that nothing stops me!
I should so like to fly until I lose myself
in the infinite depths of your desire.

A América Cermeño

De mi acento sonoro los raudales
sus aromas te ofrendan dulcemente,
lo mismo que sus cántigas la Fuente
ofrenda en el jardín a los rosales.

Yo quisiera de esencias infinitas,
al tejer estos versos perfumarlos,
porque sé que has de oír tú recitarlos
por tu amado, de amor en vuestras citas.

Cuando tú los escuches suspirante,
mientras lee el amado acariciante . . .
vuestras almas acaso confundidas,

Observa que es suprema la ventura
de dos almas que viven la ternura,
en idilio de amor por siempre unidas . . .

To América Cermeño

   Of my sonorous voice the torrents
their aromas offer to you sweetly,
just as its songs the fountain
offers in the garden to the roses.

   I should like with infinite essences,
on weaving these verses, to perfume them,
because I know you will hear them recited
by your lover, full of love each time you meet.

   When you hear them sighingly,
while your beloved reads caressingly,
your souls perhaps blended together,

   observe that the good fortune is supreme
of two souls who live out tenderness,
in an idyll of love ever united . . .

A Adelaida Pinet

    Lo mismo que las gotas del rocío
en el húmedo cáliz de las rosas,
estos versos de esencias cariñosas
para ti los guardaba el astro mío.

    Para tí que eres lirio inmaculado
que empiezan a besar las ilusiones
bajo un iris de mil irisaciones
que alumbra tu sendero perfumado . . .

    Ya que finges un lirio muy divino,
ya que emprendes de flores un camino
a la luz de bendita irisación,

    sabe ser como el lirio candorosa,
guarda el bello perfume de la rosa,
que sin él es mentira la ilusión.

To Adelaida Pinet

   Just like the drops of dew
in the humid chalice of a rose,[71]
these verses of affectionate essences
were held safe for you by my muse.

   For you who are an immaculate lily
that excitement begins to kiss,
beneath a rainbow with a thousand iridescences
that illuminates your perfumed path . . .

   Since you already seem to be a divine lily,
since you set out upon a path of flowers,
by the light of blessed iridescence,

   know how to be innocent like a lily;
keep safe the lovely perfume of your rose,
for without it, the dream is a lie.

A Rosalía Vila

Si las flores son hermosas,
y los lirios y las rosas
    son candor,
eres tú más candorosa,
más divina y más hermosa,
pues que finges tú la rosa
    del amor . . .
Si los astros son muy bellos,
esparciendo sus destellos
    en redor,
son tus ojos dos estrellas
más radiosas y más bellas
que los astros y sus huellas
    de fulgor . . .
Si desprenden, divinales,
su perfume los rosales
    tan sutil,
más divina y perfumada
fluye esencia no igualada
de tu boca circundada
    de marfil . . .
Contemplando una palmera,
una tarde placentera,
    compare,
con la palma tu altiveza,
su hermosura a tu belleza,
y aún más llena de grandeza
    te encontré . . .
Comparando aquella palma
con tu cuerpo, pensé en tu alma
    de candor,
la fingí toda ilusiones,
toda ensueños y emociones,
con las mil irisaciones
    del amor . . .
Y tal vez no me engañaba
cuando a tu alma comparaba
    la emoción,
porque es tu alma un embeleso,
porque finge el primer beso
que, al nacer, dejara impreso
    la ilusión . . .

To Rosalía Vila

If the flowers, they are lovely
and the lilies and the roses
    are candor
you are even more innocent
more divine and more beautiful
because you imitate the rose
    born of love . . .
If the stars are very lovely
scattering their gleaming sparkle
    all around,
then your eyes they are two such stars
more radiant and more lovely
than the stars and their glowing tracks
    of brilliance.
If they give off, all divinely
their perfume, all the roses
    so subtle,
more divine yet, and more perfumed
flows the essence without equal
of your mouth that is surrounded
    by marble . . .
Contemplating now a palm tree,
all on a pleasant afternoon,
    I compared,
with that palm your composed poise
its beauty to your loveliness,
and even more full of greatness
    I found you . . .
Comparing that far off palm to
your body, I thought on your soul
    all candor,
I imagined it all of dreams,
all fantasies and emotions,
with the thousand iridescences
    of love . . .
And perhaps I did not deceive
when I to your soul compared
    all emotion.
For your soul is an enchantment,
because it feigns the first kiss that,
on being born, would leave forever imprinted
    that daydream . . .

A Heliodora Toledo

   Semejas el hada que sueña atrevida
forjando quimeras intensas de amor;
tú tienes un alma de sueños henchida,
por ojos dos astros de fuego y pasión.

   Dibujan tus ojos las hondas pasiones
de un pecho que late con férvido afán:
de un pecho que encierra las mil emociones
que embargan el alma sedienta de amar . . .

   Altiva y serena, tú inspiras grandeza,
soñando, reflejas la inmensa belleza
de hada que engendra la dulce ilusión.

   Tu imagen, henchida de mágicos sueños,
parece que pide que te hablen de ensueños . . .
viviendo la vida que brinda el amor.

To Heliodora Toledo

    You resemble the fairy that dreams, full of daring,
forging intense fantasies of love;
you have a soul all filled up with your dreamings,
for eyes you've two stars of fire and passion.

    Your eyes sketch out the deep passions
of a heart that beats with a fervent eagerness:
of a heart that encloses the thousand emotions
that overwhelm the soul that thirsts to love . . .

    Proud and serene, you inspire greatness;
on dreaming, you reflect the immense beauty
of the fairy who engenders sweet daydreams.

    Your image, filled up with magical dreams,
seems to plead that they speak to you of fantasies . . .
living the life that love affords.

A Ofelia Quesada

Si unos hilos no más, rubia hechicera,
tuviese de tus mágicos cabellos,
de oro entonces formara yo con ellos
las cuerdas de una lira placentera.

Acallara mi lira plañidera
entonara de amor versos muy bellos,
e inundaran mi senda los destellos
que brotan, al surgir la primavera.

¡Unos hilos no más! y trocaría
tantas notas de cruel melancolía
por los dulces arpegios del amor.

Brotarían mis versos como flores,
lo mismo que la flor de los amores,
cuando un beso se prende de esa flor.

To Ofelia Quesada

    If but a few strands, enchanting and blonde,
I were to have of your magical hair
of gold, I would form with them
the strings of a delightful lyre.

    I would silence my plaintive lyre
and intone the loveliest verses of love,
and my path would be flooded with the flashing glitter
that bursts forth at the surging of the spring.

    A few strands, no more! and I would change
so many notes of cruel melancholy
to the sweet arpeggios of love.

    My verses would spring forth like flowers,
the same as the flowering of a love,
when that flower is sealed with a kiss.

En el teatro

    En un palco te vi. Con imperiosa
mirada respondiste no sé qué,
cuando, al verte, atrevido interrogué
a tus ojos de Hurí, mujer preciosa.

    ¿Te ofendió la pregunta cariñosa
de mis ojos quizá? . . . Yo no lo sé.
No insistí, porque pronto adiviné
que mirada indiscreta es enojosa.

    Si rehúyes ingrata, una mirada;
si por ella te sientes enojada,
—¡por la sola caricia de mis ojos!—

    ¿Qué dirías si yo me propusiera,
con el alma en los labios toda entera,
probar la miel de tus labios rojos?

In the Theater

    I saw you in your box. With an imperious
gaze you responded I know not what,
when, on seeing you, I dared interrogate
your Houri eyes, precious lady.

    Did the affectionate question in my eyes
offend you perhaps? . . . I cannot know.
I did not insist, for soon I divined
that an indiscreet gaze is brings ire.

    If you refuse, ungrateful, a look;
if by such you come so far as anger,
—by the caress of my eyes alone!—

    What would you say if I proposed,
with on my lips the whole of my soul,
to taste the honey of your red lips?

A. Cermeño—R. Miqueli

Con motivo de su enlace.

    Debajo de un cielo de rosas y flores
formasteis un nido de paz y de amor;
¡qué nunca a ese nido de vuestros amores
alcancen las brumas que esparce el dolor!

    Unidos por siempre, gozad la ventura:
de eternas caricias "la luna de miel";
bebed de la fuente de inmensa dulzura
sin mezcla de penas ni gotas de hiel.

    Vivid como viven la vida de mieles,
sin quejas, sin llanto, sin mezcla de hieles,
las almas que saben vivir para amar.

    Vosotros lograsteis, en bello concilio
trocar vuestros sueños en dúlcido idilio;
ahora ¿qué os resta? . . . Tan solo gozar.

A. Cermeño—R. Miqueli

On the occasion of their marriage.

    Beneath a sky of roses and of flowers
you formed a nest of peace and of love;
let it be that the mists that bear with them pain
should never creep into to this nest of your love!

    United forever, enjoy the happiness:
the honeymoon of eternal caresses;
drink from the fountain of immense sweetness
with no added sorrows nor drops of gall.

    Live as they live a life full of honey,
without complaints, without tears, without bitterness,
those souls who know how to live for love.

    You achieved, in your lovely council
the exchange of your dreams in a dulcet idyll;
now, what is left to you? . . . Only to enjoy.

A Agnelia López

   No sé qué de citas y sueños queridos,
quimeras y ruegos que incitan a amar,
descubro en tus ojos de pasión henchidos,
tan dulces, tan bellos, de ardiente mirar.

   Tal vez porque finges la amada que un día
del alma de un verso mi anhelo engendró;
lo mismo eres bella que la amada mía;
quien sabe, mi anhelo de ti la formó.

   Tejiendo una estrofa de amor impregnada,
la nimbo con besos, pues si eres la amada,
los besos acaso te sepan a miel.

   Que aún más que la vida son dulces los besos,
si nobles dos almas los llevan impresos
sin odios que engendren regueros de hiel.

To Agnelia López

    I don't know what dates and beloved dreams,
what fantasies and pleas that incite one to love,
I may discover in your eyes that brim with passion,
so sweet and so lovely, with their burning gaze.

    Perhaps because you look like that beloved who one day
my longing engendered from the soul of a verse;
you are just as lovely as my beloved; who knows,
perhaps my desire made her in your image.

    Weaving a stanza impregnated with love,
I give it a nimbus of kisses, for if you are her indeed,
those kisses will taste to you of honey.

    For sweeter even than life are kisses,
if two noble souls carry their imprint
without hatreds that let bile trickle in.

A Rosa Sibila

El pájaro que vierte en la enramada
infinitos raudales de armonía,
parece que se inspira en la poesía
que circunda tu imagen adorada.

El rayo en que despunta la alborada
de espléndido fulgor en bello día,
lo mismo que de amor la lira mía,
te brinda una caricia enamorada.

Y las rosas de mi jardín frondoso,
como el eco divino y melodioso
el pájaro que ensálzate cantando,

Regálante perfumes que embelesan,
lo mismo que unos labios cuando besan
con ansias de vivir siempre besando.

To Rosa Sibila

The bird who pours forth in the undergrowth
infinite torrents of harmony
takes his inspiration, or so it seems, in the poetry
that surrounds your adored image.

The ray of light which turns the dawn
of splendid brilliance into the lovely day
dedicates to you an enamored caress,
and so too of love does my lyre.

And the roses of my luxuriant garden,
like the echo, divine and melodious,
of the bird who extols you in his singing,

They gift you perfumes that bewitch
just as lips do when they kiss,
with the longing to live forever kissing.

A Gloria Sibila

   Flor de amores, gentil y primorosa,
en pos dejando perfumadas huellas:
entre tantas mujeres todas bellas,
por humilde te ensalzo y por hermosa.

   Yo no sé si con arpa cadenciosa
o con luz eternal de las estrellas,
he tejido estas notas . . . mas con ellas
deposito a tus plantas una rosa.

   Tú eres la musa que gentil me inspira,
tú la paloma que, al cantar, suspira,
virgen amada de ilusión ardiente

   Fuego desprenden tus divinos ojos,
dulzor emana de tus labios rojos,
cual si ellos fuesen del amor la fuente . . .

To Gloria Sibila

    Flower of loves, charming and exquisite,
leaving behind perfumed footprints;
among so many women, all of them lovely,
for your humility I extol you and for your beauty.

    I do not know if with a rhythmical harp
or with the eternal light of the stars,
I have woven these notes . . . but with them
I deposit at your feet a rose.

    You are the muse who charming inspires me,
the dove who, on singing, sighs,
beloved virgin with ardent dreams.

    Your divine eyes give off a fire,
sweetness emanates from your red lips,
as if they were the very fountain of love . . .

A Julieta Raga

No sé que luz destellan, artista encantadora,
tus ojos como abismos de amor y de pasión,
y si ellos son espejos de tu alma soñadora,
no más que fuego debe brotar tu corazón.

Tus labios son de grana, tu faz arrobadora,
tu cuerpo un bello nido repleto de ideal;
desprenden tus miradas la lumbre abrasadora,
lo mismo que de un hada los ojos de cristal . . .

Por eso te saludan las aves y las flores,
y en medio de mis versos de pálidos colores
yo pongo este mensaje tejido para ti . . .

Tejido a los destellos de vívidos reflejos
que vierten tus pupilas, de tu alma los espejos
que son las dos antorchas de rostro de la Hurí.

To Julieta Raga[72]

    I don't know what light they give off, enchanting artist,
those eyes of yours like chasms of love and of passion,
and if they are mirrors of your dreamer's soul,
nothing but fire should burst forth from your heart.

    Your lips they are of burgundy, your face ever enticing,
your body a lovely nest brimming with every ideal;
your glances give off a scorching heat,
just like the crystal eyes of a fairy . . .

    Because of this the birds and the flowers greet you,
and amidst my verses of pallid colors
I place this message woven just for you . . .

    Woven to the glitter of vivid reflections
that your pupils pour forth, the mirrors of your soul
that are the two torches in the face of the Houri.

A Dalia Viera

   He soñado que estabas contemplando
las olas mensajeras que traían
en sus besos amor, y parecían
ensueños a la vida despertando.

   Tú mirabas las olas suspirando,
mientras ellas llegaban y volvían
y no sé qué de amores te decían
en muy dulce lenguaje, sollozando . . .

   ¡Qué adorable allí estabas, cuando a solas
en dúlcido coloquio con las olas,
recorrías un cielo de embeleso!

   ¿Esperabas quizá las de infinitas
emociones del alma aquellas citas
que dan vida a los sueños con un beso?

To Dalia Viera

    I have dreamed of you in contemplation
of the waves, messengers that brought
in their kisses love, and that seemed
daydreams awakening to the world.

    You were watching the waves sighing,
while they came and returned
and I know not what loves they told you of
in such sweet language, sobbing . . .

    How sweet you were there, when alone
in dulcet colloquy with the waves,
as you looked out toward an enchanted sky!

    Were you hoping, perhaps, out of all the infinite
sensations of the soul, for those assignations
that give life to dreams with a kiss?

A María Boza

   Si pudiese imitar a la paloma,
la de acento fugaz y enamorado,
te ofreciera un cantar inmaculado,
todo dulce embriaguez y rico aroma.

   Si de Oriente a los rayos yo lograra
arrancarles sus vívidos cambiantes,
en estrofas de luz acariciantes,
a tu humilde belleza le cantara.

   E inundaran las bellas ilusiones
con esencia de amores mis canciones,
lo mismo que los sueños adorados.

   Porque entonces, la bella transparencia
del Oriente, con luz y grata esencia
a mis versos dejáralos nimbados . . .

To María Boza

   If I could imitate the dove,
one with a fleeting and enamored tone,
I would offer you an immaculate song,
all sweet inebriation and rich scent.

   If from the Orient's rays I could manage
to pull the vivid reflections
in stanzas of caressing light,
I would sing to your unassuming beauty.

   And those lovely illusions would inundate
my songs with the very essence of love,
just like adored dreams.

   Because then, the lovely transparency
of the Orient, with its light and pleasing essence
would leave my verses nimbused . . .

A Carolina Rivero

Entre todas las fúlgidas estrellas
de la noche apacible, rutilantes,
dos no existen de rayos fulgurantes
que tus ojos más puras y más bellas.

Infinitas de luz dejan sus huellas,
cual si fuesen inmensos dos diamantes,
y en destellos de amor, acariciantes,
diluyen mil ensueños y querellas . . .

Los ojos manifiestan los sentires
del alma, y ellos tienen sus decires
que reflejan del pecho los anhelos.

Por eso yo le canto a tu alma pura,
porque tienen tus ojos más dulzura
que los astros divinos de los cielos.

To Carolina Rivero

    Amongst all the shining stars
of the gentle night, twinkling,
no two exist that beam more brightly
than your eyes both pure and lovely.

    Infinities of light leave their tracks,
as if they were two immense diamonds,
and in the glitter of love, caressing,
they dissolve a thousand daydreams and quarrels . . .

    The eyes make manifest the feelings
of the soul, and they have their say,
reflecting the longing of the heart.

    And so I sing straight to your pure soul,
because your eyes have more sweetness
than the divine stars of the heavens.

A la Sra. P. Rolo de Simón

En sus días.

Un mensaje de dichas, desprendido
del arpa celestial de los amores,
quisiéralo tejer, y con mis flores
y mis versos mandártelo prendido.

La paloma sutil de los cantares
debía yo tener por mensajera,
que volando, volando muy ligera,
surcase hacia tu hogar los anchos mares.

Con ella te mandara melodioso,
el célico mensaje venturoso
del arpa que cantó las ilusiones.

No a ti sola: también al compañero
que formara contigo, placentero
un hogar con dos nobles corazones.

To Mrs. P. Rolo de Simón

On her birthday.

I should like to weave a message
of fortune, coaxed forth from the harp
of love celestial, and with flowers
and my verses, send it off to you.

    The dove of most delicate song
I should have as my messenger,
who flying, flying so lightly,
toward your home would cross the wide seas.

    With her I would send, melodious,
the heavenly message of joy
from the harp that sang all my dreams.

    Not to you alone: also to the companion
who would form with you, delightful
a home with two noble hearts.

A Estrella Bravo

—En su álbum—

    Tan divina te halló la mente mía,
que te iguala a las hadas misteriosas,
a esas hadas de formas caprichosas
que pueblan, al soñar la fantasía.

    Por eso, como brota la ambrosia
del broche humedecido de las rosas,
efluyen mis estrofas cadenciosas,
nimbadas por la luz de tu poesía.

    Y por eso, vertiendo mi cadencia,
como vierten las flores grata esencia,
yo persigo un laurel para tu frente.

    ¡Ojalá lo consiga! . . . Desde ahora
quisiéralo ceñir solemnemente,
orgulloso, en tu sien de soñadora.

To Estrella Bravo

—In her album—

    So divine did my mind find you,
that it equates you to fay spirits,
those fairies of capricious form
that populate dreamers' fantasies.

    Because of that, as ambrosia springs forth
from the dripping chalice of the roses,
so flows out the cadence of my stanzas,
is nimbused by the light of your own poetry.

    And for that, in pouring forth my cadence,
as the flowers pour forth their pleasing essence,
I seek out a laurel for your brow.

    God will that I find it! . . . For even now
I would like to bend it solemnly,
and full of pride, to your dreamer's temples.

A Eponine P. Rolo

En su cumpleaños.

No hay flores, ni rosas, amor ni cariños,
ni un verso más dulce ni más divina!
que el verso que inspiran sonrisas de niños,
pues son confidentes de amor y de paz

Los niños son flores que aroman la vida;
hogar sin un niño no tiene ilusión,
y allí donde acaba la niñez querida
empieza la senda que traza el dolor.

Porque eres muy niña, porque eres un broche
que apenas en perlas y en plácida noche
el néctar del cielo se atreve a besar . . .

Por eso, aureolados de bellos colores,
te escribo estos versos; son ellos las flores
que hoy vengo a tus plantas a depositar.

To Eponine P. Rolo[73]

On her birthday.

There are no flowers nor roses, love nor care,
not a single verse more sweet or more divine
than the verse inspired by a child's smile,
because she is confident in love and peace.

Children are flowers that add fragrance to life;
a home with no child is without dreams,
and there where beloved childhood ends
begins the path that pain devises.

Because you are so young, and yet the clasped brooch
of a bloom, that with pearls and in the still of the night,
the nectar of heaven scarcely dares to kiss . . .

Because of that, haloed in lovely colors,
I write you these verses; they are the flowers
that today I come to lay at your feet.

A Edelmira Acosta

   Bendícente las rosas y las flores,
los ángeles te ofrendan sus sonrisas,
y tejen para ti con sus amores
de triunfos una cántiga las brisas.

   Los astros en perpetuo centelleo
retratan tu semblante purpurino,
y el pájaro cantor con su gorjeo,
de sueños va regando tu camino.

   Los ángeles, las flores y las rosas,
los astros y las brisas rumorosas,
entonan su homenaje a tus hechizos

   Reúnen sus caricias y loores
con el célico arrullo y los amores
del céfiro que juega con tus rizos.

To Edelmira Acosta

    The roses and the flowers bless you,
the angels offer up to you their smiles,
and the breezes weave for you
a song of love and triumph.

    The stars in their perpetual sparkling
trace out your rosy countenance
and the avian singer with his warbling,
goes watering the dreams that dot your path.

    The angels, the flowers, and the roses;
the stars and all murmuring breezes,
intone their homage to your charms.

    They join their caresses and praises
with the heavenly murmur and the love,
of the zephyr that plays with your curls.

Tus ojos

Para Ana Rosa Vila.

 Lo mismo que en los cielos van los astros
dejando en pos de sí luces muy bellas
van tus ojos igual que dos estrellas,
esparciendo, al mirar, divinos rastros.

 Son estrellas de amor que resplandecen
con lumbre de caricia abrasadora;
es su luz una luz dominadora:
son antorchas que nunca languidecen.

 Sin que tú lo advirtieras, pude verlos;
me oculté temeroso de ofenderlos,
evitando quizá causarte enojos.

 Pero cuando discreto te miraba,
comprendí que perdido yo surcaba
un abismo insondable: el de tus ojos.

Your Eyes

For Ana Rosa Vila.

　　Just as in the heavens the stars go by,
leaving behind themselves their lovely lights,
your eyes are just like two stars,
scattering, with their glances, divine traces.

　　They are the stars of love that gleam
with the fire of a scorching caress;
their light is a light that dominates;
they are torches that never flag.

　　Without your knowing it, I could see them;
I hid in fear of offending them,
to avoid perhaps causing you anger.

　　But when in my discretion I watched you,
I understood that, lost, I was chartering
a fathomless abyss: that of your eyes.

A Elisa Salgado

Lo divino, lo artístico, lo bello,
representan tus formas ideales;
tus pupilas dos puntos siderales
esparciendo en redor grato destello.

Yo no sé con qué blancas ilusiones
pareces tú soñar cautivadora;
¿te impresiona quizás arrulladora
el arpa del amor con sus canciones? . . .

Si es así, no desdeñes mis acentos,
porque son bella flor de sentimientos
de un alma que soñando busca abrigo.

Sentidos para ti—yo te lo juro,—
pues brotaron al mágico conjuro
de mi noble sentir para contigo.

To Elisa Salgado

    The divine, the artistic, the lovely,
describe your form in its perfection;
your pupils are two sidereal points
that scatter all around their pleasing glitter.

    You seem to dream, all captivating,
of I know not what flights of fancy;
perhaps you are moved by the lulling
of the harp of love in its songs? . . .

    If it is so, do not disdain my words,
for they are the lovely flower of the feelings
of a soul that in dreaming seeks a safe harbor.

    And intended just for you—I swear it to you,—
for they burst forth, conjured by the magic
of my noble feelings for you.

A "Angelita" Machin

    La aurora que despierta nacarada,
tiene celos de ti, siente rencores,
porque entibia sus fúlgidos colores
con rayos diamantinos tu mirada.

    La del sol infinita llamarada,
que da vida y calor a los amores,
vierte rayos de tibios resplandores
al brillo de tus ojos comparada.

    Porque en ellos refléjase infinita
el ansia del amor que los excita
a verter en su torno los anhelos.

    Prendidos de tu rostro peregrino,
lo mismo que los astros en los cielos,
van regando de sueños tu camino.

To "Angelita" Machin

    The dawn that awakes all in robed pearl,
is jealous of you, resentful even,
because her glowing colors are made dull
by the diamantine rays of your gaze.

    The infinite blaze of the sun
which gives life and heat to all love,
shines in rays of but tepid splendor
when compared to the shine of your eyes.

    Because in them lives an infinite reflection
of the thirst for the love that excites them
to pour forth their desire all around.

    Adornments of your peregrine face,
just as the stars bejewel the sky,
they go spilling dreams across your path.

Con besos y flores

Para "Elenita" Barroso.

Quisiera a tu paso verter olorosas
las flores que embriagan de aroma y candor;
ceñir a tu frente que envidian las diosas,
muy bella corona tejida con rosas,
caricias y besos y flores de amor.

Con flores y besos y luz y colores
y nardos y rosas tu senda regar;
tener de los astros divinos fulgores,
robar a las novias sus castos amores
y un himno con ellos poderte ofrendar.

Un himno a tus ojos de intensa mirada,
que son en tu cara dos astros de amor;
de citas y ensueños tejer la balada,
cantarte lo mismo que el bardo a la amada
en versos que arrullan con dulce rumor.

En versos muy bellos, de aroma divino,
cantando de amores mi ardiente ideal;
con bellas estrofas regar tu camino,
seguir tu sendero, seguir tu destino,
trocando mis sueños en vida real . . .

Que tú de mis versos la dúlcida esencia
jamás despreciaras por otra ilusión,
que a veces de un verso la rima y cadencia
contienen el néctar no más de inocencia,
¡pero otras se cambian por un corazón! . . .

Por eso a tu paso regar olorosas
quisiera mis flores de aroma y candor;
ceñir a tu frente que envidian las diosas,
muy bella corona tejida con rosas,
caricias y besos y flores de amor.

With Kisses and Flowers

For "Elenita" Barroso.

I should like, as you pass by, to pour forth fragrant
the flowers that intoxicate with aroma and with candor;
to crown your forehead, envy of the goddesses,
with a lovely crown woven with roses,
with caresses and kisses and the flowers of love.

With flowers and kisses, with light and with colors,
and polianthes and roses to water your path;
to steal the divine flames of the stars,
to rob the chaste brides of their loves,
and offer them all up to you with a hymn:

A hymn to your eyes with their intense gaze,
which are in your face two stars of love; to weave
the ballad with assignations and daydreams;
to sing to you as the bard does to his lover,
in verses that lull with their sweet sound.

In verses so lovely, of divine aroma,
singing of loves my burning ideal;
with lovely stanzas to water your path,
to follow your path, to follow your destiny,
turning my dreams into real life . . .

That you should never disregard
as just another dream the dulcet essence of my verses,
for sometimes the rhyme and cadence of a verse
contain no more than the nectar of innocence,
but others take a whole heart in trade! . . .

For that, as you pass by to pour forth fragrant
I should like my flowers of aroma and candor;
to crown your forehead that the goddesses envy,
a lovely crown woven with roses,
caresses and kisses, and flowers of love.

No olvides mis cantares...

En el álbum de "Consuelito" Rivero.

 Mujer de mis ensueños, imagen seductora,
más bella que los rayos divinos de la aurora,
conjunto primoroso de nítida ilusión:
no olvides mis cantares de dichas y de amores;
escúchalos sinceros y tiernos como flores
que brotan fervorosos del mismo corazón.

 Escucha los acentos de la armoniosa lira;
semeja los quejidos del alma que suspira
surcando desdeñada los cielos del amor;
si piensas que te adoro con ciega idolatría,
quizá entonces comprendas la justa queja mía
que finge los lamentos del arpa del dolor.

 Ignoro las caricias, ignoro los amores;
por eso es que te ofrendo mis versos y mis flores,
y anhelo verte siempre, mirarte sin cesar;
yo busco una caricia sin lágrimas ni enojos,
buscando con los míos la lumbre de unos ojos
de célicos destellos, de fúlgido mirar...

 Mujer nido de ensueños, imagen de mi amada:
¿oirás por fin la queja de mi alma enamorada
que loca va dictando mi férvida canción?...
responde, mientras cruzas el piélago infinito,
como astro deslumbrante de dulce amor bendito,
lo mismo que la estrella feliz de la ilusión.

 Anhelo beber pura la luz de una mirada,
de fuego una caricia que diérame la amada,
la vida de sus labios, su aliento respirar;
oyendo sus acentos, tejer canciones bellas,
con ella repetirlas, soñar siempre con ellas,
dormir a sus caricias de plácido arrullar...

 El sol brilla en tu cielo por siempre esplendoroso,
te ciñen sus celajes un tinte primoroso,
más bello y más divino que el iris del amor;
por eso embriagadores fascinan tus encantos,

Don't Forget My Songs . . .[74]

In the album of "Consuelito" Rivero.

    Lady of my daydreams, seductive image,
more lovely than the divine rays of the dawn,
exquisite ensemble of sharply drawn dreams:
don't forget my songs of joys and of loves;
listen to them, sincere and tender like flowers
that burst out fervently from my very heart.

    Listen to the accent of the harmonious lyre;
like unto the complaints of the soul that sighs,
chartering disdained the heavens of love;
if you think that I adore you with a blind idolatry,
perhaps then you can understand my justified complaint
that feigns the lamentation of the harp of pain.

    I know not caresses, I know not loves;
and so I offer you my verses and my flowers,
and long to see you always, to gaze at you unceasingly;
I seek a caress without tears or anger,
seek with my own the fire of a pair of eyes
flashingly celestial, with their gaze all aglow . . .

    Lady, nest of daydreams, living image of my beloved:
will you hear at last the complaint of my enamored soul
whose madness forever dictates my fervent song? . . .
respond, while you cross the infinite deep ocean,
like a blinding star of sweet and blessed love,
just like the happy star of hope.

    I long to drink the pure light of a glance,
of the fire that a caress from my beloved would give me,
the life from her lips, to breathe again her breath;
on hearing her voice to weave lovely songs,
with her to repeat them, to always dream of them,
to sleep with their caresses as a placid lullaby . . .

    The sun shines in your sky, forever splendorous,
its cloudscapes surround you in an exquisite tint,
more lovely and more divine than the nimbus of love;
because of that, your heady charms fascinate,

y níveas las palomas te arrullan en sus cantos,
y fúlgidas estrellas te dieron su esplendor.

Quisiera de la amada velar el dulce sueño,
sus horas silenciosas de amores y de ensueño,
en noches placenteras de alegre amanecer;
sentir sobre mis labios la fiebre de sus besos,
llevarlos yo en el alma eternamente impresos . . .
de su alma con la mía formar un solo ser.
. . . .

Mujer de mis ensueños, imagen seductora,
rival de los divinos destellos de la aurora,
conjunto primoroso de encantos e ilusión:
no olvides mis cantares de sueños y de amores;
escúchalos sinceros y tiernos como flores,
que brotan cariñosos del mismo corazón.

and snowy white, the doves lull you with their songs,
and fiery stars gave you all their splendor.

    I should like to watch over the sweet sleep
of my beloved, her silent hours of love and dreams,
through pleasurable nights with joyful dawns;
to feel on my lips the fever of her kisses,
to carry them forever printed on my soul . . .
and of her soul and mine to form a single being.
. . . .

    Lady of my daydreams, seductive image,
rival of the divine light of the dawn,
exquisite combination of enchantments and fantasy:
don't forget my songs of dreams and loves;
listen to them sincere and soft as flowers,
that burst forth, affectionate, from my very heart.

A Mariana Salgado

Quizá me reproches, quizá mis canciones
perturben tu idilio de paz y de amor;
perdona si en medio de tus ilusiones,
yo mezclo mis rimas, un verso, una flor . . .

Yo nunca me callo sintiendo belleza,
por eso al mirarte, no puedo callar;
tú diste a mis versos color y grandeza:
en tu alma de artista logréme inspirar.

Quizá me reproches y acaso algún día
comprendas que tu alma refleja la mía:
yo sé que tú sueñas lo mismo que yo . . .

¿Verdad que sus rosas el arte divino
deshoja a tu paso y aroma el camino
que tu alma de artista correrlo soñó? . . .

To Mariana Salgado[75]

    Perhaps you reproach me, perhaps my songs
perturb your idyll of peace and of love;
forgive me if between your daydreams,
I lay my rhymes, a verse, a flower . . .

    I never hold my tongue on feeling beauty,
therefore on seeing you, I cannot be quiet;
you gave color and nobility to my verses:
in your artist's soul I found my inspiration.

    Perhaps you reproach me and maybe some day
you will understand that your soul mirrors my own:
I know that you dream the same dreams I do . . .

    Isn't it true that the divine art pulls the petals
off its roses at your footstep and perfumes the path
that your artist's soul dreamed of running? . . .

Tus ojos

A Pura Pérez.

　　Yo no puedo comprenderlos: son dos ascuas misteriosas;
son dos chispas encendidas en el cráter de un volcán;
son dos ojos asesinos: son dos flechas venenosas
que, al volverse, vierten ansias de herir hondo con afán,

　　Yo he soñado con tus ojos, con su intensa llamarada,
acerados y punzantes, cual las hojas de un puñal:
he soñado con tus ojos de mortífera mirada,
que fingía de pasiones una loca bacanal.

　　Con tus ojos insondables, que nacieron de una noche
misteriosa de tormentas en revuelta tempestad;
y es por eso que de celos surge báquico derroche
al través de tus pupilas de profunda oscuridad.

　　En mis horas enervantes, en mis sueños de alma inquieta,
desfilando las visiones como en loca bacanal,
mil figuras "imposibles" mi cerebro de poeta
vio prendidas en la noche de tus ojos de cristal . . .

　　¡Yo no pude comprenderlos! son dos ascuas misteriosas;
hieran pronto y queman lento incomprensibles en su afán:
hieren rápidos lo mismo que las flechas venenosas,
queman lento como chispas desprendidas de un volcán.

Your Eyes

To Pura Pérez.

    I cannot understand them: they are two mysterious embers;
they are two living sparks in the crater of a volcano;
they are murderous eyes; two poisoned arrows
that in their glance, spills an eagerness to cut deeply with desire,

    I have dreamed about your eyes, with their flares of fire,
steely and sharp, like the blades of twin daggers;
I have dreamed about your eyes, with their deadly gaze
that feigns the passion of a wild bacchanal.

    About your unfathomable eyes, born from a night
of mysterious storms, a turbid tempest;
and from all that, jealousy springs in Bacchic excess
through your pupils of profound darkness.

    In my enervated hours, in the dreams of my unquiet soul,
visions parade like in a wild bacchanal,
a thousand "impossible" figures my poet's mind
saw spill forth in the night from your crystalline eyes . . .

    I cannot understand them: they are two mysterious embers;
they wound soon and burn slowly, incomprehensible in their affection;
they wound quickly, like twin poisoned arrows,
they burn slowly like sparks that leap from a volcano.

Homenaje

A la Srita. Zenaida Barcia, Reina de la Simpatía de Tampa.

Intento un homenaje rendir a tu belleza,
tejer con mis estrofas muy bello un pedestal,
en donde se entronicen amores y grandeza . . .
tejerlo con efluvios de néctar celestial.

Con néctar de mis versos, orlados con mis flores,
ungidos con esencias de nítida ilusión,
y en medio del conjunto de esencias y primores,
lo mismo que una rosa prender mi corazón.

Mas . . . no; ¡tejer con versos sin luz, sin armonía
la ofrenda que a una reina tendré que presentar! . . .
Silencia tus cantares y escucha, musa mía,
el dúlcido preludio que siéntese sonar . . .

Escucha: son legiones de miles de querubes
que armónicos entonan gentil salutación;
¿no ves cómo pasaron las blanquecinas nubes,
prestándoles las musas sutil inspiración?

¿No sientes melodiosos sus célicos rumores?
¿no llega a tus oídos su heráldico sonar? . . .
Son regios mensajeros de Reyes trovadores,
que vienen de muy lejos; "dejémoslos pasar" . . .

¿No? . . . Calla, musa mía . . . ya empiezan los violines . . .
Desgranan ya sus notas las liras de marfil . . .
Ya cumplen su mandato de amor los serafines,
al pie del Solio regio vertiendo flores mil.

Escucha las estrofas tejidas con sonrisas,
y mira los querubes volando en rededor:
sus alas perfumadas saturan a las brisas,
de aromas que eternizan las flores del amor.

Atiende . . . ya se acercan las sílfides y ondinas
con liras de oro y plata; escúchalas tañer . . .
y aquellas de los Reyes preseas tan divinas
las ninfas y nereidas las vienen a ofrecer.

Homage

> *To Miss Zenaida Barcia, Queen of Charm in Tampa.*[76]

I attempt here to render an homage to your beauty,
to weave with my stanzas a lovely pedestal
where I can enthrone your love and greatness . . .
and to weave it from a flood of celestial nectar.

With the nectar of my verses, garlanded with my flowers,
anointed with the essence of crisply envisioned dreams,
and amidst these collected essences and beautiful things,
pour out my heart, in form just like a rose.

But . . . no; How could I weave with verses with no light,
no harmony, the offering that I present to a queen! . . .
silence your songs and listen, muse of mine,
to the dulcet prelude that you can feel sounding . . .

Listen: they are a legion of thousands of cherubs
who in harmony intone a courteous salutation;
don't you see how they float by the white clouds
offering to the muses a subtle inspiration?

Don't you feel how melodious are their celestial murmurs?
Does the heraldic sound not caress your ears?
They are sumptuous messengers of player kings,
who come from very far; "let's let them pass" . . .

No? Hush, my muse, already the violins begin . . .
Already the notes slip from marble lyres . . .
Already the seraphs fulfill their mandate of love,
at the foot of the sumptuous throne pouring a thousand flowers.

Listen to the stanzas woven with smiles,
and watch the cherubs flying all about:
their perfumed wings saturate the breezes
with aromas that make everlasting the flowers of love.

Attend . . . already the sylphs and undines come close
with lyres of silver and of gold; listen to them sound . . .
and royal, precious jewels, divine,[77]
the nymphs and nereids come to offer you.

Las ninfas y nereidas, portando fulgurantes
diademas de monarcas de célica región;
¿no ves cómo adornaron el trono con diamantes? . . .
Escucha, también ellas entonan su canción.

¡Qué bellas las estrofas en célico lenguaje!
Semejan la balada divina del amor;
parece que los Reyes tejieron su mensaje
con nardos y con rosas, con luz y resplandor . . .

Las regias embajadas, las célicas legiones
de hinojos ante el Trono, salúdanla . . . ¿la ves? . . .
Parece que terminan sus regias comisiones,
y ahora reverentes se postran a sus pies.

Y ante el sublime Trono de vírgenes amores,
en donde están de frente virtudes y placer,
sus liras perfumadas los regios trovadores
arrojan a sus plantas de reina y de mujer.
. . . .

Rindieron ya su ofrenda las sílfides y ondinas,
las musas, los querubes . . . el coro angelical;
ahora, musa mía, ¿con qué estrofas divinas
te acercas a las gradas del regio pedestal? . . .

De hinojos te saludo, mi Reina primorosa,
en medio de tus galas de regio resplandor;
muy pobre fue mi lira, no pudo cadenciosa
verter la grata esencia de un verso todo amor.

En cambio yo a tus plantas deshojo tiernas flores
de inmensa simpatía, de intensa adoración;
acepta, Reina bella, mi ofrenda y mis loores,
que brota homenaje del mismo corazón.

The nymphs and nereids, bearing shining
diadems of monarchs from the celestial realm;
don't you see how they adorn the throne with diamonds? . . .
Listen, for they too intone their song.

How beautiful the stanzas in their celestial language!
They are like a divine ballad of love;
it seems as if the Kings wove their message
with polianthes and with roses, with light and with splendor . . .

The royal embassies, the celestial legions
kneeling before the Throne, greet you . . . Do you see?
As if, now finished their royal commissions,
reverent, they prostrate themselves at your feet.

And before the sublime Throne of virgin loves,
where all virtues and pleasures are at the fore,
their perfumed lyres the royal troubadours
lay at your feet: both queen and of woman.

. . . .

The sylphs and undines already paid their tribute ,
the muses, the cherubs . . . the angelic choir;
now, muse of mine, with what divine stanzas
do you approach the steps of the royal pedestal? . . .

Kneeling here I salute you, my exquisite Queen,
amidst the finery of your royal splendor;
very poor was my lyre; it could not find the rhythm,
to spill forth the pleasing essence of a verse all made of love.

Instead at your feet I strip the petals from sweet flowers
of immense charm, of intense adoration;
accept, lovely queen, my offering and my praises,
for this tribute springs forth from deep in my heart.

Última página

   Con un ferviente esfuerzo—me decía—
he de escribir un libro malo o bueno;
fui llamando a mi espíritu sereno
cada vez que una página escribía.

   A medida que el tiempo transcurría
y los viles me daban su veneno,
aún oyendo su voz, quise ser bueno:
"a su mal con mi bien" le respondía.

   Mi conciencia una cruz asemejaba,
portadora de paz entre sus brazos,
¡y a los viles también los cobijaba!

   Y, al dar fin a la obra que intentaba,
como rasgo de bien, entre sus trazos
quiero darle el perdón al que me odiaba.

FIN

Final Page

    With a fervent labor—I told myself—
I must write a book, be it good or bad;
I cried out for a serene spirit
each time that I wrote a page.

    While time continued to flow by
and the haters would fling their venom at me,
on hearing its voice I wanted to be good:
"for their worst my best" I would respond.

    My conscience began to resemble a cross,
bearing peace in her arms, offering
shelter even to those who hate me.

    And, on finishing the work that I attempted,
as an outpouring of goodness, amidst its lines
I want to pardon those who hated me.

END

NOTAS

Conforme con lo dicho en la primera página, este libro contiene, además de algunas inéditas, mis poesías publicadas en Tampa y Key West en los tres últimos años, excepción hecha de cuatro: "A Cuba y sus mujeres," "Los Días actuales," "La Guerra Europea" y "Mirando al mar," que incluyo en mi libro *Horas de nostalgia* que pronto ha de ver la luz. Quizás alguna quede olvidada en las colecciones de periódicos.

Por lo mismo que nunca pensé reunir en un tomo muchas de estas poesías, por su imperfección, esta obrita resulta en pugna con mi deseo de publicar un libro de algo más fondo y menos descuidado en la forma; pero yo que sobre todas las cosas, amo lo único que heredé de mis mayores: el apellido, ya que hubo quien quiso mancharlo, atribuyendo mis versos, en gran parte de asunto cansado, a otros autores, cuando son de mi exclusiva propiedad, opté por publicarlos así, como fueron escritos muchos de ellos para llenar compromisos, casi sin pensarlos.

De ahí las repeticiones y disonancias que han de encontrarse en este librito, principalmente en su 2a. parte.

Además de una errata en la página 25, donde dice tejida con lágrimas, que debe leerse tejida con las lágrimas, se encontrarán otras de caja, que el buen sentido de los lectores subsanará.

EL AUTOR.

NOTES

As I established on the first page, this book contains, in addition to some previously unpublished work, the poetry that I published in Tampa and Key West in the last three years, with the exception of four poems: "To Cuba and Her Women," "These Days," "The European War," and "Watching the Sea," which I will include in the book *Hours of Nostalgia* which will be published soon. Perhaps some other remains forgotten in newspaper collections.

Just as I never thought about collecting many of these poems in one volume, due to their imperfection, this little book stands at odds with my desire to publish a book that is more profound and less careless with the form; but I love above all things the only thing I inherited from my family—my surname—and given that there was someone who wanted to tarnish it by attributing my verses, in large part on tired themes, to other authors, when they are my exclusive property, I opted to publish them here, as many of them were written to fulfill promises and almost without thinking.

From that history come the repetitions and dissonances that will be found in this little book, principally in its second part.

In addition to an error on page 25, where it says "woven with tears" and ought to say "woven with the tears," there will be others to be found, which the good sense of the reader will correct.

The Author.

APPENDIX 1

The Social World of *Lágrimas y flores*

Analyzing the patterns that emerge from among the individuals to whom Feliciano Castro dedicated the poems in *Lágrimas y flores* reveals the overlapping networks of social relations in which he was ensconced, networks that can perhaps best be described by two concentric circles: his very local web of connections on the tiny island of Key West as defined by the cigar-making industry, print journalism, and particularly the Cuba Society's theater group; and the more expansive, transnational web of connections among creative writers and journalists in the Latin American Caribbean region.

In Key West, Castro's local social network appears to have centered on the Cuba Society, a theater company in which six of Castro's dedicatees were actively involved: director Francisco Pineda; playwright and critic Octavio J. Monteresy; Santiago García, "Consuelito" Rivero, and Mariana Salgado, who may have been actors in the troupe; and Castro's close friend Rogelio Miqueli, a Key West editor with whom Castro traveled to Havana at least once and who served as a secretary for the Cigar Makers' International Union (El corresponsal 9). Given Castro's close connections to Cuban émigrés involved in performance and drama, it is no wonder that one of his poems in the *Flores* section is set and titled "In the Theater."

While Consuelito Rivero and Mariana Salgado were members of the Cuba Society, little is known regarding most of the dedicatees—almost exclusively women—in the *Flores* section, except that at least two recipients (Zenaida Barcía and Julieta Raga) can be definitively located in Tampa, where Zenaida was elected "Queen of Charm" in December of 1916, and Raga came in second. The three Rolo women—the daughters (one of whom, Sofia, would eventually marry Castro) of printer Juan Pérez Rolo, Castro's partner at Taller Tipográfico—lived in Key West, as did Antonia Pérez Rolo, their mother, the only woman to whom a poem in the *Lágrimas* section is dedicated; many if not all of the other dedicatees in *Flores* were also in Key West, an assertion supported by O.J. Monteresy, who, in a review of *Lágrimas y flores* for *El Mundo*, said that Castro, on arriving in Key West, had "sabido ganar nuestras simpatías depositando a los pies de cada uno de nuestras damitas un ramillete de rimas" [known how to earn our sympathies, by depositing at the feet of each of our little ladies a bouquet of rhymes] (15). Several surnames that appear multiple times in the *Flores* section—Bravo, López, Rivero, Salgado, Síbila, Toledo, and Vila—may also indicate family groupings, and all of the dedicatees merit further research by future scholars working to reconstruct the history of the Cuban émigré community in Key West.

Castro's broader circle of artistic connections, which spanned the Latin American Caribbean, is defined by such dedicatees in the *Lágrimas* section as Cuban poets Arturo Doreste (who dedicated a poem to Castro), F. Dominguez Pérez, and J. M. Subirats, as well as Indigenous Honduran poet, journalist, and historian Salvador Turcios.

Organized here for future literary scholars' and historians' ease of reference are the dedicatees in each section, listed in alphabetical order, in the hope that this archive of names will help recuperate and revitalize exiled voices, social networks, and poetic traditions from the past, ushering them into the ever-evolving canon of the literature of the Americas.

Dedicatees in *Lágrimas*

Alzay, R. M.

"Mensaje de lágrimas" ["Message of Tears"]
Further information on the identity of R. M. Alzay remains to be discovered.

Dominguez Pérez, F.

"Es un iris tu voz" ["Your Voice Is an Iris"]
"F. Dominguez Pérez"

F. Domínguez Pérez published a book of poems, *Cantos de vida* [Songs of Life], in Cuba in 1913 that includes the verse "La voz del poeta" [The voice of the poet] (7–8), to which Castro's poem "Your Voice is an Iris" may be responding. Pérez was also the director of the biweekly Cuban periodical *Alpha,* printed in Mayarí beginning in 1915 (Ford 194).

Doreste, Arturo

"Soñaba" ["I Used to Dream"]

Arturo Doreste (1895–1983) was a Cuban poet of Canary Island descent. In 1916, at only 21 years of age, he won the Floral Games of Santiago de Cuba along with Miguel A. Macau (Primelles 209). The Floral Games are a tradition of poetry competitions that arose in the Middle Ages in Barcelona and other cities; revived in the nineteenth century as part of the Catalán Renaixença and the century's general interest in the past, the tradition spread across the major cities of Spain and Latin America.

In 1917, Doreste—already a contributor to multiple newspapers both in Cuba and abroad—published his first book of poems, *Mis sueños y mis rosas* [My Dreams and My Roses]. Appearing shortly after the death of his mother and heavily influenced by her loss, this book is, like *Lágrimas y flores,* divided into two distinct parts, and, like *Lágrimas y flores,* it begins with a sonnet to the poet's mother. In this poem, in response to her death, the speaker turns to poetry for solace: "Como perdí mi madre idolatrada / . . . / Hacia ti, Poesía inmaculada, / me dirijo, cual triste peregrino" (21) [Given that I lost my idolized mother / . . . / Toward you, immaculate Poetry, / I turn, as a sad pilgrim]. The first half of the volume ranges from the philosophical and sentimental to explorations of nation and identity. The second part, consisting of only eight poems and dedicated to the poet's father, is a beautiful mourning sequence for Doreste's mother.

Just as Castro dedicated "Soñaba" to Doreste, Doreste in turn dedicated the poem "La voz piadosa" ["The pious voice"] to Feliciano Castro. In Doreste's poem, the memory of friendship and of this pious voice are a consolation that help the speaker to persist through the turmoil and suffering of loss: "Igual que un astro hermoso que se esfuma / trás el luctuoso velo de la bruma, / se oculta mi soñar y mi alegría . . . / Pero una voz piadosa de consuelo, / brota de lo profundo de mi anhelo / diciéndome que aguarde todavía . . . !" (119–120) [Just like a lovely star that vanishes / behind the tragic veil of the sea mist /so hide my dreams and my joy . . . / but a pious voice of consolation, / bursts forth from the depths of my yearning / telling me to keep holding on].

García, Santiago

"El derrumbe universal" ["The Universal Collapse"]

Santiago García, a Key West resident, formed part of the theater group of the Cuba Society.

Kubelik, Jan

"La eterna queja" ["The Eternal Complaint"]

Because of the devotion to music that infuses Castro's volume, his dedicatee "Kubelik" here is very likely Jan Kubelik (1880–1940), a Czech violinist and composer who toured internationally—he played dozens of times in Rome, where Castro may have seen him perform during the period when Castro resided as a student at the Pontifical Spanish College of St. Joseph in the Palazzo Altemps. Kubelik also recorded early gramophone albums, including a 1904 rendition of *Ave Maria,* a prayer that appears in Castro's poem "The Angelus."

Milord, Domingo

"El alma de Martí" ["The Soul of Martí"]

Born in Havana, Domingo Milord was the son of a Cuban cigar manufacturer and the grandson of a Cuban surgeon (both also named Domingo Milord). In 1872, Milord's father, who supported Cuban independence, moved the family to Key West, where Milord attended school at the San Carlos Institute. Later, Milord became a foreman at a cigar factory, held various official positions, and was appointed Cuban Consul of Key West.

Miqueli, Rogelio

"Una patria azul" ["A Blue Patria"]

"A. Cermeño—R. Miqueli"

The prefatory note and endnote that bracket Castro's "¡Cubanos, proseguid!" ["Cubans, Carry On!"] were also written by Miqueli.

Rogelio Miqueli served as a secretary to the Cigar Makers' International Union throughout 1912 and up to May of 1913 (Perkins vols. 36-38), and was involved with the Cuba Society theater group (El corresponsal 9). The headnote and endnote of Castro's poem "Cubans, Carry On!" suggest that Miqueli was also associated with the weekly periodical *Florida* in Key West. He would go on to edit the anarchist newspaper *Nueva Vida* in the 1920s (for which his sister Violeta wrote), and to produce antifascist theater with the Sociedades Hispanas Confederadas at the time of the Spanish Civil War and during Franco's dictatorship (Feu 36, 38).

Monteresy, Octavio J.

"Pagina gris" ["Gray Page"]

A brash and daring writer, Octavio J. Monteresy was one of the most outspoken voices for Key West in the Cuban press in the decade surrounding the publication of *Lágrimas y flores*—of which he wrote a glowing review for the Havana newspaper *El Mundo* in June of 1918. From 1911 to 1921, he served as a regional correspondent and particularly the Key West correspondent variously for *El Mundo, La Lucha,* and *El Diario de la Marina;* as more of the journalistic output of this era finds its way into digital archives, his will be a name to watch. Monteresy was also the author of at least one play, *Dolora, drama social* [*Dolora: A Social Drama*], on which he worked with several others who appear in this book and which was staged at the Cuba Society in Key West (Primelles 211).

Pineda, Paco

"El Pescador" ["The Fisherman"]

The fact that *Paco* is a common nickname for *Francisco* suggests that this poem's dedicatee is very likely Francisco Pineda, the director of the theater group of the Cuba Society in 1916 (El corresponsal 9); the numbered five-act structure of Castro's "El Pescador" resonates with Pineda's theatrical pursuits. Thematically germane to the poem, moreover, is the *Miami Herald*'s report that Francisco Pineda was one of three young men "rescued from a horrible death of thirst and starvation" after their small fishing boat capsized and went missing off the Key West coast in 1912; a fourth man died ("State News" 7). Important to recall is the community's assumption of tragedy and death that occurred when a fishing boat did not return on time, a trope common in Galician literature.

Rolo, Antonia Pérez

"Paisaje nocturno" ["Nocturnal Landscape"]

The only woman to whom a poem in *Lágrimas* is dedicated, Antonia Pérez Rolo was the wife of Castro's business partner Juan Pérez Rolo, the co-owner of Taller Tipografico. Soon to become Castro's mother-in-law, she is remembered by the family as having written for the weekly periodical *Florida,* for which she is named as the editor of the recurring section "Pagina de hogar" [Page of the home].

Subirats, J. M.

"¿Porqué despertarla? . . ." ["Why Wake Her? . . ."]
In the decade surrounding the publication of *Lágrimas y flores,* J.M. Subirats moved in the swirl of Cuba's intellectual high society, publishing his poem "Elegía" [Elegy] in the magazine *Arte* [Art] in 1917 (Ruiz 9) and hosting banquets for the literati. One such banquet honored the young writer and lawyer Manuel Antonio Varona, a future Prime Minister of Cuba, and the menu and guest list for the occasion appeared in the newspaper (Quesada 8). When Castro dedicated "¿Porqué despertarla? . . . ," Subirats was likely already, like Castro himself, a Mason, because by 1952, Subirats was the Master of the Ancient Mystical Order Rosae Crucis (Rosicrucian) lodge in Santiago de Cuba ("Directory" 45), and this mystical order is composed solely of Master-level Masons.

Torres, Leandro de

"La mano del amigo" ["The Hand of a Friend"]
Further information on the identity of Leandro de Torres remains to be discovered.

Turcios, Salvador

"Tiempo" ["Time"]
Salvador R. Turcios (1880–1973) was a Honduran journalist, poet, and historian. He spent fifteen years in El Salvador as a journalist, during which time he published a series of anti-imperialist essays which were later compiled in the volume *Al margen del imperialismo yanqui* [*At the Margin of Yankee Imperialism*] (Arrellano 275). Among his other publications was *Libro de sonetos* (1914), the act of publishing which in Central America at this time Turcios calls "no solo un *heroísmo transcendental,* sino una *audacia inaudita*" (original emphasis, scan 21) [not only a *transcendental heroism* but also an *unheard-of audacity*]. This collection of one hundred sonnets explores Turcios's indigeneity, his identity as a poet, and relationships to death, life, and the natural world. It includes a number of pieces dedicated to literary and historical entities, both European, like Cervantes, and of the Americas, like Bolívar and the Popol Vuh (the sacred text of the Maya K'iche,' preserved orally until its transcription in 1550). Like Castro's, Turcios's volume includes multiple articulations of the poet's relationship to his country's flag and to the nature of citizenship. The volume is available via Hathi Trust.

Dedicatees in *Flores*

Acosta, Edelmira

Ávalo, Celia
Ávalo, Graciela

Barcía, Zenaida, was crowned "Queen of Charm" by the Tampa illustrated magazine *Bohemia* in December of 1916, winning with 21,401 votes. Her picture appears in the December 9 issue (Soto no. 21). While the accompanying article says very little about Zenaida herself, she does appear in society pages throughout the paper's run. These mentions suggest that she was a major player in the organization of social events, that she was very generous with her time (several times, there are published notes submitted to and published in the magazine thanking her for helping people with event planning), and that she was kind (see Soto nos. 6–22).

Barroso, "Elenita"

Boza, María

Bravo, Célida
Bravo, Dulce María
Bravo, Estrella

Cermeño, América

Colón, "Teresita"

Corbett, Graciela

Fueyo, Adelaida

López, Agnelia
López, Delia
López, Georgina
López, Josefina
López, Rosa María

Machín, "Angelita"

Martínez, Antonia

Pérez, Pura

Pinet, Adelaida

Pintado, Celeste

Pita, Ofelia

Quesada, Ofelia

Raga, Julieta was a working artist in the Tampa area in 1916, who seems not only to have been a very popular local musician, but also to have supported herself as a singer (she was a comic soprano, a "tiple cómica"). There are records of multiple performances (exhibitions or revues, zaruelas and operettas) that she gave around Tampa, Ybor City, and West Tampa in the fall of 1916 in the extant volume of *Bohemia* (see Soto nos. 6-22). Raga also came in second to Zenaida Barcia in *Bohemia*'s Queen of Charm competition (see Barcia), with 8,954 votes. Because of this, her photograph appears in the December 9 issue of *Bohemia*, alongside Barcia's (no. 21). In her photograph, she is looking down at a small bouquet of flowers and smiling in a gentle way, almost laughing.

Rivero, Carolina
Rivero, "Consuelito," who formed part of the Cuba Society theater group
Rivero, Ofelia

Rodríguez, Estela

Rolo, Eponine P. was the younger sister of Sofía Pérez Rolo and the daughter of Castro's business partner Juan Pérez Rolo and his wife Antonio Pérez Rolo.
Rolo, Sofía Pérez
Rolo de Simon, Sra. P.

Saenz, "Conchita"

Salazar, Elvira

Salgado, Adolfina
Salgado, Elisa
Salgado, Mariana formed part of the Cuba Society theater group.

Síbila, Gloria
Síbila, Rosa

Toledo, Heliodora
Toledo, "Lolita"

Viera, Dalia

Vila, Ana Rosa
Vila, Rosalía

APPENDIX 2

Meter and Verse Forms

Title	Stanzas	Meter
Mi madre y mi bandera / My Mother and My Flag	Sonnet	11/ABBA ABBA CCD EED
El alma de Martí / The Soul of Martí	Sonnet	11/ABBA ABBA CCD EED
Lágrimas / Tears	17	Royal Quatrains: hendecasyllabic, chained rhyme
¡Mentira! / Lie!	Sonnet	11/ABBA ABBA CCD EED
La jauría / The Pack of Dogs	Sonnet	11/ABBA ABBA CCD EED
¿Por qué callas? / Why Do You Hold Your Tongue?	Sonnet	11/ABBA ABBA CCD EED (D is a near rhyme)
El hombre que infama / The Man Who Defames	Sonnet	12/ABBA ABBA CCD EED (agudo)
Es un iris tu voz / Your Voice Is an Iris	Sonnet	11/ABBA ABBA CCD EED
A mi padre / To My Father	Sonnet	11/ABBA ABBA CCD EED
Una patria azul / A Blue Patria	13	Quatrains: 16-syllable lines, agudo
Yo tengo aqui en mi cuarto . . . / I Have Here in My Room . . .	10	Alexandrine quatrains (Spanish Alexandrines are 14-syllable lines in two hemistichs with a middle caesura), agudo, strophic chained rhyme
Las palmas / The Palms	Sonnet	11/ABAB ABAB CCD EED
El tiempo / Time	8	Hendecasyllabic sextets, rhyme AABCCB
La eterna queja / The Eternal Complaint	Sonnet	11/ABBA ABBA CCD EED
La escuela / School	11	Alexandrine quatrains, agudo, strophic chained rhyme
Página gris / Gray Page	Sonnet	11/ABBA ABBA CDC DCD
El derrumbe universal / The Universal Collapse	10	Hendecasyllabic sextets, rhyme AABCCB
La barquilla y el alma / The Little Boat and the Soul	7	12-syllable line quatrains, strophic chained rhyme

Title	Stanzas	Meter
Mis versos / My Verses	continuous	Alternating 6- and 12-syllable lines in quatrains, strophic consonant rhyme on odd lines, strophic assonant rhyme on even lines
Mis ilusiones / My Daydreams	5	Octavilla aguda: octave in arte menor, the fourth and eighth lines agudo; stanza adheres to a set pattern. Here abbcdeec
¡Cuba y mi amada! / Cuba and My Beloved	7	Decima espinela (or classical): 8-syllable lines with consonant rhyme abbaaccddc
El pescador / The Fisherman	5 sections	Silva (alternating 7- and 11-syllable lines) with six lines per stanza, strophic consonant rhyme AbAb
Paisaje nocturno / Nocturnal Landscape	Sonnet	11/ABAB ABAB CCD EED (D is a near rhyme)
En la ausencia / In Absence	5	Octavilla aguda: octave in arte menor, the fourth and eighth lines agudo; stanza adheres to a set pattern. Here abbcdeec
¿Porqué despertarla?... / Why Wake Her?	3	Romancillo (arte menor form of the romance: continuous assonant rhyme on even verses, odd verses free) in hexasyllables, here with 9-syllables in lines 5 and 13 of each stanza
El Angelus / The Angelus	Sonnet	11/ABBA ABBA CDC DCD
Soñaba / I Used to Dream	11	Royal Quatrains: hendecasyllabic, chained rhyme
La mano del amigo / The Hand of a Friend	Sonnet	11/ABBA ABBA CCD EED
¿Te acuerdas? / Do You Remember?	11	Quintilla (quintet in arte menor), octosyllabic, consonant rhyme abaab
Yo / Self	Sonnet	11/ABBA ABBA CCD EED
En la playa / On the Beach	8	Compound septet with agudo: stanzas of seven octosyllabic lines composed of a tercet and a quatrain, with the third and seventh lines broken (4 syllables), agudo, and rhyming with each other (aabcccb). The poem begins with one introductory hendecasyllabic quatrain with ABAB rhyme)
F. Domínguez Pérez	Sonnet	12/ABAB CDCD EEF GGF (agudo in BDF)

Meter and Verse Forms · 311

Title	Stanzas	Meter
El dos de noviembre / The Second of November	4	Decima espinela (or classical): 8-syllable lines with consonant rhyme abbaaccddc
¿ . . . . ?	8	Octavilla aguda: octave in arte menor, the fourth and eighth lines agudo; stanza adheres to a set pattern. Here abbcdeec
España / Spain: Hail, Flag of Mine!	9	Quintet with 16-syllable lines (agudo), consonant rhyme ABAAB, atypically for the poet has two diereses in the first line
Año viejo/ Old Year	1	Alexandrine sextet AABCCB
Año nuevo / New Year	1	Alexandrine sextet AABCCB
Cuba	9	Quintet with 16-syllable lines (agudo), consonant rhyme ABAAB
El grito de Yara / The Cry of Yara	19	Decima espinela (or classical): 8-syllable lines with consonant rhyme abbaaccddc
¡Cubanos, proseguid! / Cubans, Carry On!	11	Alexandrine quatrains, agudo, strophic chained rhyme
Bodas de plata del Centro Español de Tampa / The Silver Anniversary of the Spanish Center in Tampa	14	Royal quatrains: hendecasyllabic with consonant chained rhyme, except for one stanza that has enclosed rhyme
Mensaje de lágrimas / Message of Tears	17	Royal quatrains: hendecasyllabic with consonant chained rhyme
Mi ofrenda / My Offering	13	Alexandrine quatrains, agudo, strophic chained rhyme
A mis hermanas / To My Sisters	Sonnet	11/ABBA ABBA CDC DCD
A las obreritas / To the Factory Girls	9	Decasyllabic sextet with caesura, strophic rhyme AABCCB (agudo on v. 3 and 6)
Quisiera . . . / I Should Like . . .	Sonnet	11/ ABAB CDDC EEF GGF
¿Por qué te escribo? / Why Do I Write to You?	5	Decasyllabic quintet, in two hemistiches, consonant rhyme ABAAB
Rimas / Rhymes	5 (numbered)	Compound septet with agudo: stanzas of seven octosyllabic lines composed of a tercet and a quatrain, with the third and seventh lines broken (4 syllables), agudo, and rhyming with each other (aabcccb). The poem begins with one introductory hendecasyllabic quatrain with ABAB rhyme)
A Dulce María Bravo	Sonnet	11/ABBA ABBA CCD EED

Title	Stanzas	Meter
A Antonia Martínez	Sonnet	11/ABBA ABBA CCD EED
A "Conchita" Saenz	Sonnet	10/ABAB CDCD EEF GGF (BDF agudo)
Tu debieras tener . . . / You Ought to Have	Sonnet	11/ABBA ABBA CCD EED (Note: In several of this variant, C and E are very similar, to the point that it seems intentional)
A Graciela Corbett	Sonnet	11/ABBA ABBA CCD EED
A "Teresita" Colón	Sonnet	12/ABAB CDCD EEF GGF (BDF agudo)
A Célida Bravo	Sonnet	11/ABBA ABBA CCD EED
A Josefina López	Sonnet	11/ABAB CDCD EEF GGF
A Rosa María López	Sonnet	11/ABBA ABBA CCD EED
A Sofía Pérez Rolo	Sonnet	11/ABBA ACCA DDE AAE
En el baile / At the Dance	Sonnet	11/ABBA ABBA CCD EED (C is imperfect)
A Graciela Avalo	Sonnet	11/ABBA ABBA CCD EED (D agudo)
Tu boca / Your Mouth	Sonnet	11/ABBA CDDC EEF GGF
A Delia López	Sonnet	11/ABBA ABBA CCD EED (D agudo)
A Celia Avalo	Sonnet	11/ABBA ABBA CCD EED
Tu caricia / Your Caress	Sonnet	11/ABBA ABBA CCD EED (A is a near rhyme, schema could also read as ABBA BCCB DDC AAC but intentionality unclear)
A "Consuelito" Rivero	Sonnet	11/ABBA ABBA CCD EED
Estela Rodríguez	Sonnet	11/ABBA ABBA CCD EED
La amada mia / My Beloved	14	Royal quatrains: hendecasyllabic with consonant chained rhyme
Ofrenda póstuma / Posthumous Offering	Sonnet	11/ABAB CDCD EEF GGF
A Ofelia Rivero	Sonnet	11/ABBA ABBA CCD EED
A América Cermeño	Sonnet	11/ABBA ABBA CCD EED
A Adelaida Pinet	Sonnet	11/ABBA ABBA CCD EED (D agudo)
A Rosalía Vila	7 septets w/o breaks	Compound septet with agudo: stanzas of seven octosyllabic lines composed of a tercet and a quatrain, with the third and seventh lines broken (4 syllables), agudo, and rhyming with each other (aabcccb). The poem begins with one introductory hendecasyllabic quatrain with ABAB rhyme)

Meter and Verse Forms · 313

Title	Stanzas	Meter
A Heliodora Toledo	Sonnet	11/ABAB CDCD EEF GGF* (BDF agudo, don't actually rhyme)
A Ofelia Quesada	Sonnet	11/ABBA ABBA CCD EED (D agudo)
En el teatro / In the Theater	Sonnet	11/ABBAABBACCDEED (agudez in B)
A. Cermeño—R. Miqueli	Sonnet	12/ABAB CDCD EEF GGF (BDF agudo)
A Agnelia López	Sonnet	12/ABAB CDCD EEF GGF (BDF agudo)
A Rosa Sibila	Sonnet	11/ABBA ABBA CCD EED
A Gloria Sibila	Sonnet	11/ABBA ABBA CCD EED
A Julieta Raga	Sonnet	14/ABAB ACAC DDE FFE (BCE agudo)
A Dalia Viera	Sonnet	11/ABBA ABBA CCD EED
A María Boza	Sonnet	11/ABBA ABBA CCD EED
A Carolina Rivero	Sonnet	11/ABBA ABBA CCD EED
A la Sra. P. Rolo de Simón	Sonnet	11/ABBA CDDC EEF GGF
A Estrella Bravo	Sonnet	11/ABBA ABBA CCD EDE
A Eponine P. Rolo	Sonnet	12/ABAB CDCD EEF GGF* (BDF mostly agudo; neither the Bs nor the Ds actually rhyme)
A Edelmira Acosta	Sonnet	11/ABAB CDCD EEF GGF
Tus ojos / Your Eyes	Sonnet	11/ABBA CDDC EEF GGF
A Elisa Salgado	Sonnet	11/ABBA CDDC EEF GGF
A "Angelita" Machin	Sonnet	11/ABBA ABBA CCD EDE (
Con besos y flores / With Kisses and Flowers	6	Hendecasyllabic quintet: agudo, consonant rhyme ABAAB
No olvides mis cantares . . . / Don't Forget My Songs . . .	8	Alexandrine sextet, agudo, strophic rhyme AABCCB
A Mariana Salgado	Sonnet	11/ABAB CDCD EEF GGF (BDF agudo)
Tus ojos / Your Eyes	5	Quatrains with 16-syllable lines in two hemistiches, agudo, strophic chained rhyme
Homenaje / Homage	15	Alexandrine quatrains, agudo, strophic chained rhyme
Última página / Final Page	Sonnet	11/ABBA ABBA CDC CDC

ENDNOTES

1 Decades later, in a 1966 profile in the *Miami Herald,* Castro would recall the rigors of standing and shouting the texts indoors in the tropical heat: "It was exhausting . . . I really used to sweat" (Smith).
2 Studies such as Gerald Poyo's 2014 *Exile and Revolution: José D. Poyo, Key West, and Cuban Independence* and Consuelo E. Stebbins's 2007 *City of Intrigue, Nest of Revolution: A Documentary History of Key West in the Nineteenth Century* meticulously chronicle the Cuban exile community's long efforts on behalf of anticolonial revolution.
3 See especially chapters 13 and 14 of Ada Ferrer's magisterial *Cuba: An American History.*
4 For work on these interconnections from the early modern period through the twentieth century, see Allyson Poska's *Women and Authority in Early Modern Spain: The Peasants of Galicia* and Kirsty Hooper's *Writing Galicia into the World: New Cartographies, New Poetics.*
5 See particularly Isabel Alvarez Borland's foundational survey *Cuban-American Literature of Exile: From Person to Persona.*
6 Odes to flags and other national symbols are an outgrowth of the nineteenth-century cultural urge toward the solidification of national identity in Latin America. This trend, visible in narrative throughout the century, as discussed in Doris Sommer's *Foundational Fictions: The National Romances of Latin America,* continued through the *fin de siècle,* as evidenced by Cuban Bonifacio Byrne's "Mi bandera" (1899) and Argentine Juan Chassaing's "A mi bandera" (1906).
7 See Lou Charnon-Deutsch, "The Naturalization of Feminine Nature," in *Fictions of the Feminine in the Nineteenth-Century Spanish Press.*
8 The first volume of editor Manuel Soto's *Bohemia,* 24 issues in total—the only known extant copies—are available thanks to the Digital Commons @ University of South Florida. This magazine, which includes much valuable literary, cultural, and photographic material from Tampa, is a recent addition to the fragile archive of the Spanish-language press of the period; its discovery postdates the bibliographic work of Kanellos and Martell. Because the magazine does not have page numbers, and has formatting that does not lead to the imposition of clear pagination, throughout this book we refer to the issue of the magazine where texts or references appear, rather than the page.

The poems appearing in this first volume of *Bohemia* that are gathered into *Lágrimas y flores* are "¡Cuba y mi amada!" [Cuba and My Beloved!] (vol. 9), "Mis Versos"

[My Verses] (no. 12), "¡El Tiempo!" [Time!] (no. 13), "España. ¡Salve bandera mía!" [Spain. Hail, Flag of Mine!] and "Cuba. ¡Salve Bandera Amada!" [Cuba. Hail, Beloved Flag!] (on facing pages, framed in red linework in no. 14), "El dos de noviembre" [The Second of November] (no. 16), "No olvides mis cantares" [Don't Forget My Songs] (no. 17), "Soñaba" [I Used to Dream] (no. 20), "El Angelus" (no. 21), "¿Por qué despertarla?" [Why Wake Her?] (no. 22), and "1916" and "1917" (in this book "Año Viejo" [Old Year] and "Año Nuevo" [New Year]) (no 24). See notes at each corresponding poem for more detail.

The poems that appear in this first volume of *Bohemia* that are not in *Lágrimas y flores* are "Cuando yo muera" [When I Die] (no. 8), "Otoñal" [Autumnal] (no. 10), "El beso" [The Kiss] (no. 15), "A Cuba y sus mujeres" [To Cuba and Her Women] (no. 18), "Página Gris" [Gray Page] (while there is a sonnet by this name in this book, it is an entirely different poem; this one is dedicated to Raúl F. Roces, one of the principal writers for *Bohemia*) (no. 19), "Hazme dueño de tu amor" [Make Me Lord of Your Love] (no. 23), and "Memorias de un huérfano" [Memories of an Orphan] (no. 24). Two prose pieces also appear: his first publication in the magazine, an essay lauding women for their domestic roles as mothers and wives and critiquing feminism, suffrage movements, and the then-controversial Puerto Rican feminist lectora Luisa Capetillo's use of male clothing, "El feminismo verdadero" [True Feminism] (no. 6); and a prose poem "¡Tan solo una alborada!" [Only One Dawn!] (no. 11).

9 Kanellos and Martell's comprehensive history of Hispanic periodicals stipulates that no extant copies of *Florida* are known (285), and the best efforts of the editors of the current collection could not locate any copies that had been recovered since the publication of their book in 2000. However, as this volume went to press, a cache of issues of the newspaper *Florida* was recovered by one of Castro's descendants and shared with the editors. A chronologically incomplete run spanning the period from January 1918 through February 1925, the issues are fragile and need to be examined, catalogued, digitized, and placed in an appropriate archive. A preliminary inspection, however, indicates that Castro published both poetry and political essays within the pages of the periodical, including such poems as "A Tampa" [To Tampa] and "La Cruz Roja" [The Red Cross] (accompanied by the image of a nurse) and such essays as "Palpitaciones: Los Obreros que Empiezan" [Palpitations: The Workers Who Begin] and "Palpitaciones: San Carlos" [Palpitations: San Carlos](all 1918).

10 If you're counting, note the synalephas between *princesa* and *está*, and *se* and *escapa*.

11 For example, see Lisa Reid Ricker's "(De)Constructing the Praxis of Memory-Keeping: Late Nineteenth-Century Autograph Albums as Sites of Rhetorical Invention" in *Rhetoric Review*.

12 The original word *patria* is used throughout this volume because the word means far more than any single translation. It is homeland, and motherland, and fatherland. It also goes beyond the level of a nation, in the way that its cognate *patriotism* does not: people can feel that their patria is their city (either birth or adopted), for example, or their region. Particularly during struggles for independence or in times

of political upheaval, the term *patria* is often used to refer to a nation or a place that is beloved and to which one feels allegiance but that does not yet exist as a geopolitical entity.

13 While it is not an uncommon phrasing, the use of "al partir" here to reference a departure from a beloved land calls up without doubt the sonnet by that title by one of Cuba and Spain's most celebrated authors, Gertrudis Gómez de Avellaneda (1814 in Puerto Príncipe, Cuba–1873 in Madrid, Spain). The sonnet, written in 1837 as the author's family relocated to Spain, and when Gómez de Avellaneda was the same age as Castro was when he published this book, details both her love of the island that she calls the "pearl of the sea," and her sorrow at being uprooted.

14 It may seem jarring for a book published within a passionately political Cuban enclave to begin with a poem about the duty and sentiment infusing the author's devotion to the red and gold flag of Spain, but this loyalty forms a counterpoint to Castro's equally fervent extolling of the Cuban flag in the following poem. Loyalties, like identities, can be hybridized, and we see Castro's careful effort to balance these twinned national and cultural allegiances again in the pairing of patriotic poems "Spain" and "Cuba" later in *Lágrimas*.

15 Born in Havana, Domingo Milord was the son of a Cuban cigar manufacturer and the grandson of a Cuban surgeon (both also named Domingo Milord). In 1872, Milord's father, who supported Cuban independence, moved the family to Key West, where Milord attended school at the San Carlos Institute. Later, Milord became a foreman at a cigar factory, held various official positions, and was appointed Cuban Consul of Key West.

16 While odes to flags and other national symbols are an outgrowth of the nineteenth-century cultural urge toward the solidification of national identity in Latin America (on this foundational myth-making in fiction, see Sommers), and can therefore be found throughout the region in the century following the independence wars, the Cuban Bonifacio Byrne's "Mi bandera" (1899), which followed his 1897 book of sonnets, *Efigíes*, lauding a series of heroes from the independence war, is a clear reference point for Castro. Byrne's poem, which was written on his return to Cuba after the war, is an anti-imperialist exploration of the author's conflicting and turbulent emotions on seeing the US flag waving alongside the Cuban one, signaling the formalization of US power on the island after the war. Like Castro, Byrne spent time in Florida (he emigrated to Tampa in 1895); like Castro, Byrne was a tobacco factory lector and contributed to the Cuban émigré press, notably collaborating on José Martí's *Patria*, among other publications.

17 This intertext comes from "A Aguascalientes" [To Aguascalientes], a poem read in the Morelos Theater at the distribution of prizes to the students of the Scientific Institute, February 5, 1905, by Juan de Dios Peza (1852–1910), who was, in his day, the most popular poet in Mexico. This popularity and his title as the "poeta del hogar" [poet of the hearth] were grounded in his connection to the common people, according to Eugenia Revueltas: "si los otros eran admirados por la población letrada, en el caso de Juan de Dios Peza, la influencia de su poesía rompía dcon las barreras del analfabetismo y el poeta era dicho y recitado por el pueblo" (qtd. in Iris 255) [if

the others were admired by the learned, in the case of Juan de Dios Peza, the influence of his poetry broke the barrier of illiteracy and the poet was quoted and recited by the people]. A member of the Mexican Academy of Language, Peza wrote broadly across poetry, drama, essay, and periodical presses, and published on both sides of the Atlantic. He was involved in the highly influential magazine *La Ilustración Española y Americana*, which fomented literary community across the hispanophone world, and he created the first anthology of Mexican verse to be published in Spain (1879). His most famous work is *Cantos del hogar* [Songs of the Hearth] (1890, New York). Peza died in 1910, just before the Mexican Revolution began (Iris 251–53).

"A Aguascalientes" is a slow build of a poem that first lauds the lovely and fertile simplicity of Aguascalientes, then ties it into a national narrative of survival and heroism, and ends in shades of Martí's "Los Pinos Nuevos" ["The New Pines"] speech, handing the future over to the students addressed in the poem. This intertextual stanza comes from the beginning of the poem, and details the enthusiasm that the speaker feels on coming to a region with "una historia que marca en honda huella / Heroísmo, valor, justicia, honores, / ¿Cómo no hablar con entusiasmo en ella?" (324) [a history that marks with a deep track / heroism, valor, justice, honors: / how can one not speak of it with enthusiasm?]. The spoken enthusiasm that follows is what Castro has referenced.

18 While the use of "drool," particularly in the quantities described here, to refer to ill-meant words may seem off-putting, it is an allusion to Clarín's *La Regenta*, the preeminent Spanish realist novel (1884). In it, gossip, and more specifically, the slander of José Zorilla's sentimental poetry, is described in just such a way: "Estos versos que ha querido hacer ridículos y vulgares, manchándolos con su baba, la necedad prosaica, pasándolos mil y mil veces por sus labios viscosos como vientre de sapo, sonaron en los oídos de Ana aquella noche como frase sublime de un amor inocente y puro que se entrega con la fe en el objeto amado" [These verses that prosaic foolishness has wanted to make ridiculous and vulgar, staining them with their drool, passing them a thousand times across their lips, viscous like the belly of a frog, resonated in (the protagonist's) ears that night like the sublime phrases of an innocent and pure love that entrusts itself to its beloved].

19 *Iris*, which we may think of primarily as a flower (as indeed, many of Castro's original readers may have) also means in English, in addition to the anatomical structure in the eye, "a rainbow-like or iridescent appearance; a circle or halo of prismatic colours; a combination or alternation of brilliant colours" ("Iris"). When it appears in the text, it encompasses these layers of meaning: the rainbow, the polarization of light, the iris of the eye, and the bloom.

20 F. Domínguez Pérez published a book of poems, *Cantos de vida* [Songs of Life], in Cuba in 1913 that includes the verse "La voz del poeta" [The Voice of the Poet] (7–8), to which Castro's poem may be responding. He was also the director of the biweekly Cuban periodical *Alpha*, printed in Mayarí beginning in 1915 (Ford 194).

21 The specific type of candelabra referenced here sounds, in English, rather ominous: the Tenebrae Hearse, a triangular candle rack used during the Tenebrae. The Tenebrae are the solemn services held in the second half of Holy Week; the literal mean-

ing of the word, the Latin for darkness, is symbolic of the spiritual darkness of the days before the Resurrection (Broderick 162).

22 Literally, a crucifixion scene or *vía crucis* (Stations of the Cross} set up in a church; figuratively, any great ordeal or suffering.

23 Castro has a tendency, as here, and in "Yo tengo aquí en mi cuarto," "Mi ofrenda," and several poems in the "Flores" section, to use the form 'dúlcido/a' instead of the standard 'dulce,' presumably for maintenance of meter, though it is worth noting that this form is quite common in the work of Castro's nineteenth-century Cuban (and broader Latin American) literary interlocutors, including in the work of Juan Cristóbal Nápoles Fajardo, Federico Rodríguez, and Andrés Cassard.

24 Rogelio Miqueli served as a secretary for the Cigar Makers' International Union throughout 1912 and up to May of 1913 (Perkins vols. 36–38), and was involved with the theater group of the "Cuba" Social Club in Key West with several other figures who appear in these pages (Corresponsal, "La Sociedad" 9). The headnote and endnote of Castro's poem "Cubans, Carry On!" suggest that Miqueli was also associated with the weekly periodical *Florida* in Key West. He would go on to edit the anarchist newspaper *Nueva Vida* in the 1920s (for which his sister Violeta wrote), and to produce antifascist theater with the Sociedades Hispanas Confederadas at the time of the Spanish Civil War and during Franco's dictatorship (Feu 36, 38).

25 Barcarolles are folk songs sung by Venetian gondoliers.

26 While the comparison of love to a prison may be a literary commonplace in the time of Castro's writing, and one derived from the long Petrarchan tradition, given the breadth and depth of Castro's literary erudition and the construction of mother-child relationships in this book, this merits a reference for the unfamiliar to Castilian author Diego de San Pedro's 1492 *Cárcel de amor* [*Prison of Love*]. This sentimental novel offers an example of courtly love that, never attained, creates strong connections between the maternal and the romantic, as Castro develops as well.

27 A much different version of this poem appears in the Tampa magazine *Bohemia* (1916) (see Soto no. 13), illustrated with a line drawing of a palm tree. There, it has no dedication. While some elements are retained—such as the opening line referring to an atom, and the question to the philosopher—very few individual verses remain the same. However, the meaning and the theme are very similar; it is an interesting instance of two radically divergent iterations of the same poem.

28 Salvador R. Turcios (1880–1973) was a Honduran journalist, poet, and historian. He spent fifteen years in El Salvador as a journalist, during which time he published a series of anti-imperialist essays that were later compiled in the volume *Al margen del imperialismo yanqui* [At the Margin of Yankee Imperialism] (Arrellano 275). Among his other publications was a book of sonnets (1914), the act of publishing which in Central America at this time Turcios calls "no solo un heroísmo transcendental, sino una audacia inaudita" (original emphasis, scan 21) [not only a transcendental heroism but also an unheard-of audacity]. This collection of one hundred poems explores Turcios's indigeneity, his identity as a poet and relationships to death, life, and the natural world. It includes a number of pieces dedicated to literary and historical entities, both European, like Cervantes, and of the Americas, like Bolívar

and the Popol Vuh (the sacred text of the Maya K'iche', preserved orally until its transcription in 1550). Like Castro's, Turcios's volume includes multiple articulations of the poet's relationship to his country's flag and to the nature of citizenship. The volume is available via Hathi Trust.

29 Because of the devotion to music that infuses Castro's volume, his dedicatee here is very likely Jan Kubelik (1880–1940), the Czech violinist and composer who toured internationally—he played dozens of times in Rome; Castro may have seen him live—and recorded early gramophone albums, including a 1904 rendition of *Ave Maria*, a prayer that appears in Castro's poem "The Angelus."

30 A brash and daring writer, Octavio J. Monteresy was one of the most outspoken voices for Key West in the Cuban press in the decade surrounding the publication of *Lágrimas y flores*—of which, as it happens, he wrote a glowing review for the Havana newspaper *El Mundo* in June of 1918. Monteresy was more interested in giving his stories punch than necessarily finishing his sentences, a style that must have been popular, because from 1911 to 1921, he served as a regional correspondent and, in particular, the Key West correspondent variously for *El Mundo, La Lucha,* and *El Diario de la Marina*; as more of the journalistic output of this era finds its way into digital archives, his will be a name to watch. Monteresy was also the author of at least one play, *Dolora, drama social* [Dolora: A Social Drama], on which he worked with several others who appear in this book and which was staged at the "Cuba" Society in Key West (Primelles 211), an institution mentioned in conjunction with Castro's poem "Cubans, Carry On!"

31 Santiago García formed part of the theater group of the "Cuba" Society in Key West in 1916, along with several other figures who appear in this volume (El corresponsal 9).

32 This poem appears in the Tampa magazine *Bohemia* (1916). There, it has a dedication: "Para 'Acacia', contestando a su pregunta: '¿De qué haces tus versos y canciones?'" [For "Acacia," answering her question: "What do you use to make your verses and songs?"] There are only two words changed in the body of the text between the two versions: in line 12, "vívido" [bright] was previously "férvido" [fervent]; in line 29, "Pedazos" [Pieces] was previously "Gemidos" [Wails]. See Soto, no. 12.

33 While Castro has dated this poem 1917, he did publish it in the fall of 1916 in the magazine *Bohemia* in Tampa. This version of the poem is very similar to that earlier version, with a few notable changes. In the sixth stanza, where it reads "esa patria" [that patria], it previously had "ese suelo" [that soil], a shift that signals a growing allegiance to Cuba as an adopted patria. The other point of change is the final stanza, which has several shifts in word choice. For example, the former version had "en ese adorado suelo" [on that adored soil] and "En ese edén de consuelo, / de amores dulce morada" [In that Eden of comfort, / the home of sweet loves] where this version has "sobre su virgen suelo" [over her virgin soil] and "en la embriaguez de mi anhelo / por la caricia soñada" [in the euphoric intoxication of my yearning / for the long-dreamt-of caress], where we can see the replacement of one element of innocence (virginity from Eden), and one element of sensual pleasure (intoxicated caresses from the home of loves), increasing the intensity of the affection displayed.

These shifts also seem to move the poem's rendering of love, yearning, and affection from the domestic register more decidedly into the realm of the erotic. See Soto no. 9.

34 This intertext comes from the poem "A Méjico. En las últimas desgracias de España" by Juan de Dios Peza, 1885. (For author, see note on "Soñaba" [I Used to Dream]). The poem is a narration of the end of the Spanish Reconquest with the taking of Granada by Spanish forces. Rather than trumpeting Spain's glory, however, the poem highlights the suffering and bloodshed of the battle on both sides as "Cada fosa sepulcral / Abrese ante fuerza extraña, / Y parece que en España / Comienza el juicio final" (249) [Every sepulchral grave / opens before a strange force / and it seems that in Spain / Judgement Day begins]. It ends with an invocation of the importance of humanity, and the dignity of all, with a reference to Fray Bartolomé de las Casas. The lines from the poem that Castro has referenced are part of a description of Andalucía as it was before this bloodshed: "esa region que encierra / tantos recuerdos de gloria" (247) [that region that encloses / so many memories of glory]. It is, however, a very sad and bloody poem to connect to this one. Tellingly, in terms of the accusations of theft that Castro responds to in the prologue, the quotation marks around this intertext do not appear in the original publication of this poem, in *Bohemia* (Soto no. 9); while it is not always standard to put intertexts in quotation marks, he clearly wanted to delineate his borrowings sharply.

35 The fact that Paco is a common nickname for Francisco suggests that this poem's dedicatee is very likely Francisco Pineda, the director of the theater group of the "Cuba" Society in 1916, of which many figures mentioned in these pages were members (El corresponsal 9); the numbered five-act structure of Castro's poem resonates with Pineda's theatrical pursuits. Thematically germane to the poem, moreover, is the *Miami Herald*'s report that Francisco Pineda was one of three young men "rescued from a horrible death of thirst and starvation" after their small fishing boat capsized and went missing off the Key West coast in 1912; a fourth man died ("State News" 7). This event is not unique, and there was good reason to for the community to assume that a fishing boat that did not make it home was a sign of tragedy and death. This is also a common theme in Galician literature.

36 Antonia Pérez Rolo was the wife of Castro's business partner Juan Pérez Rolo, the co-owner of Taller Tipográfico. Soon to become Castro's mother-in-law, she is remembered by the family as having written for the weekly periodical *Florida,* for which she is named as the editor of the recurring section "Pagina de hogar" [page of the home].

37 This poem appears in the Tampa magazine *Bohemia* (1916), framed by the illustration of a lyre, and accompanied by the sketch of a naked male child. There, it is dedicated to José Santaella, who wrote the theater reviews for *Bohemia*. The dedication is the only change. See Soto no. 22.

38 In the decade surrounding the publication of *Lágrimas y flores*, J.M. Subirats moved in the swirl of Cuba's intellectual high society, publishing his poem "Elegía" [Elegy] in the magazine *Arte* [Art] in 1917 (Ruiz 9) and hosting banquets for the literati. One such banquet honored the young writer and lawyer Manuel Antonio Varona, a fu-

ture prime minister of Cuba, and the menu and guest list for the occasion appeared in the newspaper (Quesada 8). Subirats was likely already a Mason, like Castro, when Castro dedicated this poem to him, because by 1952, Subirats was the Master of the Ancient Mystical Order Rosae Crucis (Rosicrucian) lodge in Santiago de Cuba ("Directory" 45), and this mystical order is composed solely of Master-level Masons.

39 Unlike the other instances in this volume where Castro uses quotation marks to denote an intertext—an assiduousness perhaps linked to the accusations of plagiarism that prompted the publication of this book—the original source of this quotation remains to be discovered. These quotation marks were present in the version of this poem published in *Bohemia* in 1916 (Soto no. 20).

40 The Angelus is a set of prayers honoring Mary and her conception. Performed at 6:00 a.m., noon, and 6:00 p.m., it includes three Hail Marys (in Spanish, the Ave María) and the words that Mary spoke when she was visited by the angel Gabriel. Moreover, the term *angelus* also refers to the bell that is rung at these times of day (Broderick 8–9).

This poem appears in the Tampa magazine *Bohemia* (1916). Unlike the majority of those poems that are compiled from that magazine, the text of "El Angelus" is not changed at all. See Soto vol. 21.

41 This poem appears in the Tampa magazine *Bohemia* (1916). There, it is framed by black line work and art nouveau lilies. It does not include the dedication that it has here, but is otherwise the same. See Soto no. 20.

42 Arturo Doreste (1895–1983) was a Cuban poet of Canary Islands descent. In 1916, at only 21 years of age, he won the Floral Games of Santiago de Cuba along with Miguel A. Macau (Pimelles 209). The Floral Games are a tradition of poetry competitions that arose in the Middle Ages in Barcelona and other cities; revived in the nineteenth century as part of the Catalán Renaixença and the century's general interest in the past, the tradition spread across the major cities of Spain and Latin America.

In 1917, Doreste—already a contributor to multiple newspapers both in Cuba and abroad—published his first book of poems, *Mis sueños y mis rosas* [My Dreams and My Roses]. Appearing shortly after the death of his mother and heavily influenced by her loss, this book is, like *Lágrimas y flores*, divided into two distinct parts, and, like *Lágrimas y flores*, it begins with a sonnet to the poet's mother. In this poem, in response to her death, the speaker turns to poetry for solace: "Como perdí mi madre idolatrada / . . . / Hacia ti, Poesía inmaculada, / me dirijo, cual triste peregrino" (21) [Given that I lost my idolized mother / . . . / Toward you, immaculate Poetry, / I turn, as a sad pilgrim]. The first half of the volume ranges from the philosophical and sentimental to explorations of nation and identity. The second part, consisting of only eight poems and dedicated to the poet's father, is a beautiful mourning sequence for Doreste's mother.

Just as Castro dedicated this poem to Doreste, he in turn dedicated the poem "La voz piadosa" [The Pious Voice] to Feliciano Castro. In Doreste's poem, the memory of friendship and of this pious voice is a consolation, and helps the poetic voice to carry on through the turmoil and suffering of loss: "Igual que un astro hermoso que

Endnotes to Page 115 · 323

se esfuma / trás el luctuoso velo de la bruma, / se oculta mi soñar y mi alegría . . . / Pero una voz piadosa de consuelo, / brota de lo profundo de mi anhelo / diciéndome que aguarde todavía . . . !" (119–120) [Just like a lovely star that vanishes / behind the tragic veil of the sea mist /so hide my dreams and my joy . . . / but a pious voice of consolation, / bursts forth from the depths of my yearning / telling me to keep holding on].

43 Castro uses the idea of whiteness to refer to purity several times: here, in the poem "Cuba," and in the sonnet "To Elisa Salgado." This use of whiteness as a stand-in for purity, in addition to permeating post-Victorian Western consciousness, is likely an allusion to the poem "Tú me quieres blanca" [You Want Me White] (1911) by the Argentine modernist Alfonsina Storni. In this poem, Storni articulates societal expectations around female chastity through a series of white images: a beam of moonlight, seafoam, the nacre inside a shell, and a flower's bud furled too tightly to allow any light to pass through it.

Here, *pure* is used because the phrase "a white, very white thought" has different connotations for readers today than it would have had for Castro and his audience—though it was still infused then, of course, with centuries of white-supremacist ideology.

44 The intertext is from "Oda (Leída en la session que el Liceo Hidalgo celebró en honor de doña Gertrudis Gómez de Avellaneda)" [Ode (read at the session that the Hidalgo Lyceum held in celebration of Doña Gertrudis Gómez de Avellaneda)] by Manuel Acuña, June 20, 1873. Acuña (1849–1873) was one of the greats of Mexican Romanticism, though he only saw one book of his poetry published. Other collections were published posthumously. He was also a playwright and cofounded the Literary Society Nezahualcóyotl, a tertulia of which Juan de Dios Peza was a member. Acuña's status as a legend is inextricably tied to his death. He died by ingesting cyanide six months after reading this poem—a fate caused in part, perhaps, by his unrequited love for a woman, and deriving also from his long-held interest in the esoteric and the morbid. His best-known poems are "Nocturne" and "Ante un cadáver" [Before a Cadaver]; the first that he published was to the death of a friend (Ortega 234–240).

The poem referenced here is also in part an ode to death: that of its interlocutor, Gertrudis Gómez de Avellaneda (1814–1871), one of the best and best-known Romantics. Claimed by both Cuba—Camaguey was her beloved birthplace—and Spain, where she spent most of her life and died, she was one of the first two women to publish a volume of poetry in Spain, an act that precipitated a wave of female writers entering the public sphere. Her most famous work is the anti-slavery novel *Sab*, published in 1841, but she wrote extensively in drama, prose, and poetry. Avellaneda was bold, decisive, loud, and open about her romantic entanglements. Her societal privilege almost allowed her to live the life of academic leisure but for the limits placed on her by her gender, perhaps most notably her rejection by the Royal Academy of the Spanish Language, which never admitted a woman during her lifetime. In praise of Avellaneda, and in the light of a literary tradition that saw female authorship as inferior and frivolous, José Martí wrote, "No hay mujer en Gertrudis

Gómez de Avellaneda; todo anunciaba en ella un ánimo potente y varonil; era su cuerpo alto y robusto como su poesía ruda y enérgica" (97) [There is nothing of woman in Gertrudis Gómez de Avellaneda; everything about her announced a potent and virile spirit; her body was tall and robust like her poetry, sharp and energetic].

Acuña's poem is about youth, how la Avellaneda's poetry opened his eyes to beauty and wonder beyond a mother's kiss, the world of poetry, and his experience of her death from afar. He thanks her for making him a poet and offers his work as a tribute to her. The stanza from which Castro's quotation is drawn reads, "Tu voz fue la primera / que me habló en la dulzura de ese idioma / que canta como canta la paloma / y gime como gime la palmera" [Your voice was the first / that spoke to me in the sweetness of that language / that sings like the dove sings / and moans like the palm moans] (201). The whole volume is available on Hathi Trust.

45 Further information on the identity of Leandro de Torres remains to be discovered.
46 See note on "Es un iris tu voz" [Your Voice Is an Iris].
47 November second is the Commemoration of All the Faithful Departed (Día de los fieles difuntos), also known in English as All Souls' Day, which follows after and continues the focus on remembrance of All Saints' Day (Día de todos los santos) on the first of the month. Within the Catholic tradition, All Souls' Day particularly commemorates those who are trapped in purgatory.

This poem appeared in the magazine *Bohemia* in November of 1916, illustrated with a line of dark trees that also appeared on the cover of the magazine's fifth issue, earlier that fall. The two versions are the same but for two things. First, the version in *Bohemia* includes a full stanza in quotation marks—likely an intertext—that was cut for this version. Second, this version changes half of one verse, from "do no brota ni una flor" [where grows/springs forth not even one flower] to "que no tiene ni una flor" [that has not even one flower]. See Soto no. 16.

48 The Parcae (plural) are the Fates of ancient Roman lore. This is the singular form: only one of the three is traitorous, impious, and terrifying here.
49 This poem and its companion piece, dedicated to Cuba, appear on facing pages of the magazine *Bohemia*, framed in red linework (the only color in the magazine apart from similar decorations on the cover surrounding a photograph of a woman). The text of that version is radically different from what appears here. While many of the references are retained, the language has been heavily rewritten. In contrast, the poem to Cuba remains almost entirely intact. See Soto no. 14.
50 The myth of Pelayo at Covadonga is the story of the beginning of the Reconquest, the period between the Umayyad conquest of Hispania (what would later be Spain) in 722 C.E. and the fall of the final Iberian Muslim Kingdom, the Nasrid Kingdom of Granada, in 1492. That year, of course, also saw Columbus's famous voyage. The myth of Covadonga relates that a Muslim force confronted a small Christian force led by the local leader Pelayo in 718 or 722 in a place called Cova Dominica (Covadonga) and that Pelayo's Asturian forces received help from the Virgin Mary to defeat the Muslims. In the 900s, when the kings of Asturias had extended their territory in the face of the Andalusian Emirates to the point of relative safety, they located their legitimacy and their origin in Pelayo's triumph; the story attained cul-

tural cachet during the reign of Alfonso III (ruler of León, Galicia, and Asturias, and the first to be called "Emperor of Spain") via his *Chronica Adefonsi tertii regis* [*Chronicle of Alfonso III*], which the king composed with the goal of demonstrating a continuity between Visigothic Spain and the later Christian medieval Spain, so as to justify the ongoing Reconquest. Under the auspices of this text, the story of Pelayo at Covadonga becomes one of the cornerstones of Spanish history (Fontana and Villares, 2: 65, 109–110).

51 Another foundational myth, the story of the siege at Numancia is, ironically, a story of decided defeat. The Roman general Scipio Africanus took control of Numancia after a siege in 130 C.E. Because it coincided with the fall of Carthage and the control of the Hellenic peninsula, the taking of Numancia constituted an important milestone in the consolidation of the Roman Empire. The stories we have of the Numantine War come from authors who knew of it firsthand, and their writing elegizes the resistance of the population with a general tone of imperialist satisfaction and a hagiographic admiration for Scipio (Fontana and Villares, 1: 1280). Different narratives of the siege supply very different outcomes: either Scipio easily enslaved enough of his enemies to warrant a triumph on his return to Rome, or the Numantines quickly gave way to the invaders, or most of them killed themselves to avoid capture, or not a soul remained alive in the city at the end of the battle; the *Primera crónica general* [*First General Chronicle*], composed at the behest of Alfonso el Sabio [the wise] in the thirteenth century, affirms that not one soul escaped.

In 1585, Cervantes wrote a play about this fabled city, largely based on the *Primera crónica* and potentially also upon later sources that were even more dramatic. In Cervantes's play, the Roman general is unable to enjoy his victory, a clear signal that by the sixteenth century, historical accuracy about this event was far less important than its use in the construction of the ingrainedness of Spanish bravery in the face of certain death (Marrast 24–25). With the Napoleonic invasion of Spain in 1808 came a huge resurgence in the popularity of the Cervantine play; a possibly apocryphal account claims that it was staged in Zaragoza at the height of the suffering of that city under the French invasion as a means of inciting resistance among the population. The play enjoyed continued popularity through the next decades because the tragic end of the fabled city resonated with the suffering of the Second of May and the bloody episodes of the Spanish War of Independence that allowed Spaniards to identify with the brave but doomed Numantines in their moment of need (27).

52 The "Despot of the Seine" is a reference to José Bonaparte, the brother of Napoleon Bonaparte, who was installed by Napoleon as King of Spain following their invasion of the peninsula in 1807. The second of May of 1808 saw a huge uprising in Madrid against the French interlopers, and the backlash against this civilian uprising (depicted in Goya's famous painting *El dos de mayo*, 1814) was the fuse that set off the War of Independence. While the "Despota del Sena" is not a particularly common nickname for Bonaparte, it appears in several places, including the 1878 poem "A S.M. el Rey Católico D. Alfonso XII, en la muerte de su augusta y malograda esposa" [To his Majesty the Catholic King Don Alfonso XII, on the Death of his August and Departed Wife] by Gaspar Bono Serrano. In that poem, as in Castro's, Serrano uses

the Second of May and the Despot of the Seine as markers for Spanish fortitude: "Contemplad ese pueblo madrileño, / El pueblo, joven Rey, del Dos de Mayo, / Que obligó a Europa a despertar del sueño, / Y de luengo y letárgico desmayo, / Cuando amagaba el déspota del Sena / A un hemisferio con servil cadena" (2) [Contemplate that populace of Madrid, / the people, young King, of the Second of May, / who obliged Europe to awaken from its sleep, / and from a lengthy and lethargic faint, / when the Despot of the Seine threatened / a hemisphere with a servile chain].

53 Earlier versions of these two poems appear in the Tampa magazine *Bohemia* (1916), under the titles "1916" and "1917." The structure and tone of these poems remains the same, but Castro did substantial rewriting, including the references to atoms (which also appear in "¡El tiempo!" [Time!]). See Soto no. 24.

54 This poem appears with its companion piece, dedicated to Spain, in the magazine *Bohemia* (1916), on highly decorated facing pages. While the text of the poem to Spain is radically different here, the text of this poem is very close to identical. The few changes that Castro made here lead to a poem that is now more apostrophic (changing "que" [that] to "tú" [you]), more impassioned ("cariñoso" [caring] to "fervoroso" [fervent]), and shifts the last line from something that the poetic voice gives to Cuba "fui depositar" [I went to deposit], to something that Cuba, as a new mother or patria, offers him: "fui a encontrar" [I came to find]. See Soto no. 14.

55 For Agramonte, see note on "El Grito de Yara" [The Cry of Yara].

56 With his Cry of Yara—which alludes to indigenous Taíno chief Hatuey, who rebelled against the Spaniards in Cuba in the 1500s and was burned at the stake in Yara—Cuban plantation owner Carlos Manuel de Céspedes freed his slaves and proclaimed rebellion against Spain on October 10, 1868, igniting the Ten Years' War. By 1870, the twinned goals of this rebellion became clear: full emancipation of all Cubans from enslavement, and anticolonial Cuban independence from Spain. Cubans in eastern Cuba supported the effort, which did not spread to the richer, whiter, western Cubans who still held allegiance to Spain, which protected their ability to use slave labor on sugar plantations. The Ten Years' War ended in a stalemate with a peace treaty in which Spain promised some autonomy to Cubans. Emancipation would not occur until 1886, and Cuba's independence from Spain was not achieved until 1898. October 10, which heralded both visions of freedom, remains a national holiday in Cuba, holding a significance comparable to that of the July 4 holiday in the United States—with the difference, of course, that the U.S. revolution included no provision for emancipation.

The San Carlos Institute, founded in 1871 by Cuban exiles in Key West, was a mutual aid society and social club that included a bilingual, racially integrated school, a theater, and a ballroom. It functioned as the center of émigré social life and political organizing for Cuban independence; José Martí spoke there in 1892.

57 Ignacio Agramonte was a leader of the Ten Years' War. Once Céspedes had begun the war with the Cry of Yara in October 1868, Agramonte led the revolutionary uprising from within the city of Camagüey in November; he was also, like Castro, a Mason. Francisco Vicente Aguilera y Tamayo collaborated with Céspedes, despite

hailing from one of the wealthiest families in Cuba, and served as the vice president of the democratic government established during the Ten Years' War. He left Cuba during the war on a doomed mission to seek international aid and died in exile.

58 The brigadier Julio Sanguily was wounded and captured by Spanish forces in 1871. His successful rescue, enacted by Agramonte, spread both of their names far and wide.

59 This reference to glory, along with the one in the following stanza, is "palma" in Spanish, the same word as the palm trees that sing the song of the victory. Castro is playing with the double meaning here, as well as continuing the correlation between palm trees and positive attributes—in people and actions—that is visible throughout the volume.

60 The taking of Las Tunas in 1897 was a potentially definitive victory for Cuba's Liberation Army. While the battle had several heroes—including José Martí's son, the general Calixto García, and the spy María Machado ("La toma")—it can be assumed that Castro is speaking here about Mario García Menocal, who was present at the battle and was, at the writing of *Lágrimas y flores*, the president of Cuba; Menocal had just aligned with the Allies, and declared war on Germany a day after the United States joined World War I. The comparison to Martí is generously aspirational in this case, as Menocal was heavily invested—for the sake of his own financial gain—in the promotion of U.S. economic interests on the island (Ferrer 188–92).

61 Carlos Manuel de Céspedes was killed by Spanish troops in San Lorenzo in 1874.

62 Several of Castro's friends in Key West were involved in this club, including Octavio J. Monteresy, Santiago García, Rogelio Miqueli, "Consuelito" Rivero, and Mariana Salgado (El corresponsal 9). It holds the resonance, if not the actual political activity, of the revolutionary clubs of the 1890s.

63 Founded in 1891, the Spanish Center in Tampa was the city's first mutual aid society. It was both a social club and a provider of economic security. Members paid twenty-five cents a week for social privileges and death and injury benefits. The Center provided a social outlet, held dances, offered a library and classes in Spanish and English, and hosted theater and other community events. (Mormino and Pozzetta, *The Immigrant* 178). The anniversary celebration for which this poem was written preceded Castro's first poem publication in *Bohemia* by one week. He would go on to publish verses in every issue (save one) of the magazine's first volume (the only volume currently recovered). While causality is impossible to determine definitively, this poem may have opened that opportunity for him.

64 Further information on the identity of R.M. Alzay remains to be discovered.

65 A *cantiga* is a type of lyric particular to Galician Portuguese, the medieval Romance language of the northwestern part of the Iberian peninsula. This distinctive style of music was used in Marian miracles, as well as in secular *cantigas de amor* [cantigas of love] and cantigas de amigo [cantigas of friends (written from the female perspective)]. The form was also used in the Renaissance ("Cantiga").

66 The diminutive "Conchita" derives from "Concepción" (Conception), though *conchita* has several regional colloquial uses as well.

67 *Polianthes tuberosa* is a perennial with elongated spikes of white, waxy flowers. Said to be the most fragrant plant in the world, it is commonly used in perfume, where its rich, creamy scent is in a family with other high-powered white flowers of the world of perfumery, like orange blossoms and ylang ylang. Polianthes are no longer found in the wild, though they were native to Mexico. *Polianthes* is used here instead of the common name *tuberose* for aesthetic reasons—perhaps the same reasons that led to the plant's alternate common name, the Polyanthus lily. According to Florencio Jazmín's 1878 *Lenguaje de las flores* [Language of Flowers], polianthes signify a date (a romantic meeting, not a calendar entry) and voluptuousness (156, 159).

68 Sofía Pérez Rolo and Castro married in 1920.

69 "Consuelito" Rivero formed part of the theater group of the "Cuba" Society in 1916, along with Mariana Salgado, Librada Vargas, Santiago García, Manuel Ochoa, Rogelio Miqueli, Pedro Acevedo, Mateo Salgado, Aníbal Castellanos, Armando Salazar, master of music Luis Salazar, director Francisco Pineda, scenographer José Ortíz, and playwright Octavio J. Monteresy (El corresponsal 9).

70 This intertext comes from Don Ramón de Campoamor's *El drama universal* (1869), an extensive poem in eight acts with around six scenes each. It is in part a tragic story of courtly love and in part a religious allegory in the long shadow of Calderón de la Barca's 1717 *Autos Sacramentales*: highly symbolic theatrical productions in verse in which figures like Jesus and Mary join the Sun, the Moon, Time, and other archetypes to assist in the creation of a moral story. The auto sacramental is a specifically Spanish tradition, though it has some similarities to medieval English morality plays.

This quotation appears in the second scene of the first act of Campoamor's poem, in which, near the death of the two male rivals in a love triangle, a figure called Jesus mago (Jesus the Wise Man), who was a witness to the death of Jesus Christ, comes down from heaven to talk to them about penitence (Campoamor 536). This excerpted stanza follows a description of two columns of angels forming a bridge of light across the sky, which allows Mary to appear (537).

71 This is a potential reference to Carolina Coronado's (1820–1911) poem "A una gota de rocío" [To a Drop of Dew], which similarly constructs female sexual desire through the visual and tactile description of water on petals.

72 Julieta Raga lived in Tampa and seems to not only have been a very popular local musician but also to have supported herself as a singer (she was a comic soprano, "tiple cómica"), thus the "artista encantadora" [enchanting artist] with which Castro begins this sonnet. There are records of multiple performances (exhibitions or revues, zaruelas and operettas) that she gave around Tampa, Ybor City, and West Tampa in the fall of 1916 in the extant volume of *Bohemia* (see Soto nos. 6-22). José Santaella describes one such performance so: "El público acogió con frenéticos aplausos a los rasgueos de guitarra del señor Llorente, que acompañaba a Julieta Raga en unos cantos andaluces que llegaron hasta donde deben de llegar: el alma. Este número fue muy aplaudido" (Soto no. 22) [With thunderous applause, the audience embraces the guitar strumming of Sr. Llorente, who accompanied Julieta

Raga in some Andalusian songs that touched what they should touch: the soul. This number was very much applauded]. Raga also came in second to Zenaida Barcia in *Bohemia*'s Queen of Charm competition (see "Homenage" [Homage], the poem dedicated to Barcia), with 8,954 votes. Because of this, her photograph appears in the Dec. 9 issue of *Bohemia*, alongside Barcia's (no. 21). In her photograph, she is looking down at a small bouquet of flowers, and smiling, in a gentle, almost laughing way.

73 Eponine Pérez Rolo was the younger sister of Sofia Pérez Rolo and the daughter of Castro's business partner Juan Pérez Rolo and his wife Antonio Pérez Rolo.

74 A very different version of this poem appears in the Tampa magazine *Bohemia* (1916). There, it is not dedicated to "Consuelito" Rivero. Furthermore, while the theme and structure are the same, the two versions have few concrete commonalities, with whole lines and stanzas changed. It is, additionally, framed in terms of memory "recuerdos" rather than Castro's usual oneiric second world "daydreams" in the first verse. See Soto no. 17.

75 Mariana Salgado formed part of the theater group of the "Cuba" Society in 1916, along with "Consuelito" Rivero, Librada Vargas, Santiago García, Manuel Ochoa, Rogelio Miqueli, Pedro Acevedo, Mateo Salgado, Aníbal Castellanos, Armando Salazar, master of music Luis Salazar, director Francisco Pineda, scenographer José Ortíz, and playwright Octavio J. Monteresy (El corresponsal 9). Thence, clearly, his reference to her artistic ability, and perhaps the position of this poem in the collection, right after one of the poems dedicated to "Consuelito."

76 The tradition of holding competitions for local Queens of Charm (also translated as *likeability, niceness,* or *popularity*) dates back to the earliest days of the Cuban communities in Tampa and Key West, where it formed part of the diverse and constant efforts to fundraise for the cause of Cuba Libre. A number of Tampa newspapers held such competitions, including *Nueva República* in 1897, *La Revista* in 1904, and *Bohemia*, the illustrated weekly directed by Manuel Soto and José de la Grana for which Castro wrote. Throughout its first volume, this paper ran a "Queen of Charm" competition that garnered tens of thousands of cast votes (in part, probably, because Soto offered ten votes in exchange for each person a young woman could convince to sign up for a six-month subscription). This magazine is heavily illustrated, both with drawings and photographs, and the photographs of several competitors for "Queens of Charm" appear in issues that precede the final tabulation of votes by a local notary. Barcia, of course, was crowned queen, with 21,401 votes, and her picture appears in the December 9 issue (no. 21). Her photograph makes her seem forthright, straightforward, and through the simplicity of her hair, dress, and jewelry, not particularly engaged with the performative elements of the sartorial expectations placed on women. While the accompanying article says very little about Barcia herself, she does appear in society pages throughout the paper's run. These mentions suggest that she was a major player in the organization of social events, that she was very generous with her time (several times, there are published notes submitted to and published in the magazine thanking her for helping people with

event planning), and that she was kind (see Soto 6-22). The known issues of *Bohemia*, this first run from the fall of 1916, are available in the University of South Florida's Digital Commons. The institution of the Queen of Charm extended across Latin America and Spanish-speaking communities in the United States, particularly in the first half of the twentieth century and generally tied to patriotic festivals.

77 As "preseas," these jewels can also be medals or other accolades that come with accomplishment.

WORKS CONSULTED

Acuña, Manuel, and José Farias Galindo. *Manuel Acuña: Biografía, obras completas, epistolario y juicios.* Grupo Editorial "Mexico," 1971.
Alvarez Borland, Isabel. *Cuban-American Literature of Exile: From Person to Persona.* UP of Virginia, 1998.
Arrellano, Jorge Eduardo. *Literatura Centroamericana. Diccionario de autores centroamericanos.* Colección Cultural de Centro América, 2003.
Bécquer, Gustavo Adolfo. "Rima XXI." *Biblioteca Digital Ciudad Seva,* ciudadseva.com/texto/rima-21/. Accessed 1 Aug. 2022.
"Bird's Eye View of Key West, Fla., Key West Island, C.S. Monroe Co., 1884." Library of Congress, www.loc.gov/resource/g3934k.pm001142/?r=-0.177,0.015,1.369,0.64,0. Accessed 2 Aug. 2022.
Broderick, Robert. *Concise Catholic Dictionary.* The Bruce Publishing Co., 1944.
Campoamor, Don Ramón de. *Obras completas de Don Ramón de Campoamor.* Montaner y Simon, Editores, 1888.
"Cantiga." *Dolmetsch Online,* dolmetsch.com/index.htm. Accessed 1 Aug. 2022.
Charnon-Deutsch, Lou. "The Naturalization of Feminine Nature." *Fictions of the Feminine in the Nineteenth-Century Spanish Press.* Penn State UP, 2000, pp. 13–51.
Clarín [Leopoldo Alas]. *La Regenta. Project Gutenberg*, 12 Dec. 2020, https://www.gutenberg.org/ebooks/17073.
El corresponsal. "La sociedad 'Cuba' y su brillante sección de declamación." *El Mundo* [Havana], 6 Sept. 1916, p. 9. *Readex.*
Darío, Rubén. "Sonatina" (1895). *Poemas del alma,* www.poemas-del-alma.com/sonatina.htm. Accessed 2 Aug. 2022.
"De Colón. Una boda." *Diario de la Marina* [Havana], 12 May 1914, p. 10. *Readex.*
"De Key West." *La Lucha* [Havana], 25 Dec. 1909, p. 2. *Readex.*
"Del Puerto." *El Mundo* [Havana]. 27 Dec. 1921, p. 11. *Readex.*
"Demanda de divorcio." *El Mundo* [Havana], 22 Oct. 1915, p. 5. *Readex.*
"Directory." *The Rosicrucian Digest,* May 1952, pp. 44–45.
Domínguez Caparrós, José. *Diccionario de métrica Española.* Paraninfo, 1895.
Domínguez Pérez, Francisco. *Cantos de vida.* Imprenta de El Liberal, 1913. *Digital Library of the Caribbean.*
Doreste, Arturo. *Mis sueños y mis rosas.* El Camagueyano, 1917. *Hathi Trust.*
Dralyuk, Boris. *My Hollywood and Other Poems.* Paul Dry Books, 2022.
Ferrer, Ada. *Cuba: An American History.* Scribner, 2021.
Feu, Montse. "Violeta Miqueli's Direct Action Against State Violence." *The International Journal of Information, Diversity, & Inclusion,* vol. 6, no. 4, 2022, pp. 32–46.

Fontana, Josep, and Ramón Villares, editors. *Historia de España*. Crítica / Marcial Pons, 2009. 12 vols.
Ford, Jeremiah D.M. *A Bibliography of Cuban Belles-Lettres*. Harvard UP, 1933. Hathi Trust.
Gómez Castellano, Irene. "El discurso líquido en *Don Juan Tenorio*." *Miríada Hispánica*, no. 18, 2021, pp. 61–82.
Gopnik, Adam. "The Rules of Rhyme." *The New Yorker*, 23 May 2022, https://www.newyorker.com/magazine/2022/05/30/the-rules-of-rhyme-daniel-levin-becker-whats-good-notes-on-rap-and-language. Accessed 3 April 2023.
Hooper, Kirsty. *Writing Galicia into the World: New Cartographies, New Poetics*. Liverpool UP, 2011.
"Iris." *OED Online*, Oxford UP, 2022.
Iris, Manuel. "Vindicación de Juan de Dios Peza." *Historia crítica de la poesía Mexicana*, edited by Rogelio Guedea, Fondo de Cultura Económico / Consejo Nacional para la Cultura y las Artes, 2015, vol. 1, pp. 251–263.
Jazmín, Florencio. *El lenguaje de las flores y de las frutas, con algunos emblemas de las piedras y los colores*. M. Saurí, 1878.
Kanellos, Nicolas, and Helvetia Martell. *Hispanic Periodicals in the United States, Origins to 1960: A Brief History and Comprehensive Bibliography*. Arte Publico Press, 2000.
"Key West Real Estate Market Brisk." *The Miami Herald*, 1 Aug. 1944, B1. *Readex*.
Kronik, John W. "Influencias francesas en la génesis del Modernismo: Parnaso y Simbolismo." *Actas del Congreso Internacional sobre el Modernismo Español e Hispanoamericano*, edited by Guillermo Carnero, Córdoba: Diputación Provincial, 1987, pp. 35–51.
Lista, Alberto. *Poesías de don Alberto Lista*. 2nd ed., Imprenta Nacional, 1837. Hathi Trust.
Marrast, Robert. Introduction. *Numancia*, by Miguel de Cervantes Saavedra, 6a ed, Cátedra, 2013, pp. 11–33.
Martí, José. "Boletin." *Crítica y libros*, edited by Gonzalo de Quesada, Imprenta y Papelería de Rambla, Bouza y co., 1914, vol. 13, pp. 95–100.
———. "Our America." *Selected Writings*, edited and translated by Esther Allen, Penguin, 2002, pp. 288–296.
Monteresy, Octavio. "'El Mundo' en la emigración." *El Mundo*, 16 Jun. 1918, p. 15.
Mormino, Gary R., and George E. Pozzetta. *The Immigrant World of Ybor City: Italians and Their Latin Neighbors in Tampa, 1885–1985*. U of Illinois, 1987.
———. "Spanish Anarchism in Tampa, Florida, 1886–1931." *Hidden Out in the Open: Spanish Migration to the United States (1875–1930)*, edited by Phylis Cancilla Martinelli and Ana Varela-Lago, UP of Colorado, 2018, pp. 91–128.
Navarro, Tomás. *Métrica española. Reseña histórica y descriptiva*. Labor, 1983.
Ortega, José. "Manuel Acuña o el otoño anticipado." *Historia crítica de la poesía Mexicana*, edited by Rogelio Guedea, Fondo de Cultura Económico / Consejo Nacional para la Cultura y las Artes, 2015, vol. 1, pp. 234–250.

Pérez Rolo, Juan. "My Memories." Translated by Grey Castro. Typescript.
Perkins, G. W., editor. *Cigar Makers' Official Journal*, vols. 36-38, 1912–1914. *Hathi Trust*.
Peza, Juan de Dios. *Poesías escogidas. Nueva y única edición ilustrada autorizada por el autor y aumentada con varias composiciones inéditas.* Carlos Maucci, 1905. *Internet Archive*.
Poska, Allyson. *Women and Authority in Early Modern Spain: The Peasants of Galicia.* Oxford UP, 2005.
Poyo, Gerald. *Exile and Revolution: José D. Poyo, Key West, and Cuban Independence.* UP of Florida, 2014.
Primelles, León. *Crónica cubana 1915–1918.* Talleres Tipográficos de Editorial Lex, 1955.
Quesada, C. "Camagüeyanas: un homenaje muy merecido." *El Mundo* [Havana], 19 June 1923, p. 8. *Readex*.
Rábade Villar, María do Cebreiro. "*Spleen,* tedio y *ennui*. El valor indiciario de las emociones en la literatura del siglo XIX." *Revista de Literatura,* vol. 74, no. 148, 2012, pp. 473–496.
Ricker, Lisa Reid. "(De)Constructing the Praxis of Memory-Keeping: Late Nineteenth-Century Autograph Albums as Sites of Rhetorical Invention." *Rhetoric Review,* vol. 29, no. 3, 2010, pp. 239–256.
Romero Luque, Manuel. "El soneto modernista: Manuel Machado como paradigma." *Rhythmica. Revista Española de Métrica Comparada,* no. 15, 2017, pp. 113–145.
Ruiz, Alberto. "Mundo habanero." *El Mundo* [Havana], 25 Aug. 1917, p. 9. *Readex*.
Sebold, Russell P. "'Una lágrima pero una sola': Sobre el llanto romántico." *Trayectoria del romanticismo español,* by Sebold, Editorial Crítica, 1983, pp. 185–194.
Serrano, Gaspar Bono. "A S.M. el Rey Católico D. Alfonso XII, en la muerte de su augusta y malograda esposa. Elegía" (1878). *Biblioteca Virtual Miguel de Cervantes,* 2012.
Smith, Anne. "He Read Romance into Tough Life of Cigar Workers." *The Miami Herald,* 3 June 1966, p. B1. *Readex*.
"Sobre divorcio." *El Mundo* [Havana], 17 Sept. 1915, p. 9. *Readex*.
Sommer, Doris. *Foundational Fictions: The National Romances of Latin America.* U of California, 1993.
"State News Notes: Key West Journal." *Miami Herald,* 3 May 1912, p. 7. *America's Historical Newspapers*.
Soto, Manuel, editor. *Bohemia. Revista Semanal Ilustrada.* Vol. 1, nos. 1-24, Tampa, 1916. *Digital Commons @ University of South Florida.* https://digitalcommons.usf.edu/bohemia/
Stebbins, Consuelo E. *City of Intrigue, Nest of Revolution: A Documentary History of Key West in the Nineteenth Century.* UP of Florida, 2007.
"Three Key West Lodges Hold Installations." *The Miami Herald,* 30 Dec. 1943, p. B1. *Readex*.
Tinajero, Araceli. *El Lector: A History of the Cigar Factory Reader.* Translated by Judith E. Grasberg, 2007, U of Texas P, 2010.

"La toma de las Tunas del 28 de agosto de 1897: Golpe letal a España." *Portal José Martí,* www.josemarti.cu/la-toma-de-las-tunas-del-28-de-agosto-de-1897-golpe-letal-a-espana/. Accessed 1 Aug. 2022.

Trelles, Carlos Manuel. *Bibliografía cubana del siglo XX tomo primero.* Imprenta de la Vda. de Quirós y Estrada, 1916. *Internet Archive.*

Turcios, Salvador R. *Libro de sonetos.* San Salvador, Imprenta Nacional, 1914. *Google Books.*

Varela-Lago, Ana. "Working in America and Living in Spain: The Making of Transnational Communities among Spanish Immigrants in the United States." *Hidden Out in the Open: Spanish Migration to the United States (1875–1930),* edited by Phylis Cancilla Martinelli and Ana Varela-Lago, UP of Colorado, 2018, pp. 21–65.

Westfall, L. Glen. *Key West: Cigar City USA.* The Historic Key West Preservation Board, 1984.

Feliciano Castro (1892–1982), a Galician Cuban American poet, printer, news editor, and lector (cigar-factory reader), was born into a farming family in the village of Villalba in the province of Lugo in Galicia, Spain, and emigrated to Cuba with his godfather at the age of nine. After receiving a classical education at the Pontifical Spanish College of St. Joseph, a Jesuit seminary in Rome, he returned to Havana at the age of nineteen. In 1916, he moved to Tampa, where he wrote for the magazine *Bohemia,* and he relocated in 1917 to the vibrant Cuban community of Key West, where he spent the rest of his life. Author of *Lágrimas y flores* (Taller Tipográfico, 1918), he also may have written two additional collections of poetry, *Horas de nostalgia* and *La Ruta negra,* though their publication is uncertain and there are no known extant copies. He wrote for the Spanish-language weekly newspaper *Florida,* was named the honorary vice consul to Spain for Key West and Monroe County in 1926, and in 1934 became the administrator of the Spanish-language newspaper *Cayo Hueso.* In 1937, Castro was elected unanimously as an honorary member of The Social Club Martí in Key West, and for several decades, he ran The Florida Press, a Spanish-language print shop, behind his home at 311 Elizabeth Street.

Joy Castro is the author of the 2023 historical novel *One Brilliant Flame*, about Cuban Key West in the 1800s; the Appalachian novel *Flight Risk*, a finalist for a 2022 International Thriller Award; the post-Katrina New Orleans literary thrillers *Hell or High Water*, which received the Nebraska Book Award, and *Nearer Home*, which have both been published in France by Gallimard's historic Série Noire; the short fiction collection *How Winter Began*; the memoir *The Truth Book*; and the essay collection *Island of Bones*, which received the International Latino Book Award and was a finalist for the PEN Center USA Literary Award. She is also editor of the craft anthology *Family Trouble: Memoirists on the Hazards and Rewards of Revealing Family*, and the founding series editor of Machete, a series in innovative literary nonfiction at the Ohio State University Press. Her fiction, essays, and literary, film, and cultural criticism have appeared in venues including *Ploughshares, The Brooklyn Rail, Senses of Cinema, Salon, Gulf Coast, Brevity, Afro-Hispanic Review, Seneca Review, Los Angeles Review of Books,* and the *New York Times Magazine*. A former writer-in-residence at Vanderbilt University, she is currently the Willa Cather Professor of English and Ethnic Studies (Latinx Studies) at the University of Nebraska–Lincoln, where she directs the Institute for Ethnic Studies.

Rhi Johnson is assistant professor in the department of Spanish and Portuguese at the University of Indiana Bloomington, doing interdisciplinary work on materiality, gender, and the social imaginary in the cultural production of the eighteenth and nineteenth centuries in the Iberian peninsula and its transatlantic network of influence. They are the editor and translator of an ecocritical anthology of poetry by Galicia's premier Romantic poet, *Because I Want to See the Sea: Poems by Rosalía de Castro*, and have translations in *Latin American Literature Today* and *As cantigas de Martin Codax en 55 idiomas*. Their academic work appears in venues such as the *Revista Canadiense de Estudios Hispánicos, Romance Quarterly, Decimonónica,* and *Dieciocho*. The current focus of their research is how new materialisms impact our understanding of the relationship that female agency and autonomy have with bodies of water, explored in the monograph *Women and Water: Fluxes of the Feminine in the Nineteenth Century*.

Printed in the United States
by Baker & Taylor Publisher Services